KEEPING THE
JEWEL IN THE
CROWN

Other books by Walter Reid

A Volunteer's Odyssey: Arras 1917
(*second edition*, Arras 1917: The Journey to Railway Triangle)
Architect of Victory, Douglas Haig
Churchill 1940–1945: Under Friendly Fire
Empire of Sand: How Britain Made the Middle East

KEEPING THE JEWEL IN THE CROWN

CROWN

The British Betrayal of India

WALTER REID

BIRLINN

This book is for Flora and Arthur

First published in 2016 by
Birlinn Limited
West Newington House
10 Newington Road
Edinburgh
EH9 1QS

www.birlinn.co.uk

Copyright © Walter Reid 2016

ISBN 978 1 78027 336 5

British Library Cataloguing-in-Publication Data
A catalogue record for this book is available from the British Library

Facsimile origination by Hewer Text (UK) Ltd
Printed and bound by Gutenberg Press, Malta

CONTENTS

LIST OF ILLUSTRATIONS

ACKNOWLEDGEMENTS

The question which this book is intended to answer began to form in my mind during my first visit to India. It was, 'Did the British mean to leave all this?', and it was prompted by architecture.

The buildings in question were – perhaps surprisingly – not the magnificent, triumphalist monuments of Delhi. Lutyens' concept of New Delhi was certainly an extravagant, public assertion of the grandeur and permanence of the imperial project, and interestingly it was a statement made later than might have been expected. New Delhi only became India's capital in 1911, and the great Lutyens' buildings were completed twenty years after that. The Viceroy's House, for long the largest Head of State's residence in the world, wasn't ready for occupation until 1929. All of this building for a continuing imperial future was therefore going on at the same time as the Montagu Declaration and the Irwin Declaration led Indians to think that there wasn't going to be an imperial future.

But Lutyens' creations were inherently exotic, extraneous to India. What struck me more forcibly was the organic nature of Mumbai's architecture and what it revealed. The British influences are obvious. The University looks familiar to a Scot, because the architect Sir George Gilbert Scott had a hand in it as well as in Glasgow University. The Law Courts look very like the Courts in the Strand. The Victoria Railway Station could be in any great British city. But this huge financial centre is not a political statement. The array of the commercial buildings of the city in all their wealth of western styles, including an enormous art deco element, represents a continuing capital investment and commitment that looks far into the future. Did the British honestly mean to leave all this?

I approached the question without prejudice. Indeed, as I started from the view, to which I adhere, that the Indian Civil Service, the men who administered India from India, as opposed to the Indian Office, chiefly in

Britain, which ruled India in a more political sense, were highly-principled and motivated by a powerful sense of duty, I rather expected to end up accepting the traditional British view of an honourable commitment to leading the subcontinent to independence as early as possible. Alas, as I proceeded on my journey I came increasingly and inescapably to a much more sombre conclusion.

Sad though that is, the journey was fascinating. I wish to take the opportunity of thanking some of those who helped me along the way. Sir Dickie and Lady Stagg were generous hosts at the High Commissioner's Residence in Delhi, where the journey began. I am particularly grateful to Arabella for sharing with me her enthusiasm for some contemporary Indian writers. Paul Addison of Edinburgh University and John Hussey, OBE, very kindly read this work in typescript, and I am hugely indebted to them for their comments and recommendations. I must also record my gratitude to Lawrence James and John Keay. Their own works on India are essential reading.

My thanks go to Dawn Broadley, whose input in terms of research and generally making the text fit for the publishers has been essential and has made the writing process much more fun than it otherwise would have been. Fun is the word I'd associate too with my publishers, Birlinn. Hugh Andrew presides over a very large list without losing his enthusiasm for its components, and the Editorial Director, Andrew Simmons, copes with an immense work-load without ever making it seem like work. Helen Bleck was a very kind copy-editor, gently excising innumerable errors and solecisms without communicating any sense of exasperation.

Indian history was the research area of my younger daughter, Bryony, and I am grateful to her for reading the text at an early stage and for valuable comments in regard to structure and argument. As a journalist, my wife, Janet, also sharpened my dialectical edge as well as brushing away infelicities in the course of more proof-reading than anyone should be asked to undertake. Because it is so true, I have no embarrassment in summing up my gratitude to her by saying again what I have said before: life is great fun, but it wouldn't be without her.

Argyll
April 2016

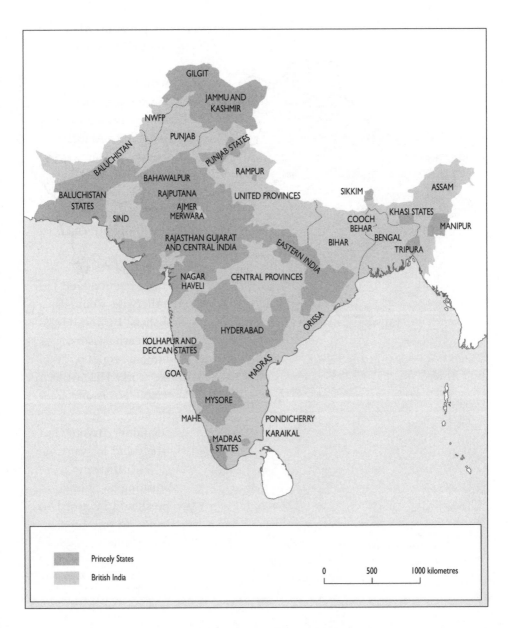

British India and the Princely States

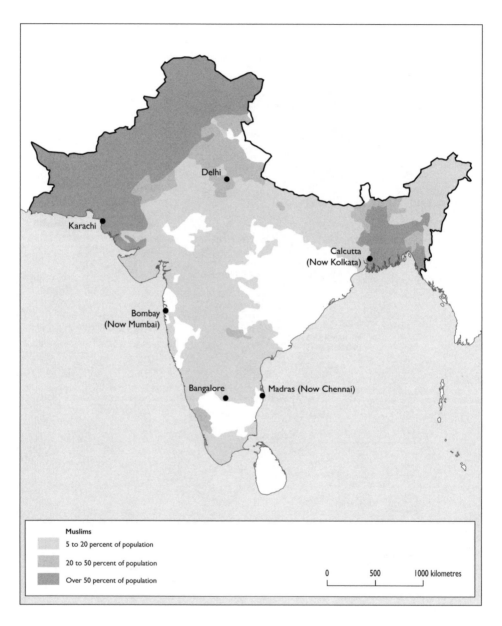

Distribution of Muslim population in 1909

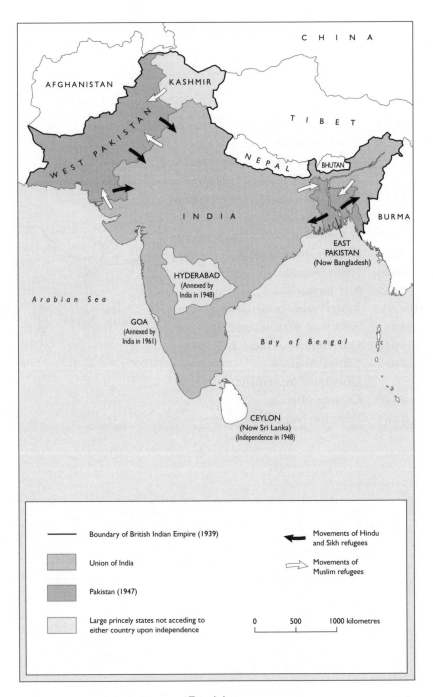

Partition

Principal Events

POLITICAL FRAMEWORK

Year	Government	Prime Minister	Secretary of State	Viceroy
1916	December – Coalition	Lloyd George	Austen Chamberlain (from May 1915)	April – Chelmsford
1917			July – Montagu	
1918 E	December – Coalition	Lloyd George		
1919				
1920				
1921				
1922 E	November – Conservative	Bonar Law	March – Peel	April – Reading
		Baldwin (1923)		
1923 E	December – Labour minority	MacDonald		
1924 E	October – Conservative	Baldwin	January – Olivier	
			November – Birkenhead	
1925				
1926				April – Irwin
1927				
1928			October – Peel	
1929 E	May – Labour minority	MacDonald	June – Wedgwood Benn	
1930				
1931 E	October – National Government	MacDonald	August – Hoare	April – Willingdon
		Baldwin (1935)		
1932				
1933				
1934				
1935 E	November – National Government	Baldwin	June – Zetland	
1936				April – Linlithgow
1937		Chamberlain (1937)		

Year	Government	Prime Minister	Secretary of State	Viceroy
1938				
1939				
1940	May – Coalition	Churchill	May – Amery	
1941				
1942				
1943				October – Wavell
1944				
1945	May – Conservative	Churchill		
E	July – Labour	Attlee	August – Pethick-Lawrence	
1946				
1947			April – Listowel	February – Mountbatten
E = general election				

I

INTRODUCTION

The End of Empire

There is nothing sadder in this story than the way it ended. At three minutes before midnight on 14 August 1947 the unity of the Indian subcontinent was broken. Pakistan was established as an independent, sovereign state. Exactly five minutes later India too became independent. Later that day, King George VI wrote his regular letter to his mother, adding after his signature as usual the letter 'R', for *Rex* or King, to remind her that he was her monarch as well as her affectionate son. But Queen Mary was saddened to see that he had omitted the customary 'I', for *Imperator,* Emperor of India. The British Raj had ended.

It ended horribly. Between August 1947 and the spring of 1948 millions of Indians, perhaps fourteen million, perhaps sixteen million, were forced to leave their homes. No one knows the true numbers of those killed. At the time a very conservative figure of 200,000 deaths was bandied about on the basis of formal notifications. The true figure may be around a million. But whatever the figure, the deaths alone do not speak of the horror of the times, the mutual hatred, the extravagance of the violence, rapes and mutilation. This was not a case of communities at war, Sikh, Hindu, Muslim, one seeking victory over the others. It was bloodlust, the crystallisation of hatred.

Women and children suffered appallingly. Babies were picked up by the feet and their heads were smashed against walls. Female children were raped. Older girls were raped and then their breasts were chopped off. If they were pregnant they were disembowelled. Trains arrived in Lahore station full of dead passengers, messages scribbled on the sides of the carriages reading 'A present from India'. Trains of dead Sikhs and Hindus were sent in the other direction with the legend, 'A present from Pakistan'. One convoy of Sikhs and Hindus from West Punjab was seventy-four miles long and the raiders who attacked it knew it was coming by its smell of death.[1]

This was not how British rule was intended to end. The historian Thomas Babington Macaulay was intimately involved with India. He resigned his seat in the House of Commons to go to India from 1834 until 1838 as Law Member on the governor-general's council. He was involved in the formulation of the Criminal Code, and in Indian education. He believed passionately what would nowadays be unacceptable: that the route to improvement for Indians lay in adopting the English language and assimilating European culture. Before he went to India he made a famous speech in the House of Commons on 10 July 1833 on the second reading of the India Bill. He set out his views on the development of India and ended with his vision of how Britain might finally retire from the subcontinent:

> The destinies of our Indian empire are covered with thick darkness. It is difficult to form any conjecture as to the fate reserved for a state which resembles no other in history, and which forms by itself a separate class of political phenomena. The laws which regulate its growth and its decay are still unknown to us. It may be that the public mind of India may expand under our system till it has outgrown that system; that by good government we may educate our subjects into a capacity for better government; that, having become instructed in European knowledge, they may, in some future age, demand European institutions. Whether such a day will ever come I know not. But never will I attempt to avert or to retard it. Whenever it comes, it will be the proudest day in English history. To have found a great people sunk in the lowest depths of slavery and superstition, to have so ruled them as to have made them desirous and capable of all the privileges of citizens, would indeed be a title to glory all our own.

Why was the British legacy so very different from what Macaulay had envisaged for that proud day?

* * *

As Independence came to India, with its accompanying intercommunal violence and ethnic cleansing, the case of *United States of America v Karl Brand et al* was coming to a conclusion in Nuremberg. This was the so-called 'Doctors' Trial', the first of the trials of war criminals before national military tribunals. The Nazi leaders had been tried by an international military tribunal, also at Nuremberg, two years earlier. The doctors were charged, like their leaders, with crimes against humanity.

Of course, what happened in India cannot be equated with the enormity of the Holocaust. Even allowing for all who died in India over the period of British rule, the scale of suffering is not comparable, and neither the evil nor the motivation of the Nazi regime was paralleled in British India. But the fact remains that death and suffering were – and still are – the consequence of how Britain discharged her responsibilities to a now divided subcontinent.

The question that no one tried to answer at Nuremberg, and that remains unanswered, relates to those who were *not* in the dock, the compliant German people. How much were they to blame? Professor Sir Ian Kershaw has used the phrase 'a willing complicity' to describe their role. This book is about a willing complicity too, about the failure of Britain to take real, purposeful steps to prepare India for Independence, and about deliberate blindness to the consequences of the desperate scuttle which flowed from that lack of preparation.

The book seeks to show that there was a willing collusion by the political classes in a policy, or a series of policies, amounting together to a lack of steady, consistent policy, which had as its inevitable outcome the condition in which India was left in 1947 – the terrible intercommunal hatred which was distilled in the events which I have just described, together with an absence of the established political institutions and governmental organisations which are the basis of the harmonious society which Macaulay envisaged.

There was no intent to bring this about, but there was a silent connivance in holding back political progress for as long as possible – until finally Britain could postpone it no longer and finally had to scuttle out at short order, leaving chaos behind.

The story of the last thirty years of the Raj reveals little evidence of goodwill or wholehearted commitment to India's well-being. On the contrary, it is an unsettling story of deceit and double-speak. These squalid political years were not a part of her history of which Britain can be proud.

The Argument

Amongst the things this book is not, is a history of India. It covers in detail just the last thirty years of British rule. It's not even a history of the Independence movement, because it largely ignores the Indian side of the struggle. It is not an economic history. It is a study of British politics in the period as they affected India. I shall show that the political classes made no genuine, committed attempt to prepare India for Independence. Maybe *realpolitik* entitled them to try to hang on to the jewel in the crown as long as they could. The Romans had tried to hang on to what they had, after all, and Churchill was frank enough to say that this was what he was trying to do. What was not acceptable was that almost all the policy-makers pretended that they were doing what they were not: discharging the duty of trustee-ship, of making India capable of controlling her own destiny.

This is an interpretative study, based for the most part on the letters and documents of those involved and drawing on public records and state papers. The narrative largely covers the last three decades of the British Raj, the years from 1917, when the Montagu Declaration* was made, appearing to promise some form of Independence, to August 1947, when self-rule in a half-discussed form was thrust on unprepared peoples. The *uniting* of India under imperial rule had been declared to be the great British achievement, and retaining that unity had been the aim of British administrators; but in the final despairing desire to be quit of responsibility, Britain accepted the fracturing of the subcontinent, with all the consequences that persist to this day. The delineation of the new frontiers was carried out in just five weeks, and the lines of the boundaries were not announced until *after* Independence had been granted, in order not to upset Britain's last days.

Thirty years is conveniently taken by many historians as the span of a generation, very roughly the period between an individual's birth and that of the next generation. If the idea of imminent self-government was born in the Montagu Declaration of 1917, with careful nurture that idea might have reached maturity in 1947. What this book argues is that while there were men and women of good will who did seek to promote the concept of Independence, most politicians and senior administrators, for good reasons, bad reasons or out of indifference, were concerned to do nothing to move India steadily and purposefully towards her destiny. Some thought that British mercantile prosperity still required privileged access to Indian markets. Some simply wished to retain a symbol of world domination and couldn't countenance the acknowledgement of a shrinking authority. Many of these people, and Churchill was at their centre, deliberately sought to obstruct any moves of which they disapproved in any way they could. Others, far greater in number, were less overtly hostile to Independence, but

---

* Dealt with in Chapter 5.

found the concept infinitely remote from their mindset. They publicly applauded the idea of Independence and even appeared to work for it, but finally took care to pitch the day on which Independence would be attained at an indefinable date far in the distant future.

The first chapters of the book contain a fairly brief account of the background to 1917 and the Montagu Declaration. Even progressive administrators in these years, like Curzon and Milner, regarded it as axiomatic that the notion of self-rule for India was absurd (Chapter 2). But after the First World War, it became a political necessity to appear to clarify her future. The Montagu Declaration was the outcome. Its critical significance, as will become clear, lay in the fact that it referred to eventual dominion status – but it was carefully vague about when it would be attained; and it would be a dominion within the Empire. Anyway, no one knew what dominion status meant. Governments could hide behind the fact that the status was a vague concept which meant very little (Chapter 12). When in 1931 the Statute of Westminster defined dominion status as implying the right to secede from the Empire, that was not accepted as being the kind of status India would have.

In the inter-war years, there was no emphasis on the economic development of India or the creation of a responsible middle class. Instead Britain tightened its control, as was reflected in the Rowlatt Act and the Amritsar Massacre (Chapters 5 and 7). There had always been an element of 'divide and rule' in Britain's handling of the Muslim and Hindu communities and the princes, but there was a conscious development of the policy in these years and until the very end, when its consequences in the fracture of the subcontinent into India and Pakistan were apprehended. The policy was finally indicted in the inter-communal atrocities of 1947 and afterwards (Chapters 50 and 51). Initially the Congress party embraced Muslims as well as Hindus, but by 1947 the two communities were effectively locked in confrontation: Congress *versus* the Muslim League, with the princes detached. As late as 1940 Churchill, as a Cabinet minister but not yet prime minister, planned to sit on this 'tripos' as the basis of an indefinite presence in India. His views did not change when he became prime minister.

The major piece of Indian legislation in the period this book covers, the Government of India Act of 1935, was designed to keep the Congress party from effective power (Chapter 23). The Act provided for a federal system which was unacceptable to India's political interests and reserved real power to the viceroy. It could never be implemented.

The Second World War concentrated Britain's thoughts. Particularly after the fall of Singapore in February 1942, India became a critical part of Britain's Eastern strategy. It was essential, at a minimum, to keep India quiet. Various policy initiatives involving promises for the future took place, including the Cripps Mission of March of that year, which was unsuccessful – and, as I argue, inevitably so (Chapters 32–34). But in any event, Churchill, now prime minister, felt himself able to abjure promises made against the exigencies of war (Chapter 33).

The war over, Britain no longer had the means, financial or otherwise, or indeed the strength of will, to hold on to India. But the Labour Government which was elected in 1945 had no wish to let go of India entirely. For geo-strategical and prestige reasons India was to be kept in the Commonwealth and tied in to defence commitments (Chapter 42). Empire would continue under another name. It was envisaged that an area around Delhi would not pass out of British control and that there would be a continuing British presence (Chapter 36).

Not many men emerge well from this story. One who does is Archibald Wavell. This highly intelligent soldier, appealing if pathologically reticent, was appointed viceroy in September 1943. He was chosen precisely because he was no politician. He seemed the ideal man to sit tight and keep India quiet through the war, which was exactly what Churchill wanted. But like a good soldier should, he made an appraisal of the situation based on the facts he found and – to the great irritation of Churchill and later of Attlee – did something his predecessors and political masters had never done, and came up with a policy (Chapters 37–39, 42). It was precisely the opposite of what his history and instincts would have suggested, but it was correct and it was what his successor, Mountbatten, would do.

Wavell saw that nothing the politicians had been doing had prepared India to look after herself. In particular there had been no economic preparation. The choice was to stay for another generation – which was impossible – or to leave now, accepting that there would be disorder, chaos, illiteracy, corruption, all the deprivation that we now associate with the third world, not what Macaulay had envisaged. His analysis of British dishonesty (Chapter 38) encapsulates what I shall demonstrate: 'I have found HMG's attitudes to India negligent, hostile and contemptuous to a degree I had not anticipated'.

The history of these thirty years is one in which Britain obfuscates and misleads. We shall repeatedly find Indians being offered a form of words which is known to mean one thing to them and quite another to those making the promise. These weasel statements, these deliberate misunderstandings, are difficult to excuse. They are the reason that Indian politicians then and now accused and accuse the British of bad faith.

The Scottish judge Lord Shaw of Dunfermline wondered if the legal maxim *res ipsa loquitur*, the facts provide the answer, would have carried the weight it does if the words had not been in Latin. But the maxim has a value. It means that in certain circumstances the facts are so clear that they raise a presumption of negligence. In assessing the sincerity of the Declarations that British politicians made in the last years of the Raj, and their claim that they were discharging the duties of trusteeship, of preparing India for her Independence, the maxim will be useful to keep in mind. I have described briefly the violence surrounding the British departure. The disorder and chaos that Wavell foresaw has not even now been eliminated.

If India was not ready to go, after two centuries of British presence, whose fault was that? Why did the British period end so badly? Why had Britain not prepared to make an inevitable outcome a happy one? That is what this book is about.

2

THE BACK STORY

This book looks in detail at just the last thirty years of British rule. But neither the history of the British Empire nor the history of British India began in 1917, and I shall start with a brief introduction to both.

The Reasons for Empire

A 1950 Colonial Office paper[2] disarmingly says that Britain 'as a seafaring and trading nation . . . had long been a "collector of islands and peninsulas"'. In a much-quoted remark, Sir John Seeley, the Regius Professor of Modern History at Cambridge, said something similar in 1883: 'We seem, as it were, to have conquered and peopled half the world in a fit of absence of mind'.[3] That didn't mean quite what it seemed to say: what Seeley meant was that there had not been a *coherent* policy behind Britain's imperial expansion. There had been an incoherent set of policies. The 1950 paper explained that the collection of islands and peninsulas was assembled to protect trade and the sea routes. The motive for Empire was selfish.

The early territories were acquired in a search for valuable raw materials. Mercantilist policy involved closing off routes and markets against competitors. The importance of synergy was exemplified in the slave trade.

After the loss of the American colonies, a briefly distinct and cohesive policy was adopted. It was a policy to establish what was called a Second British Empire. Acquisitions were made in the first place for commercial reasons; but as other nations, such as the Netherlands and France, were at the same game it was also important to acquire points of strategic importance from which to defend the acquisitions. Later, coaling and re-fitting stations also became important. Of the dependencies with which the 1950 paper was dealing, three-quarters had been obtained in little more than the previous fifty years. The African acquisitions were largely made as part of the European scramble for a place in the sun. The motives for that burst of activity are less obviously mercantile than in the earlier periods of acquisition: it *was* assumed that Africa would have resources worth having, but more importantly there was a collective view that no self-respecting European power could be without an empire, even though latterly the expenses of Empire were greater than its financial benefits. The final period of expansion, the creation of what might be called the Third British Empire, took place long after the Empire was thought to be in decline. At the end of the First World War Britain acquired what were called mandates, which effectively brought new colonial possessions in the shape of Palestine, Jordan and Iraq. Between 1914 and 1919 the superficial area of the Empire expanded by roughly 9 per cent, and in the twenty-one years from 1901 its population increased by some 14.5 per cent.

In all three periods the motivation consisted of desires which interlocked: desires for wealth, for strategic possessions from which to defend the wealth, and for prestige, the inevitable concomitant of wealth. In the process, numberless hundreds of thousands of native populations were slaughtered, usually by deploying modern firepower against peoples armed for a Stone Age battle. Other numberless hundreds of thousands were consigned to slavery, enduring the most degrading and inhumane of conditions. Almost always, the subject races, even the most sophisticated and educated amongst them, were regarded as and made to feel inferior to the ruling caste.

The colonial administrators must be judged by the standards and attitudes of their times, and not those of later periods. Even the cruelty which we find most shocking was, in its time, regarded as acceptable. Well-meaning administrators unhesitatingly considered that they and their fellows were, and probably always would be, superior to the native population. Practices like suttee – the burning of a widow on her husband's funeral pyre – and the viciousness of dacoits and thuggees were noted; the many respects in which the West could learn from the East were not.

By the nineteenth century young British men of ability went into the Colonial Service and the Indian Civil Service not only to make more money than they could have done at home, but also because they were animated by a sense of duty. They attempted to improve the lot of the subject peoples at the cost of taking themselves far from home and family, returning only infrequently in the course of twenty years, seeing wives and children as well as their own colleagues buried in dusty cemeteries in the subcontinent.

If the actions of the British in their Empire are judged by the standard of the times, the story of these administrators will not, I believe, be found to be an ignoble one. It is not the purpose of this book to argue otherwise. The book is not about the executives, but their political masters, and it is about just one chapter of Britain's imperial history, the response of the British to the demands of the Indians for Independence. I attempt to judge what Britain did in that fairly brief period against the standards of that same period. I also judge what was said against what was done, and that is a valid and revealing test.

The Indian Background

Why did Britain want to get involved in India? As early as 1608, a settlement had been established in what is now Gujarat, and in the course of the century other settlements followed, notably in Bengal. From the outset, as in America, British expansion into India was not carried out by the British Government at all, but by merchant adventurers, 'the East India Company, the Governor and Company of Merchants of London trading into the East Indies', otherwise the Honourable East India Company or, colloquially, John Company.

There was no initial intent to occupy, and when occupation took place it began indirectly. The post-American policy involved looking very closely at ways of repositioning the trading system on which Britain's prosperity depended. There was not initially any appetite for large-scale colonisation. The experience and the expense of the American experiment demonstrated that the benefits of the mercantilist system would be eroded by the costs of policing extensive territories. The preferred approach was to establish a network of entrepôts, like the Straits Settlements of Malacca, Penang and Singapore in South-East Asia. Initially the same approach was followed in India.

The extent of the Company's possessions in India increased dramatically in the course of the eighteenth century in competition with France, in the vacuum created by the collapse of the Mughal Empire. The East India Company had three independent armies, largely composed of local mercenaries, but under the command of British officers who had been trained at the Company's own military training school. By the end of the eighteenth century these armies had defeated both the French and the Indian potentates, notably the rulers of Mysore, and effectively controlled most of the subcontinent, either directly or by way of treaties with local princes.

All this was done by a company in which the British Government owned not a single share. Despite that, the government exercised an increasing degree of control. The Regulating Act of 1773 provided that whatever the Company acquired was acquired on behalf of the Crown. Although Warren Hastings, governor-general of Bengal from 1772 till 1785, was only a Company employee, he was ultimately under the authority of the Crown and could be impeached by the House of Commons, as he was in 1787.

As the British presence in India became increasingly important, so governmental control was tightened. There was legislation in 1784, 1786, 1793, 1833, 1835, 1853 and finally 1858. The detail of these Acts need not be examined here, but the effect of all but the last was incremental, and their cumulative result was to reduce the powers of the Company enormously, and to impose detailed parliamentary control on how India was run, providing for the establishment of a British judiciary in the subcontinent; for education; and requiring, as early as 1833, that there would be no colour bar within the Company or discrimination on the basis of religion, a provision which had no practical effect.

There was a seismic change with the passing of the 1858 Government of India Act. This Act followed the outbreak in the previous year of what was usually called in Britain the Indian Mutiny. How the events of that year are viewed depends on where one stands. At the time there was no such thing as a united India. Amongst Indians, a consensus view only developed in the following century, when the Mutiny became known as the War of Independence of 1857, or the First War of Indian Independence. In Britain, on the other hand, there was an immediate public reaction. The rising was called variously the Indian Mutiny, the Sepoy Mutiny, the Great Mutiny, the Rebellion of 1857, the Mahommedan Rebellion. The predominant reaction in Britain was of anger in the face of treacherous ingratitude. There *were* many atrocities, and public opinion was outraged by reports of rape, of assaults on 'fragile female bodies' both adults' and children's. Civilians and wounded soldiers were killed. But what the British did after suppression of the Mutiny was no less atrocious, and more Indians than Britons were killed in the Mutiny and its aftermath. There was little justice in the search for revenge. Both mutineers and those who were merely fugitives were shot, hanged and hacked to pieces. Some men were tied over the muzzles of cannons and reduced to atoms.

Parliament treated the Mutiny as an indictment of the Company's role, and the 1858 Act was more or less the end of the Company. It carried on, as a tea trader, until 1874, but as no more than that. From 1858 the whole of India and its armies was controlled directly by the British Government. The government had already had a role in the moral aspects of British rule, and had sought to ensure that the liberal, cultural benefits of education were extended to the natives of the subcontinent and that the spread of Christianity was encouraged. Now it had to formulate a wholesale and systematic policy for the huge area and vast population for which it was directly responsible.

It is important to remember that while Britain prided itself on having united the divided parts of a subcontinent that lacked cohesion, there was always a distinction between British India and Indian India. The Indian part was ruled by the princes, landed potentates. Even fifty years after the nation-building that started in 1858, a small British presence ruled just two-thirds of the subcontinent directly, and the remaining third, the princely states, only indirectly. In 1900 there were 674 princely states, with a population of 73 million, one-fifth of all India. The princes in general governed in the British interest. They were paid to do so, and British political officers made sure that they did so. The princes were treated with deference. Their orders were given to them, so to say, in the supplicating optative mood ('Would that you might do such and such'). But whatever the appearance, it was Britain that ruled in the princely states. She ruled by the optative mood, but with the Gatling gun in the background. In British India Indians did not even appear to rule. In British India there were in 1909 no Indians at all on the Viceroy's Council. A quarter of a century later, Indian representation on the council was minimal.

The viceroy presided over the government of India. He was what his title suggested: the substitute for the king. His personal powers were far in excess of anything that his royal master possessed, and he enjoyed surroundings of splendour and luxury far in excess of his king. During the nineteenth century the viceroys could to a great extent ignore London. On the other hand, in these years they were not charged with the development of policy, and were administrators rather than innovators. As communications improved, they were controlled in increasing detail by the government in London. Even so, many of the twentieth-century viceroys made a significant personal contribution to political events, for good or bad. We shall look at some of them in detail. The viceroy administered on behalf of the imperial government, but he was always subordinate to London, where his immediate boss was the Secretary of State for India.

The change from a passive to an active viceroy took place under a number of viceroys (or governors-general as they were known until 1858).* It concluded with the appointment of Lord Curzon, who was viceroy from 1899 to 1905. Curzon's attitude to India was complicated. Much about India appealed to him emotionally. On the other hand, he resented the evidence he saw of the growth of a confident nationalism. 'I have observed the growing temper of the native. The new wine is beginning to ferment in him, and he is awaking to a consciousness of equality and freedom'.[4] He saw the growth of nationalism as a reaction to arrogant and ignorant English people who did not attain his own lofty ideals. He was distressed to find that although in the last twenty years there were eighty-four examples of known killings of Indians by Europeans, in these twenty years and indeed the twenty years before them only a total of two Europeans had been hanged. 'You can hardly credit the sympathy with wrong-doing that there is here – even amongst the highest – provided that the malefactors are Englishmen.' He publicly punished the Ninth Queen's Royal Lancers for failing to deal with the alleged killing of an Indian by troopers of the regiment.

Curzon is not an easy man to like, but he is difficult not to admire. Here is his concept of the imperial role:

> Let it be your ideal to remember that the Almighty has placed your hand on the greatest of his ploughs, in whose furrow the nations of the future are germinating and taking shape, to drive the blade a little forward in your time, and to feel that somewhere among these millions you have left a little justice or happiness or prosperity, a sense of manliness or moral dignity, a spring of patriotism, a dawn of intellectual enlightenment, or a stirring of duty where it did not exist before – that is enough. That is the Englishman's justification in India.[5]

The grandeur of that purpose and its immense scale simultaneously glows with vision and declares that the vision would not be accomplished within a hundred years.

The change in the viceregal role arose more because of Curzon's dynamic personal approach than because of any instructions that were given to him by the government. Curzon was stiff, haughty and ambitious. That impression was reinforced by his stance: he had a weak back and was required to wear a

---

* For instance, Dalhousie (1848–56), Lytton (1876–80) and Dufferin (1884–88).

steel corset.* He is still remembered in a piece of undergraduate doggerel, the *Balliol Masque*:

> My name is George Nathaniel Curzon.
> I am a most superior person.
> My cheeks are pink, my hair is sleek.
> I dine at Blenheim twice a week.

Curzon was a distinguished Orientalist and by far the most knowledgeable Conservative statesman to be charged with the administration of India. He split Bengal into a Hindu western half and an eastern 'Bengal and Assam' – a largely Muslim area. Despite his unbending appearance and uncompromising statements, he was a humane viceroy, who travelled huge distances in the aftermath of a dreadful cholera epidemic, trying to bring relief to the devastated areas; he had no interest at all in anything approaching Independence for India and regarded any such notions with disdain and repugnance. His object throughout was efficient administration. That was the motive for splitting Bengal. Above his tomb at Kedleston there hangs a Curzon medieval war banner and the flag of the Indian Empire.

It is worth noting that the Hindus understood his motive for the Bengal split to be part of a 'divide and rule' policy. Dividing and ruling was not part of Curzon's purpose, but his successors, who unlike him faced immediate demands for Independence and separation, undoubtedly found it convenient to play one community against the other. The policy of divide and rule consisted in a whole range of manoeuvres. One of them, a response to the Great Mutiny of 1857, was to divide every Indian regiment into separate communal battalions, Hindu, Muslim and Sikh, so that there would always be at least one which remained loyal.

---

* At the Lausanne Conference his steel back brace broke, and his valet got drunk and lost his dress trousers. Mussolini, who also attended Lausanne, wore an unlikely combination of white spats and black shirt, but at least he did not part company with his trousers. Other British foreign secretaries have had trouble with their trousers. Sir Geoffrey Howe, as he then was, lost his in the course of a sleeper train journey in the United Kingdom sixty years later. Douglas Hurd, also still a commoner, rushing from his shower to meet an Arab potentate, broke his zip, and had to conduct his audience with his legs crossed, a solecism in the Arab world, but one that he judged preferable to the alternative.

Even when not overtly dividing and ruling, Britain did see the two communities in very different lights. Many Britons found the Hindus – and the majority of the Independence movement leaders were Hindus – unappealing. No great effort was made to look into the subtleties of the Hindu religion. At a superficial level a multiplicity of gods – elephant gods, monkey gods and so on – were to a Victorian mind almost a caricature of paganism, savagery and idolatry. The monotheistic Muslims, on the other hand, held to a religious philosophy which was much more akin to Christianity, and indeed recognised common Abrahamic roots, venerating Jesus as a great teacher. British civil servants tended, although there are countless exceptions, to find the Muslims easier to get on with. They seemed to be more socially welcoming as well as less arrogant. British officials knew that if they were admitted into Hindu houses for a meal, there would be a ritual of 'purification' carried out after their departure: they were regarded as unclean.

The Muslims were thought of as brave and intrepid warriors. They gained points in the Second World War, when for political reasons the largely Hindu Congress party refused to cooperate, unlike the Muslims. Sixty-five per cent of the Indian Army soldiers who fought for Britain were Muslims, although they constituted only 27 per cent of the population.

The Cultural Divide

Curzon was a reforming proconsul, who took no account of his political self-interest in doing justice for the native population. And yet this humane and hard-working viceroy, who had the advancement of the circumstances of his Indian subjects at heart, flatly refused to consider more Indian participation in government. When Romesh Chunder Dutt, the president of the Congress party in 1901, pressed for the appointment of Indians to the vice-regal council, Curzon summarily rejected the request. In his view, self-government on the white colonial model would mean 'ruin to India and treason to our trust'. Salisbury, Secretary of State for India from 1874 to 1878 and later prime minister, thought it axiomatic that the Hottentots, the Hindus and even the Irish could never be suitable races for self-government. The Duke of Wellington was even more forthright about ludicrous colonial pretensions: 'A Constitution for Malta! I should as soon think of elections for an army or a parliament on board ship!' This sort of prejudice proceeded from the enduring conviction that, Hindu or Muslim or Sikh, an Indian was always inferior to a white man.

In 1895 the British Army replaced the single-shot Martini-Henry rifle with the new magazine-fed Lee Enfield. It was a much superior weapon, but its bullet was narrower, at .303 inches, than its predecessor's .457 inches. Some military men were concerned that the new ammunition did not have adequate stopping-power. A controlled experiment was therefore carried out. A number of Muslim tribesmen, sentenced to death after proper trial, were executed by firing squads using the different types of ammunition, and their bodies were then opened up to see which bullets had done most damage.

The men were lawfully executed and they were dead when their bodies were opened up, but it's impossible to imagine the same thing happening to the bodies of British Tommies: Indians were regarded as a lower form of life. A duty was owed to them, but it would not do to confuse them with Europeans. Indeed many believed it was not ultimately in the interests of the Indians themselves that their political aspirations should be achieved.

Sir Michael O'Dwyer, an able but tough paternalist, served in the Indian Civil Service from 1885 to 1919. We shall meet him again in connection with the Amritsar Massacre. After his retirement, he campaigned as a die-hard opponent of reform: at a meeting of the Royal Central Asian Society in London in March 1940 he was shot at close range and died in Caxton Hall.* He represented informed specialist opinion of the Conservative school when he spoke of 'the demon of discord' that could unleash 'all the latent feuds and hatreds' in the country, which were only held down by constant vigilance.[6] Major General Sir George Younghusband served in the Indian Army at various times between 1878 and 1918. He wrote, 'It is never wise to stand studied impertinence, or even the semblance of it, from any Oriental. Politeness, and courtesy, by all means, and even camaraderie, as long as these are reciprocated, and all is fair and square, and above board. But the moment there is a sign of revolt, mutiny, or treachery, of which the symptoms not unusually are a swollen head, and a tendency to incivility, it is wise to hit the Oriental straight between the eyes, and to keep on hitting him thus, till he appreciates exactly what he is, and who is who.'[7]† It is

---

* His assailant was a Sikh, Udham Singh, who was exacting revenge for Amritsar. At his trial he said he had waited 21 years for revenge. He was convicted of murder and hanged.

† A more enlightened appraisal is contained in a note which the future George V, then Prince of Wales and aged 40, wrote in 1905 after a visit to India: 'No doubt the

essential not to be misled by hindsight. Well into the twentieth century intelligent, well-meaning people, liberal in most matters, and versed in the politics of India, could sincerely be incapable of conceiving that Indians could ever exercise self-government.

Natives are better treated by us than in the past, but I could not help being struck by the way in which all salutations by the Natives were disregarded by the persons to whom they were given. Evidently we are too much inclined to look upon them as a conquered and down-trodden race & the Native, who is becoming more and more educated, realizes this. I could not help noticing that the general bearing of the European towards the Native was to say the least unsympathetic. In fact not the same as that of superiors to inferiors at home.' (Nicolson, *King George V*, p.88.)

3

THE MORLEY–MINTO REFORMS

Curzon's first five-year term as viceroy was a success, but his second, shorter term was less happy, undermined by scheming by Kitchener, the commander-in-chief, and unsupported by the home government. When he returned to Britain the trajectory of his brilliant career was checked.

He was replaced by Gilbert Murray, the fourth Earl of Minto. As a young man Minto had been a sportsman, racing with some success in the French Grand National and elsewhere under the name of 'Mr Rolly'. After that he entered the army. As a result of family connections rather than obvious ability, he became Governor-General of Canada. His time there was fairly unremarkable and it was accordingly, as his wife said, a 'bolt from the blue' when he was appointed viceroy.

Just two weeks after he reached India the Conservative administration in London was replaced by Campbell-Bannerman's Government following the great Liberal victory of 1906. As a result of the change of government, Mr Rolly found himself in harness with the fairly radical John Morley as Secretary of State. Morley was bookish and earnest; proud, as he said, to have been made Secretary of State as a 'humble man of letters'. Because of his record as an unimpeachable radical with a contempt of jingoism, it was expected that he would be acceptable to nationalist Indian opinion. It was not evident that he and Minto would get on well. In the event, they generally did: preserving the rule of law tempered Morley's radicalism. Together they made the first systematic attempt to reform the government of India.

The two men worked together on what became known as the Morley–Minto Reforms, more correctly the Indian Councils Act of 1909. Morley believed that the British were in India 'to implant . . . those ideas of justice, law, humanity which are the foundations of our own civilisation'. He hoped that limited reforms would separate the moderates from the extremists. The

Act extended the franchise and increased the numbers of Indians on the provincial and central legislative councils, but it was in essence a device to devitalise Indian nationalism by the promise of progress towards responsible government. Responsible government was not self-government, though the distinction was rarely spelled out: responsible government meant devolution of certain functions to elected representatives but with overall control firmly retained by Britain. The Morley–Minto promise was undated and meaningless. The true effect and purpose of the reforms was to strengthen British control without conceding anything in return.[8]

The idea of adopting representative principles in India was essentially a way of putting an end to demands for something that was held to be manifestly impossible – truly independent government. Lord Kimberley, Liberal Secretary of State for India for most of the period 1882 to 1894, said that 'the notion of a parliamentary representation of so vast a country almost as large as Europe containing so large a number of different races is one of the wildest imaginations that ever entered the minds of men'. Minto thought the same way. He wrote to Morley in 1907: 'We are no advocates of representative government for India in the Western sense of the term. It could never be akin to the instincts of the many races composing the population of the Indian Empire. It would be a Western importation uncongenial to Eastern tastes'. Morley heartily agreed and rejected 'the intention or desire to attempt the transplantation of any European form of representative government to Indian soil'. Both men conceived this impossibility of establishing representative government in India as a truth without limitation of time. In 1909 Minto told the House of Lords that he thought it neither desirable nor possible nor even conceivable that British political institutions should be extended to India. At the cost of some logical contortion he declared: 'If I were attempting to set up a parliamentary system in India, or if it could be said that this chapter of reforms led directly or necessarily up to the establishment of a parliamentary system in India, I, for one, would have nothing at all to do with it'. This is a sentiment, spoken or unspoken, that was implicit in British policy till the very end, till practical considerations required precipitate scuttle; but it was not a sentiment that was shared with Indians. They saw responsible government, self-government, home rule all as much the same thing, and all a short step from Independence.

There was correspondence between Morley and Minto about which Indians should sit on the Viceroy's Executive Council. Minto wanted S. P. Sinha, and got him, rather than Mookerjee: 'Sinha is comparatively white, whilst Mookerjee is as black as my hat!'[9] At lower levels, too, Indians were effectively excluded. Entrance to the Indian Civil Service, the ICS, was open to Indians, but the entrance examinations were held in the United Kingdom. Entrance to the ICS was open to all in the same way as was entry to the Ritz. There was hostility to the 'educated native'. Very few Indians were admitted to the Indian Civil Service before the First World War.

Curzon had resigned the viceroyalty in 1905. He looked at the proposed Morley–Minto reforms with horror: 'It is often said, why not make some prominent native a member of the Executive Council? The answer is that in the whole continent there is not an Indian fit for the post'. Milner was equally forthright: 'the idea of extending what is described as "colonial self-government" to India . . . is a hopeless absurdity'.[10]

Much later – in the 1940s – self-government was seen as a prerequisite for membership of what by then was increasingly being referred to as the Commonwealth. Earlier, that was far from the case: excellent and efficient administration was seen as the benefit that Britain brought to her possessions. This was the attitude of men like the titanic Joseph Chamberlain, whose vision of an Empire bound together by preferential tariffs inspired voters but damaged the fortunes of the Tories for a generation; like Cromer, who ruled Egypt for thirty years and was convinced of the futility of allowing native races to administer their own affairs; and like Lord Milner, the great proconsul whom I shall shortly introduce. For them, good government was not self-government, but well-administered control. This is what was wonderfully described by the philosopher James Mill as a vast system of outdoor relief for the upper classes.

Having mentioned Alfred, later Lord, Milner it might be as well that I outline his role in the development of twentieth-century imperialism at this point. No one except Joseph Chamberlain, to whom he was close, had as much influence on twentieth-century British colonial policy. From his Oxford days he looked for a role of public usefulness, and it was in the development of the concept of an imperial economic and political system, 'a Southern British World, stretching from Africa to Egypt, to the Middle East, to India and to Australia and to New Zealand' that this remarkably high-minded and ambitious youth was to find it.

He went to South Africa as High Commissioner for Southern Africa and Governor of Cape Colony before the South African war. After the war he became civil administrator of the Orange River and Transvaal colonies. Throughout the period he remained High Commissioner. During his work on reconstruction he inspired the group of young and able assistants that gathered round him, and through them, 'Milner's Kindergarten', and in his subsequent political roles he enormously influenced events. Members of the Kindergarten went on to found a magazine known as the Round Table to promote the concept of imperial unity. Milner was at the centre of the group associated with it, also known as the Round Table. He also used a loose grouping at All Souls' College, Oxford, to promote his opinions and the idea of a 'forward' imperial policy, a policy of positive advancement of his Southern Empire that would span the globe. His views, like those of many others, including Churchill, as I shall show, were influenced in part by the contemporary and significant theories of social Darwinism.

It is important to take into account the intellectual influence of thinking such as Milner's. Opposition to Indian Independence didn't only flow from crass ideas of white supremacy, but also from the theories, economic, political and anthropological, of serious thinkers. Often the respectable arguments were used to camouflage prejudice, but that was certainly not always the case.

4

The Impact of the First World War

In the course of the First World War over a million Indians fought overseas for Britain in addition to those who served in the subcontinent. Some 54,000 died. About 13,000 were decorated and 11 VCs were awarded. India also provided £1m of cash.

The scale of the subcontinent's contribution to the war inevitably invigorated and revitalised Indians' expectations. Things were never the same again. Britain had to adapt to the new demands and appear to respond to them. The argument of this book is that the response was equivocal and misleading. India increasingly wanted Independence. Britain *seemed* to be saying that she would have it. In reality, Britain did not radically change her position. Some Britons thought that India would ultimately be independent, but even those who believed this were working on a very different timescale from the Indian nationalists. The *majority* of British policymakers thought that Independence would never come or, if it did, would come at a time in the future so distant that the practical implications needed no consideration.

In 1916 General Sir Edmund Barrow, then Military Secretary to the India Office, a man who had worked in India all his life, wrote, 'By bestowing liberty, justice and education in India we have done much to emancipate it from the shackles of caste and prejudice but it will take generations yet to reach the ideals of the philanthropists and philosophers and to satisfy the longings of an awakened India'.[11] Britain never admitted that everything she said was based on the premise that Independence, if it occurred, would be 100 years more distant than the Indians thought.

Prior to the First World War the only support in parliament for a liberal response to Indian demands came from elements of the still politically insignificant Labour party, such as Keir Hardie and Ramsay MacDonald. In 1909 the Labour party had condemned the limited scope of self-government envisaged in the Morley–Minto Reforms. The party was in contact with the London branch of the Indian Congress party. Congress was to become the most important political motor for Independence in India. Eventually it was overwhelmingly Hindu and partisan, but that was not the case in its early years. Its origins lay in a proposal in 1883 that Indian local magistrates should have jurisdiction over Europeans. There were widespread protests and the viceroy, Lord Ripon, withdrew the measure. The withdrawal was as unpopular with the Indians as the measure had been with the English. The consequence was the formation in 1885 of the Indian National Congress.

It was founded in December of that year by Allan Octavian Hume, a retired ICS official. He believed that he was guided from the spirit world by a variety of 'Mahatmas' and 'Gurus'.[12] At the first meeting, there were seventy-one Hindus and two Muslims. The party split in 1907, with the foundation of the New party, which stood for direct confrontation and boycott. The rift was later mended. Soon afterwards Mohandas Gandhi came on the scene.

Gandhi, M.K. Gandhi or Mahatma Gandhi (a Sanskrit adjective, 'the high-souled', applied to Gandhi from his forties onwards) will be introduced more fully in later pages. He is now so much a part of legend – hugely so of course in India, but in the world-mind too – that it is difficult to separate reality from myth. There were certainly some who in his lifetime regarded him as a hypocrite rather than a saint. Without going as far as that, it was possible to find his elliptical utterances and his obstinacy over side-issues profoundly irritating. But the power of his personality, stemming from a fundamental simplicity and goodness, has never been denied, and it is impossible to imagine how India would have found its way to Independence without him.

His influence on Congress turned it into an activist, populist movement. For many British the growth of Congress was the crystallisation of unacceptable ambitions on the part of what Ripon's successor, Lord Dufferin, called the 'Bengali Babu'. An analogy was detected between Indian aspirations and the pretensions of the unruly Irish at home.

At the Lucknow session of the Congress party in 1916 a resolution was passed asking Britain to confirm that it was her 'aim and intention . . . to confer self-government on India at an early date'. Britain ignored the resolution but could not afford to ignore the aspirations behind it and the unrest that they provoked. Britain was at war with the Turks, and needed substantial elements of the Indian Army to help to dismember the Ottoman Empire, particularly in Mesopotamia, which bordered India's frontiers. Muslim opinion in India was at risk of being alienated by the fact that Britain was fighting Muslims in the Ottoman Empire.

This combination of British need and Indian demand resulted in a perception that things were on the move. In the Imperial Legislative Council* in 1917 Madan Mohan Malaviya said that the War had 'put the clock . . . fifty years forward'. It was assumed that there would be extensive reforms after the War to allow Indians to take their legitimate part in the administration of their own country.

Austen Chamberlain was the current Conservative Secretary of State. He wanted India to be represented at the Imperial War Conference. That seemed not unreasonable, as so many Indians had been taken half a world away to die in the mud and the cold of the Western Front and in Palestine and Mesopotamia; but when India took her seat at the conference (and later at the peace conferences, and when she became a founding member of the League of Nations) she did so in a very different capacity from the other dominions who also debated at the peace conferences and founded the League of Nations. *Their* sacrifices had been made in their capacity as self-governing and independent countries, voluntarily part of the British Empire. India was no more than an administrative component of Britain's overseas possessions and her representatives at these international gatherings were Britain's puppets. She was only there to increase British influence.

Chamberlain devised a formula to allow India to participate at a conference which was really designed for the self-governing parts of the Empire. He defined the British goal in India as developing 'free institutions with a view to ultimate self-government within the empire'. But that was not enough. Publication of the report of the Mesopotamia Commission had already underlined the fact that the governance of India needed attention.

---

* The viceroy ruled with the assistance of a Legislative Council from 1861 until the end of the British period. The 1909 Morley–Minto Act provided that there were to be sixty members, of whom twenty-seven were elected. For the first time there were Indian members. The Government of India Act of 1919, the Montagu–Chelmsford reforms, which are discussed in Chapter 5, made further changes. The Council became bicameral, with the Imperial Legislative Assembly and the Council of State respectively the lower and upper houses. Until the end the powers of members were so limited, and the extent of the viceroy's powers to suspend and override the body so extensive, that its role was nugatory.

In May 1917 Chamberlain asked the Cabinet to give their attention to the matter. Nothing happened for two whole months, until Montagu succeeded Chamberlain as Secretary of State and Chelmsford became viceroy. They combined to enact what are known as the Montagu–Chelmsford reforms, a significant change in the system of India's government which will be looked at in detail in Chapter 5.

As an indication of how the British regarded India, and before leaving India's sacrifice in the Great War, let us note what happened to her sons who did not return. Britain took trouble in deciding how to bury her own dead. The response was the creation of the Imperial War Graves Commission, and the principle of uniform headstones: comradeship in death. It was an important part of the plan that no distinction should be made in regard to rank, and that individual names should be recorded. The names even of those whose bodies were never found were recorded, as on Lutyens' great Memorial to the Missing of the Somme at Thiepval, those 72,000 men with no known grave.

But not for the Indian dead. For them there were just mass graves, no individual names. Many Indians fought in Mesopotamia, in Britain's extremely successful campaign against the Ottoman Empire. The Memorial of the Missing at Basra lists by name all the British soldiers, about 8,000, and the 665 Indian *officers*. But 33,222 Indian other ranks are no more than numbers.[13]

5

THE MONTAGU–CHELMSFORD REFORMS

India After the War

Before we look at the Montagu–Chelmsford reforms themselves, we start with a brief look at the condition of India as she came out of the war. That condition was deplorable. The Khilafat, or Caliphate, Movement promoted the Muslim cause and demanded the restoration of the Caliph, formerly the Sultan of Turkey. It was supported by Hindus as well as Muslims. Symbols of British rule were attacked. The Punjab was in disarray. The publication of *Mother India* by an American writer, Catherine Mayo, revealed the appalling social conditions in India, particularly for women. The 1921 census showed that about two million girls were married before the age of ten and about 100,000 of them widowed before the same age. No progress had been made towards Indianising the armed services of the subcontinent. By 1930 there was still not one Indian officer with a rank higher than that of captain.

All this was despite responses from Britain that amounted to platitudes or bad faith. The Conservative Stanley Baldwin said that India would be given 'equal partnership with the dominions – in the fullness of time'. Lord Birkenhead proclaimed that India would become 'on equal terms an honoured partner in the free community of British dominions'.[14] We shall see how far this was from what Birkenhead really believed.

The Indian Civil Service was in its time a finely engineered administrative machine. Its members, originally entirely British, were an elite. It was a career that allowed able Britons of relatively modest backgrounds to enjoy a status and a standard of living that would have been impossible at home. But its ethos was not of buccaneers looking for a quick killing. On the contrary, it was infused with ideals of service and duty, and many who entered the service did not live to enjoy a moneyed retirement in the Home Counties. Overgrown cemeteries throughout the subcontinent are full of their graves and those of their wives and – poignantly – of countless infants. In the course of the 1920s Britain committed itself to Indianising the civil service, the police and the army. As ever, appearance and reality diverged. The 1924 Royal Commission on Indianisation recommended that the Indian Civil Service should be half Indian – *only* half Indian – by 1939, the police force half Indian by 1949. Indianising the army was more difficult and senior British officers resisted more generous proposals. Finally, in 1926 it was agreed that the army would be *half* Indianised by 1952!

The number of British applicants wanting to join the Indian Civil Service fell dramatically from 1919 onwards. As Denis Judd puts it, 'That members of Britain's ruling elite so evidently believed that the game was up in India must be set against the contra-indication that the British Government, British industry and British investors were conspiring to fight a rear-guard and covert action against Indian demands for self-rule'.[15]

Montagu

It is now, with the publication of the Montagu Declaration in 1917, that the study of the last thirty years of British rule in India begins. In 1917, the Secretary of State for India, Edwin Montagu, made a Declaration about the government's policy for India. On a quick reading it appeared to reassure nationalists. Looked at more closely it promised much less. What did it mean? No one in Britain could agree on that. Twelve years later, the viceroy of the time, Lord Irwin, made a further Declaration, which I shall examine later, to clarify the earlier one. As we shall see, the intent of Irwin's Declaration was equally obscure.

In the history of twentieth-century politics, Edwin Montagu's image is a sad and lonely one. He was not hugely distinguished intellectually, but he was a good debater who turned aside from possible careers in medicine and law in order to concentrate on political ambitions that would finally remained unfulfilled.

He was a protégé of Asquith and served as his parliamentary private secretary when the latter was first chancellor of the exchequer and then prime minister. In 1910, after he had been just four years in parliament, his mentor appointed him Under-Secretary of State at the India Office under Morley and Crewe. He made himself a master of the Indian brief

and visited the subcontinent in 1912. In domestic politics what interested him were rural issues and land reform. That may have been the link
with India. He hoped, unrealistically, to become viceroy when Hardinge
retired in 1915. He declared that Indian problems attracted him and his
only ambition was to go to India as viceroy. That ambition was never
fulfilled, but in 1917 he became Secretary of State. He had already
revealed something of his thinking, saying that 'the government of India
is too wooden, too iron, too inelastic, too antediluvian for the modern
purposes we have'.[16]

As Secretary of State he made a second, and extensive, tour of the subcontinent, the first visit by a Secretary of State (other than Crewe, briefly in
1912 when he accompanied the king to the Delhi Durbar). He went for this
protracted stay to learn from the people he met, mostly officials and Anglo-
Indians. He consulted closely with the viceroy, Lord Chelmsford.

But his time as Secretary of State was cut short – and indeed his political
career was ended – when he was obliged to resign from office in 1922.
Under pressure from the Indian Government he had published a memorandum which criticised the London Government's revision of the Treaty of
Sèvres, which gave effect to the dismemberment of the Muslim Ottoman
Empire. The prime minister, Lloyd George, was closely associated with the
treaty, which was unpopular with Indian Muslims. Montagu published the
memorandum without consulting his Cabinet colleagues. This was not just
a technical breach of collective Cabinet responsibility: it was disloyalty to
his boss. Montagu had no constituency of support, and without Lloyd
George he was lost.

He had already alienated his early sponsor, Asquith, by defecting to the
Lloyd George camp after the latter dethroned Asquith. Not only that: he
had married Venetia Stanley. The prime minister was besotted by Venetia,
thirty-five years his junior and the friend and contemporary of his daughter Violet; he wrote to her three times a day, including missives written
while his Cabinet considered the carnage on the Western Front. At the
same time Montagu's criticism of General Dyer, who presided over the
Amritsar Massacre,[*] alienated Tory backbenchers, who had a soft spot for
the general. They felt too that he was soft on Gandhi's non-cooperation
policy. He even lacked support within his domestic circle. Relations with
his very rich banking father were tempestuous because he did not embrace
Orthodox Judaism. In an example of the unpleasant undertones of

---

* Dealt with in Chapter 7.

anti-Semitism of these days, he was sometimes called 'Monty Jew' and faced anti-Semitic attacks – partly because of his family's supply of silver to the Indian Government, something with which he had no connection. His marriage didn't amount to much. His relationship with Venetia had never been straightforward and she was as indiscreet in her relationships after she was married, including one with Beaverbrook, as she had been before. He was unhealthy as well as unhappy and died young, at the age of forty-five.

That was Montagu. The fruits of his time as Secretary of State were the report which he and the viceroy, Lord Chelmsford, produced in July 1918, and his Declaration, which was a separate but associated initiative, a statement to the Commons in August 1917 (in which Curzon had a hand). This statement had a pivotal significance, and it was repeatedly looked back to throughout the following thirty years. Supporters of Independence read it as a promise of Independence. Supporters of the status quo looked to the last words of the critical sentence as a guarantee that not much would change:

> The policy of His Majesty's Government, with which the Government of India are in complete accord, is that of the increasing association of Indians in every branch of the administration, and the gradual development of self-governing institutions with a view to the progressive realization of responsible government in India *as an integral part of the British Empire.*

I have stressed these last words, because they meant that India was not, as might have been thought from the foregoing part, to be self-governing and independent. Unlike the dominions, a self-governing India was to be bound in permanently to the Empire, without the sovereign freedom of choosing her own destiny. Curzon's revisal of the Declaration was to insert 'responsible government' in the place of what had originally been 'self-government'. Thus there were to be self-governing institutions, not a self-governing country. There is an immense difference. Any village in the Empire could have responsible government.

The Declaration was examined repeatedly in the years that followed, and it is clear that many had taken it at face value and were subsequently embittered because so little followed from it; but while the Declaration had some significance as the first British proposal for any form of representative government in a non-white colony, it meant less than appeared to be the case.

Chelmsford

Frederic Thessiger, Lord Chelmsford, was a former London County Councillor. As viceroy he sought to give the Indians some of the rights that he had enjoyed on the London County Council. He had also governed Queensland and New South Wales. His appointment to the latter post was less interesting than that of Lord Lundy (who, according to Hilaire Belloc, 'was too freely moved to tears and as a result ruined his political career'.)*

In 1916 Chelmsford advised London that the Government of India needed to be more responsive to Indian opinion. At the end of 1916 he recommended various practical measures, including the announcement of Britain's plans for the future, together with a specific indication of the practical steps that would be taken. Montagu thought Chelmsford was unimaginative, but Chelmsford was constrained. He had to sell his reforms to senior officials in India and those they spoke to in England. He had only limited success in this and he was frustrated by the lack of enthusiasm amongst Indian politicians.

Montagu–Chelmsford

The crystallisation of the collaboration between Montagu and Chelmsford, the Montagu–Chelmsford reforms, were put into effect in the autumn of 1919 as the Government of India Act. The proposals represented a movement forward from Morley–Minto. The electorate was extended to five and a half million for the provincial authorities and one and a half million for the central legislature. (The total population of India at the time was probably around 263 million.) An amnesty for political prisoners was announced. The legislation created what was known as diarchy – two separate and parallel levels of government. Eleven provinces were created in which 'safe' responsibilities in areas such as Public Health, Education and Agriculture were placed in the hands of elected Indian representatives. Irrigation, police, press, finance and justice were 'reserved' from these devolved powers. The

---

*   We had intended you to be
                 The next Prime Minister but three:
                 The stocks were sold; the Press was squared;
                 The Middle Class was quite prepared.
                 But as it is! . . . My language fails!
                 Go out and govern New South Wales!'

officials who administered the reserved functions might be Indian but what was certain was that they were appointed by the viceroy.

Examinations for the Indian Civil Service were now to be held in Delhi as well as in London. The Viceroy's Legislative Council was enlarged, and domestic portfolios were given to Indian ministers. Every ten years there was to be an enquiry to establish 'whether and to what extent it is desirable to establish the principle of responsible government'. This provision was important. But for this, there would never have been the later Simon Commission, which as we shall see had important policy repercussions.* These repercussions were ultimately more important than anything within the reforms themselves.

Montagu–Chelmsford meant that three out of the seven ministers on the Viceroy's Executive Council were now Indian. The enlargement of the electorate created Indian majorities in various councils. But the appearance was misleading. Critical roles were retained by the British. Legislative majorities were not of great consequence when the viceroy could still veto legislation, suspend councils and if he wished fall back on arbitrary power enforced by the armed forces. Devolution was intended to tie in a larger element of society to the status quo. But giving powers to local communities meant that energies which could have been applied against the imperial power were dissipated into communal rivalry. Division always worked for Britain's benefit. Lord Birkenhead, whose time as Secretary of State will be discussed later, didn't like the reforms, and thought that the communal division meant that they would never work. 'All the conferences in the world cannot bridge the unbridgeable.'[17]

The Thinking behind the Reforms

The effect of the First World War was to propel the white dominions towards complete Independence and equality with Britain. The effect on India was not the same. In 1869 Sir Charles Adderley divided the British Empire into national settlements such as Canada and Australia, which were bound for self-government as a matter of right; and, by contrast, 'occupations for use', which were, as the label suggests, entirely utilitarian, to be disposed of when they no longer served their purpose. There the Crown governed absolutely: 'Stations merely occupied for war, debtors of trade, and subjects of inferior race are fitly so governed'. India, however, fitted into

---

* See Chapters 11, 13 and 14.

neither category. It would neither be abandoned nor would it move toward self-government.

The trigger for further change contained in Montagu–Chelmsford ('Montford' as it was sometimes called), arose from its criticism of parliament's failure in the past to make timely alterations in the system of government of India. The need was to create a system of administration which would put an end to talk of Independence, far from paving the way to it. As Adderley had said, self-government was not the general and invariable aim. In Montford despotism proclaimed its benevolence.

The Reaction in India

The remarkable Annie Besant, an English Fabian, the first woman publicly to support birth control ('checks on conception'), was also a very prominent Theosophist. Because Theosophy had its headquarters in India she arrived there in November 1893. From the outset she combined her work in Theosophy with support for the nationalist movement. In December 1917 at the party meeting in Calcutta she became the first woman president of Congress. In the same year, just after the Declaration of 1917, she met Montagu at the Viceregal Lodge. 'If only,' he said, 'the Government had kept this old woman on our side! If only she had been well handled from the beginning!'

Mrs Besant dismissed the reforms scathingly: they were 'unworthy of England to offer and India to accept'. But it was all that India would get. Even the support of the parliamentary Labour party had its limits. Labour had liberalised the 1919 legislation to an extent, but fell significantly short of advocating dominion status. Progress was to be by Fabian 'stages'. India was not yet fit for self-government. India must not be able to secede from the Empire.

Gandhi saw British 'reforms' as being ultimately aimed at the consolidation of British power. When Reading arrived as viceroy in 1921, he pressed Gandhi hard on his policy of non-cooperation. '[E]ventually he stated that he had some time ago arrived at the conclusion that every action of the government which appeared good, and indeed was good, was actuated by the sinister motive of trying to fasten British dominion on India. This was his answer to all the arguments about the new reformed councils, and in my judgement is the root cause of his present attitude to the government.'[18]

Furthermore, in March 1919, just six months before the reforms were announced, the Defence of India Regulations Act, which had been passed during the war as an emergency measure, was extended indefinitely under the Anarchical and Revolutionary Crimes Act, known as the Rowlatt Act, and based on the recommendations of a committee on revolutionary activity in India chaired by a judge, Sir Sidney Rowlatt. His report recommended that activists should be deported or imprisoned without trial for up to two years. Having possession of seditious newspapers, for instance, would be adequate evidence of guilt. Most of the Rowlatt recommendations stemmed from proposals put forward by the Indian police.

Chelmsford accepted Rowlatt's advice, and the necessary legislation went through the Executive Council against the opposition of the twenty-two elected Indian members, a minority over-ruled by the official nominees. The Act was wide-ranging. In addition to imprisonment without trial, it contained various powers to deal with anything the authorities chose to regard as terrorism or revolutionary tactics. There was strict control of the press and trial without jury. Gandhi described the Rowlatt Act as 'the Black Act'. There was widespread opposition to it – which perversely triggered its application.

The limited scope of the Montagu–Chelmsford reforms and their accompaniment by the Rowlatt Act meant that Indians who had expected a huge advance as a reward for their contribution to the war felt that they had been cruelly let down. No wonder: they faced oppression on an unprecedented scale. It was as an expression of this reaction that Gandhi unleashed *Satyagraha*. *Satyagraha* was a subtle and elusive Gandhian doctrine which I shall try to explain in the next chapter, but for hundreds of thousands of people its predictable practical consequences were riot, disorder and violence. Alongside the mystic force of *Satyagraha*, Gandhi also announced a nationwide *hartal* on 6 April 1919. *Hartal* is a traditional expression of mourning or regret. All shops and schools and offices were closed, public transport came to a standstill, and in the streets demonstrations and processions took place. Gandhi had started something which he could not control, and the violence appalled him. He admitted to an Australian journalist in April 1942 that Indians were unable to appreciate what *Satyagraha* required.[19] I'm not surprised.

A much bigger blow to any hopes that might have attended the reforms resulted from the massacre at Amritsar on 13 April 1919, more usually known in India as the Jallianwala Bagh massacre.* That ill-judged exercise of force and the measures associated with it were such a calamitous lapse of

---

* See Chapter 7.

British policy that it deserves a chapter of its own, in order that we can understand the extent to which it destroyed confidence in British good faith. The insubstantial nature of the reform agenda was exposed by the Rowlatt legislation and its spectacular crystallisation at Amritsar. A sincere move towards liberalisation could not exist concurrently with this degree of oppression.

The Reaction in Britain

But what seemed too little in India seemed too much to the forces of repression in Britain. There some retired officials and those with a financial interest in India opposed the modest moves and formed the Indo-British Association, which worked against the reforms.

Like the unofficial Indo-British Association, the official Conservative response was negative. Baldwin, who became prime minister in 1922, announced a policy of something like stasis and said that the Conservative party would favour progressive self-government, but firmly within the British Empire. He said that the progressive grant of constitutional liberties was dependent on the loyalty of the people and that the Conservative party was opposed to agitation and extremist methods. This was how the party went forward to the general election of October 1924, which it won. This was the grudging and negative basis under the various governments that controlled Indian policy during the coming years.

6

GANDHI

With the arrival of *Satyagraha*, it's appropriate to return to the man who deployed this weapon.

The simple loincloth that Gandhi affected in the latter half of his life contrasted with the formality of the young man's dress when he trained as a lawyer in London wearing a high white collar and dark suit, learning to play the violin and, deliciously, taking dancing lessons. He was a stretcher-bearer at Spion Kop during the South African War. He had been invited to go to South Africa in 1894 by Indian immigrants who had established the Natal Indian Congress and wanted his help in the struggle to protect their rights. By 21 January 1914 he had achieved an agreement with Jan Christian Smuts, the Boer commander who accommodated so well to the outcome of the South African War that he was a member of the British War Cabinet in the First World War and of the Imperial War Cabinet in the Second: he was the only man to sign treaties that ended both of these global conflicts. In 1914 he was well on his way to becoming Prime Minister of the Union of South Africa, which he was from 1919 to 1924, and again from 1939 to 1948.

Gandhi returned to India in 1914 wearing his egregious cotton garment and surviving on vegetables, to argue first for home rule and then for total Independence. The British never really understood him, never knew whether he was a saint or a hypocrite. He made them uncomfortable. When he left South Africa, Smuts said, 'The saint has left our shores – I sincerely hope forever.'

Gandhi was entirely comfortable with the English and claimed to like them. He said that if he had been English he would have done exactly what the English were doing in India. 'Hardly ever have I known anybody,' he said, 'to cherish such loyalty as I did to the British constitution . . . [In my youth] I vied with Englishmen in loyalty to the throne.'

In India his authority became immense. The unsophisticated believed him to be almost a god, performing miraculous feats. Even the sophisticated acknowledged his spirituality. There were few as sophisticated as Nehru, who said that 'the unknown looked out at us through his eyes'.

Satyagraha is an impossible word to translate and not easy to understand. Gandhi first used the weapon in South Africa. *Satyagraha* means literally 'the force of truth'. It's sometimes referred to as the truth-force, but a better description is the force of the absence of force: non-violence, the withdrawal of cooperation, boycott. It was based on some elements of Indian tradition, but Gandhi moulded it to meet his requirements. He looked to the Christian requirement of turning the other cheek, the philosophy of Tolstoy, who said that evil could best be countered by non-violent resistance. He looked at the techniques of the suffragettes in Britain. He was insistent that there should be no physical threats. His followers were to stand aside from *participation*. They were not to pay taxes. They would decline honours and positions of authority. They would not cooperate. For Gandhi himself it was personalised in his fasts to death, which the cynical British pointed out never actually got there.

As ever, there is the faintest whiff of hypocrisy: although *Satyagraha* was specifically non-violent, it inevitably led to violence. The application of the Rowlatt Act was a reaction to Gandhi's campaigns. He prescribed opposition to the Act and that opposition was manifested in violence and met by further repression and savagery.

Satyagraha was most famously expressed in the Salt March which he undertook in March 1930. Initially Congress thought the plan was laughable, and Irwin, the viceroy, dismissed the scheme as a 'silly salt stunt'. 'At present,' he said, 'the prospect of the salt campaign does not keep me awake at night.'

Salt is a basic necessity of life. The bounty of the ocean was there for the taking, where the Arabian Sea lapped on the shores of Gandhi's native Gujarat. But it was taxed under the 1882 Salt Act. The tax mattered: it bore heavily on the poorest and it made up 8.2 per cent of the government's revenues. The campaign was exquisitely simple. Gandhi had a letter delivered to Irwin by one of his British supporters, Reginald Reynolds, saying that as the government would not support a scheme of immediate full dominion status, he had 'to convert the British people through non-violence and thus make them see the wrong they have done to India'. He then set off on a march of twenty-four days, covering 240 miles. Everyone understood the message. Crowds of up to 60,000 people came out to meet him, and he addressed huge meetings.

On 5 April he reached the seashore, where he boiled some water and made some salt. The government held its hand; but when he told Irwin that he now planned to advance on a government salt plant, action was taken. Gandhi was arrested as he slept in a mango grove and was imprisoned without trial at Poona. He had achieved what he wanted. There was no direct gain from the campaign, but it was enormously effective, simple to understand and a vivid metaphor that raised tension, charged the atmosphere and demonstrated the power of civil disobedience.

7

AMRITSAR

The Jallianwalla Bagh is a large open area in the centre of Amritsar, the Punjab city which contains the specially sacred Sikh shrine, the Golden Temple. Gandhi's reaction to what happened there was that cooperation with a 'satanic regime' was now impossible.

Amongst the pilgrims at the shrine on 13 April 1919 were some protestors complaining about two arrests. Emotions were strong but there was no particular threat to public order. Then without warning, in the middle of a recital of a poem about liberty, armoured cars arrived. Soldiers deployed, knelt, took aim and, on command, shot into the crowd at point-blank range. They continued to fire. Six minutes later the soldiers withdrew. Three hundred and seventy-nine people were dead and another 1,500 were wounded.* At ten o'clock the curfew came into force and the dead and wounded were left in the Jallianwalla Bagh, the latter watching the pi-dogs gnawing at the remains of the former.

The events at Amritsar are well remembered in India and are not forgotten in Britain, but in neither India nor Britain is it now possible to recapture the impact which the news of the massacre had at the time. Though far from the only, or even the worst, of those atrocities which are inevitable when one country is held down by the force of another, Amritsar seemed particularly to undermine Britain's moral authority and her right to rule. The massacre illustrated the deficiencies of British administration; and it informed the political debate, so far as India was concerned, for the rest of the British period.

Tough measures had been taken to control India during the First World War. The use of the iron hand after the war was confirmed under the Rowlatt Act. The response to Gandhi's advocacy of his all-India *Satyagraha* was

---

* Some accounts report much higher figures.

widespread protests which, alarmingly, were not confined to one community: indeed Amritsar, in the Punjab, had a mixed community of Hindus, Muslims and Sikhs. Britain was rattled by Gandhi's success. His methods could not be countered by the usual techniques of buying support from local potentates, playing one group off against another or, finally, even by use of superior firepower. Gandhi had mobilised the subcontinent, and Britain was no longer dealing with either irregular groups of Dacoits or elite Oxbridge-educated barristers in three-piece Western suits. The British were particularly irritated because they couldn't understand Gandhi, couldn't categorise him. Harold Laski wrote almost admiringly: 'It was fascinating to see Gandhi at work and try and penetrate his secret. It comes, I think, from what the Quakers call the inner light – the power of internal self-confidence which, having established its principles, is completely impervious to reason. At bottom, it is an incredible egoism . . . sweetened by an indescribable sweetness of temper . . . [T]he basis of it all is, I think, the power of an ascetic over Eastern minds who resent the feeling of inferiority they have had for 150 years'.[20]

The most violent protests against the Rowlatt Act took place in the Punjab, where Sir Michael ('Micky') O'Dwyer, the tough but able administrator whom we have already briefly met, and who was to be shot at Caxton Hall in 1940, was Lieutenant-Governor. O'Dwyer had used aircraft against rioters in April 1919 when he was attempting to quell the effects of Gandhi's *hartal*. The violent effects of non-violence were dramatic. Chelmsford watched and reflected: 'Dear me, what a nuisance these saintly fanatics are!' O'Dwyer thought that for the Punjab, and solely for the Punjab, only the severest punishments would work. Chelmsford confirmed that these methods were 'only for the Punjab'.[21]

This was the background in the Punjab. Within the province, the worst riots were in Amritsar, where the senior British officer, with a confusingly similar name, Brigadier-General Reginald Dyer, C.B., was under orders to impose martial law and restore civil order. He had been described twenty years earlier, at Staff College, as 'happiest when crawling over a Burmese stockade with a revolver in his mouth'[22] (presumably *carried* in his mouth, rather than pointing into it). If that was his disposition twenty years earlier, it was not sweetened by the fact that in 1919 he was suffering from a painful illness.

O'Dwyer was in a highly nervous state. He thought that only the most extreme action could avert a second mutiny. Dyer too thought that the *hartal* was no more than a cover for a mass rising. It has to be remembered that the first mutiny was only little over half a century in the past, a horror story which informed the thinking of the small number of British officers who had to control a vastly superior number of native troops. Young officers were constantly reminded of the need for vigilance. There was real tension. In Amritsar five Englishmen had already been killed and there had been an assault on an English woman missionary on her bicycle. In the aftermath, Indians were forced to crawl on their stomachs down the road on which she had been attacked, saluting if they saw a white face.

For what he did at Amritsar Dyer has rightly been execrated by history. But he wasn't universally execrated at the time. The split of opinion was remarkable, and not only English commentators applauded what Dyer had done. Churchill thought the episode monstrous. But Churchill, as usual, was stirred by a sense of humanity which was beyond the reach of many of his contemporaries: the House of Lords passed a motion in Dyer's support. There is a myth widely accepted in modern India that the House of Commons presented him with a Sword of Honour. They did not do so, though the officials of the Golden Temple enrolled him into the brotherhood of Sikhs: Dyer went out of his way to court the Sikh community after the massacre.

The Scottish judge, Lord Hunter, was sent out to India to investigate the massacre. Churchill was Secretary of State for War and it fell to him to review the Hunter report. As always, when charged with authority, Churchill was far more moderate and considered than when he had no responsibility. Churchill said that Amritsar had been a 'monstrous event' and rejected the suggestion by Dyer's fans that he had saved the Empire. He readily concluded that Dyer was a dangerous man who could not be left in post. The Cabinet agreed, and their decision that Dyer should be summarily dismissed was conveyed by Churchill to the Army Council. The decision didn't meet with universal approbation. Sir William Joynson-Hicks, who was to be remembered as 'Jix', an outstandingly blinkered and reactionary Home Secretary, said that Dyer had been the country's saviour and that he was universally supported by Europeans. Jix was one of the less attractive members of an unattractive generation of Conservative MPs, but his views were not unique.

Dyer was recalled to England. He and his supporters, including O'Dwyer, demanded a legal enquiry to review the Hunter Commission's conclusions. The Commission had condemned public floggings for such minor offences as 'the contravention of the curfew order, failure to *salaam* to a commissioned officer, disrespect to a European, taking a commandeered car without leave, refusal to sell milk, and for similar contraventions'. Dyer was censured because he hadn't warned the demonstrators that they must disperse; nor had he offered medical aid. The enquiry upheld Hunter and rejected paranoid allegations of conspiracy by 'Bolsheviks and Egyptians'.

Dyer had supporters amongst the *Morning Post*'s readers and the Right-wing members of the Conservative party. In a seven-hour debate in the House of Commons on 8 July 1919 he was vigorously defended by Sir Edward Carson. India was 'seething with rebellion and anarchy', there was an underground conspiracy to destroy the Raj and drive Britain out of Egypt.[23] The House supported the government and not Dyer by 247 votes to 37. But the *Morning Post* raised the sum of £26,000 (a million pounds today) for Dyer: the views of MPs were not necessarily the view of the country at large. The most famous contributor to the fund was Rudyard Kipling. In the House of Lords debate a majority of peers supported Dyer and passed the motion supporting him to which reference has been made. No legal action was taken against him. He remained on half pay and received his army pension. After Dyer returned to England he suffered a stroke. Immensely poignantly, and revealing a sensitivity which history does not ascribe to him, he told his family that he didn't want to get better. 'I only want to die, and to know from my Maker whether I did right or wrong.'

The situation *was* dangerous and complex, and no one was wholly in the right. The Gurkha soldiers who shot down the demonstrators in Amritsar later admitted that they had enjoyed killing people of the plains.[24] In the same way, Hindus were delighted by air raids on Pathan villages on the north-west frontier in 1923. In 1943 an army enquiry concluded that, 'the Sikh would at heart enjoy nothing more than hammering Muslims'. But Britain's use of force was grossly excessive, the consequence of fear. As well as the massacre itself on that unlucky day, 13 April 1919, there were numerous public floggings and humiliations under martial law between 11 April and 9 June 1919.

Nehru thought that what had happened was 'absolutely immoral, indecent [and] to use public school language, it was the height of bad form'.[25] Others took a different view. For instance, the writer Maud Diver, an English woman who lived in India, now almost forgotten but in the first half of the twentieth century a best-selling author, and a favourite of the royal family, said: 'Organised revolt is amenable only to the ultimate argument of force. Nothing, now, would serve but strong action and the compelling power of martial law . . . At Amritsar strong action had already been taken . . . The sobering effect of it spread in widening circles, bringing relief to thousands of both races.' Both races? Maud Diver believed that many Indians agreed with her that a strong crackdown would restore the peace they wanted:

> No more trouble here or at Amritsar . . . Martial law arrangements are being carried through to admiration . . . and in no time the poor deluded beggars in the city were shouting – 'Martial law *ki jai!*' [Long live martial law!'] – as fervently as ever they shouted for Gandhi and Co. One of my fellows said to me; 'Our people don't understand this new talk of *Committee ki Raj* [government by committee] . . . Too many orders make confusion. But they understand *Hukm ki Raj* [government by order]. In fact, it's the general opinion that prompt action in the Punjab has fairly well steadied India – for the present at least.[26]

On 18 April 1919, five days after the shooting at Amritsar, Gandhi called off the *hartal*, but two months later he said that it had revealed 'a new force and a new power – a force that could prove irresistible under every conceivable circumstance provided that the truth was on our side'. Gandhi could be extraordinarily naive or hypocritical or both. Although he was the paramount advocate of non-violence, the only reason that his new force and new power was so effective was that it resulted in violence. He claimed that Indian crowds were 'the easiest in the world to disperse' but even he was patently not capable of controlling the rioters.

The significance of Amritsar was that it revealed what many privately knew, that British rule depended finally on nothing but force. That revelation was powerful ammunition for Congress, but it was not something which the diehards wanted to hear. Montagu was against Dyer and defensive of the notion that there was some sort of contract between Britain and India which would see the latter steadily advancing. He satirised the thinking of Dyer's supporters: 'An Indian is a person who is tolerable so long as he obeys your orders, but if he thinks for himself, if once he takes advantage of the educational facilities which you have provided for him, if once he imbibes the ideas of individual liberty which adhere to the British people, why then you class him as an educated Indian and an agitator'.[27]

Montagu was speaking in a House of Commons debate in July 1920 in which he was attacked for being too weak with Indian rioters and too tough with Dyer. Although the government won the vote, the degree of support for 'firmness' was interesting. And it is doubtful whether Montagu's liberal view of the rights of the educated Indian were widely shared in the country at large. In December 1919 the *Spectator* argued that 'The Oriental temperament and Oriental History' disqualified Indians from self-government. British rule was an 'absolute necessity'. It protected Hindus and Muslims from each other and India from propulsion into anarchy at the hands of 'the Brahminical caste'.[28] O'Dwyer continued to support Dyer until his death at Caxton Hall and always argued against any further fooling around with self-government, the desire for which was contained within a small and unrepresentative group. 'The fact is, as everyone, British or Indian, who understands the East will, if honest, admit, that 99% of the people do not care a brass farthing for the "forms of government" about which Congress lawyers are always arguing'.[29]

8

Rufus Isaacs, First Marquess of Reading

Rufus Isaacs, who succeeded Chelmsford as viceroy, is a fascinating example of the small but significant phenomenon of men from unlikely and slightly suspect backgrounds who flourished in public and political life in Edwardian England despite the superficial appearance of a society regulated by convention. Other examples were Horatio Bottomley, Max Aitken (Lord Beaverbrook). F.E. Smith (Lord Birkenhead), could be squeezed in too, even if he was slightly more of an insider.

Isaacs was the son of a fruit importer. His grandfather, a Hispanic Jew, had emigrated from Spain to London. He had a disruptive and unconventional background at school, from which he was removed at the age of thirteen to start working in the family business. Legend said that he ran away to sea; he didn't, but his father tried to instil some discipline into the boy by having him sign up for a two-year apprenticeship on a sailing ship. Rufus refused to sign but agreed to complete a round voyage as a ship's boy. Discipline didn't suit him: he jumped ship at Rio de Janeiro. He was caught and continued the voyage, touching land at Calcutta his first contact with the subcontinent which he was later to rule.

After further adventures, including being 'hammered', declared insolvent, on the floor of the Stock Exchange with debts of £8,000 and coming close to banishment to Panama, he found his vocation and settled to a career at the Bar, where he was immensely successful. By the turn of the century he was a young QC, earning the phenomenal amount of £30,000 a year – about £3.25 million in today's money. He became a Liberal Imperialist MP (Liberal Imperialists were a significant group within the Liberal party, who rejected what they saw as the soppy deviations of the party under Gladstone and opted for tough policies centring around what was called the New Imperial Spirit), and in turn Solicitor General, Attorney General and Lord Chief Justice, where he might have spent the rest of his life.

But during the First World War he enjoyed a number of high-profile diversions – he was a sort of unofficial ambassador to the United States when America's material aid was much needed. He said that the war spoiled him. Thereafter he found it difficult to settle back into judicial life. At the end of the war, walking in Paris with F.E. Smith, who had just been appointed Lord Chancellor by Lloyd George at the age of forty-seven (the *Morning Post* had described his appointment as 'carrying a joke too far'), Isaacs, aged fifty-nine, said: 'Look here, F.E., you and I are both too young to be stuck for the rest of our lives as judges. Let's go back to the Bar!' He didn't do that, but he did press for various appointments, including that of Ambassador to the United States. In 1921 his frustration ended when Lloyd George appointed him viceroy. 'I will never look at another law report again if I can help it!'

He went to India meaning well. He wanted the Indian Councils Act to achieve its objective of promoting the role of Indians in the civil service and army, and he was convinced that discrimination on the grounds of race was the central flaw in British rule. But despite his genuine liberalism and determination to be fair – he met both Gandhi and Jinnah, the rising spokesman for the Muslims, and visited Amritsar in an attempt to atone for the massacre – he had to face the fact that the 1919 Act had hopelessly failed to meet nationalist aspirations.

Isaacs, who became Marquess of Reading, had numerous meetings with Gandhi. He proposed 'full provincial autonomy' in return for a suspension of *Satyagraha*. Gandhi refused to buy. Finally, in 1922, Reading was obliged to have Gandhi arrested and tried for sedition, for which he was sentenced to six years in prison. In February 1922, Gandhi announced the suspension of civil disobedience. He was released from prison in February 1924, and turned his attention from directly political matters to practical improvements in the welfare of the peasant classes, campaigned to liberate the Untouchables, and promoted the production of hand-spun cloth. His attention soon returned to politics.

Reading struggled over the Hindu–Muslim split. He could see that it was dangerous. Although it was tempting to use the existence of the two communities to divide and rule, he perspicaciously pointed out to the Secretary of State in 1924 that conflict between the two communities was 'a menace to the peace of the country. Some, doubtless, think that this is to our advantage, but, if so, they fail to realise how grave the situation might become if the feeling between the two communities continues to grow more antagonistic and fails to be alleviated by some compromise'.[30]

On the other hand, the London Government had been concerned by the effect of the Lucknow Pact of 1916, which established some cooperation between Congress and the Muslim League. Since then Muslims had been active in the campaign against the British. Britain considered that the Muslims were their natural supporters and Reading was told to separate the two communities. At his request Gandhi gave up his support of the Khilafat movement, the Muslim campaign of support for the Ottoman Caliph. He also intervened to secure what turned out to be only a brief commitment from two leaders of the campaign, the Ali brothers, that they would stop inciting violence. Reading declared that he had started to work for a 'collapse of the bridge over the gulf between Muslim and Hindu'.[31] That was what the government wanted, even if the final outcome of the policy would be so terrible, far worse than he had foreseen.

He had retreated from the benign light of liberalism to the traditional device of setting Hindus and Muslims, the Congress party and the League respectively, against each other in order to neutralise both. But not entirely: he was concerned by Muslim reaction to Britain's dismemberment of the Ottoman Empire. This prompted the dispatch of the message to Montagu, formally requesting a revision of the post-war Treaty of Sèvres, which gave effect to that dismemberment. This was the document that Montagu published without authority from the prime minister. That ended Montagu's career, and Reading came close to resignation himself. When his term in office did come to an end a viceroyalty which had started with creditably good intentions had delivered very little.

9

BRITISH POLITICS BETWEEN THE WARS

Although there is little evidence of imaginative policy initiatives by British governments, it would be wrong to put the blame entirely on the political classes. Public opinion was not greatly interested in India and there was certainly no general support for the cause of Independence.* These were years in which crude racism was rife. It is wrong to apply retrospective judgements in such matters, and there is no point in criticising a society at one point in time for views that would be abhorrent in later years. The fact is, however, that in the 1920s and 1930s the majority of voters, insofar as they had any view about Indians, would not have thought them capable of governing themselves, either then or perhaps ever.

Indeed, some of the political classes were in advance of the body of the electorate. Many of the Indian leaders, particularly Congress party politicians, were highly educated, sophisticated and in some ways members of the same world as British politicians. Gandhi, Nehru and Jinnah, for instance, whom we shall meet often in these pages, were markedly Westernised: all three were barristers, members of English Inns of Court. Such men could talk easily to viceroys, cabinet ministers and parliamentarians. In particular there was a bond between Congress and the Labour party. Both sets shared liberal assumptions and progressive views and thought they understood each other.

There was an important qualification to this apparent cohesion of views. Despite the apparent consensus, there was an underlying difference of approach between the British politicians and the Indian. However agreeable the weekends at Boar's Hill, outside Oxford, where Nehru stayed with E.J. Thompson, the high-minded authority on India and father of the Marxist historian, E.P. Thompson, or when Congress party politicians joined Stafford

* Evidence of this is contained in figures quoted in Chapters 32 and 42.

Cripps, whose intimate association with India will emerge in these pages, at his home, Goodfellows in Gloucestershire, different views about the tempo of change amounted at the end of the day to a chasm in political terms. The Labour men were essentially gradualists. Some were members of the Fabian Society and some were not, but all were constitutionally incrementalist. They were prepared to amend the institution of Empire, but not to tear it down. The Indians, on the other hand, might appear to be governed by reason and logic, but for them Independence and home rule was something of the heart, something spiritual, which would justify inconsistency, obfuscation and deviousness. Thus some of the bitterest passages in this story are perhaps not conflicts between, say, Churchill and Gandhi, but the hurt that followed when Cripps and Nehru each felt betrayed by the other.

Moreover even Labour party politicians of this period, however progressive, should not be thought of as men and women of markedly advanced views. The '30s particularly, but the '20s too, made up an unappealing era: W.H. Auden described the later years as 'a low dishonest decade'. Its stifling conservative character perhaps derives mostly from the Conservative party, which tended to dominate parliament in these years, but the Labour party was not at its best either. In order to understand the political background against which the Indian debate took place, it's helpful to look briefly at the politics of these years.

When the economist J.M. Keynes looked at the parliament of 1918, he described the members as 'A lot of hard-faced men who'd done well out of the war'. This was the parliament which followed the 'coupon election'. During the war the Liberal party had split. Lloyd George brought down Asquith, his party leader, and became prime minister in a coalition with the Conservatives. At the end of the war the coalition gave an endorsement – the 'coupon' – to its candidates, who won a landslide, with a majority of 238, at the expense of the Asquithian Liberals. But Lloyd George and his Liberal followers were the prisoners of the Conservatives, who dissolved the coalition in 1922. At the 1923 election a minority Labour Government was formed under Ramsay MacDonald. A year later the Conservatives came back under Baldwin with a large majority of 210. Although Labour were returned in 1929, they were again a minority government. Following the 1931 election Labour entered into coalition with the Conservatives in the National Government.

MacDonald remained prime minister, but he was, as Lloyd George had been, at the mercy of the Tories. MacDonald had been an active member of one of the Royal Commissions that had visited India, and he had many

Indian friends. As a result he regarded himself as an expert in Indian matters. Despite that, he shrank from taking any positive decision about India, although he was ready enough to take negative ones. Gandhi had no time for him.[32] Churchill called him 'The Boneless Wonder'.

MacDonald was attacked, as Lloyd George had been, by party purists who declined to follow him into coalition: he was vilified as the Lost Leader. The idealism of the Socialist dream was betrayed. In 1935 the National Government was again returned, but openly under Conservative leaders, Baldwin and then Neville Chamberlain. The Tory hegemony persisted until – and indeed through – the war.

So for most of these years the hard-faced men who'd done well out of the Great War remained in power. The Liberals, who in 1906 had appeared to be the party of the century, were fractured, insignificant and demoralised. It appeared that they would never again enjoy power. After the 1931 election Lloyd George was personally increasingly marginalised. Additionally, he had just undergone a serious operation. He saw Sir Herbert Samuel elected Liberal leader and Sir John Simon leader of the Liberal Nationals, and reflected that he himself 'might be only half a man, but he was a bloody sight better than two Jews'. This racist pronouncement came from the former prime minister whose government had issued the Balfour Declaration.* Simon, as a matter of fact, was not Jewish. The Labour party, the obvious beneficiaries of Liberal decline, had split, and thus handed power to their class enemies.

The good fortune the Conservatives enjoyed did not make them a nicer party. They were rattled by events. There was a continuing fear of Communism. It had brought down the Russian Government in 1917 and radical movements had swept away the old regimes in Germany and throughout the Habsburg Empire. Capitalists were worried by events at home. Between 1914 and 1920 trades union membership doubled to 8.3 million. The general strike of 1926, when 1.3 million workers struck in support of the 1.2 million coal miners who had been locked out by their employers, and which was supported by the Comintern in Moscow, was seen by many people as an omen of the civil dissolution that lay ahead. In the following year the government legislated to outlaw general strikes.

---

* In 1917 the British Government issued a declaration promising to attempt to establish a national home for the Jewish people in Palestine. The document was the work of many hands, but Balfour, who was a convinced Zionist, was very much behind it, and the declaration has always borne his name.

Britain's post-war economy had never boomed as had those of other countries, including the United States, and was all the more vulnerable to the
effects of the Great Depression. By the start of the 1930s more than 3
million people were out of work – in some areas 70 per cent of the work-
force. It was impossible not to be aware of a sense of national decline. The
heavy industries that had been the motor of Victorian prosperity were
stricken, and the ship-building industry, the symbol of British industrial
pre-eminence, was manifestly in crisis.

In an inward-looking period, most people contrived to avert their eyes
from what was happening on the continent of Europe, It was indicative of
the mood of the times that, sapped by the sacrifices that had been made in
the Great War, and by the disappointments of the peace, the reaction to
the rise of fascism was to seek to buy off aggression, rather than to address
it with force.

And yet, for those in secure employment the 1930s were comfortable
years. Even the historian A.J.P. Taylor, no friend of the Conservative governments of the times, said that for people in his position, deflation made life
good. The middle and upper-middle classes, whom the Conservatives represented, were snug and smug. The fact that they could perceive threats to
their comfort made them all the more determined to secure it. With hindsight we can see that governments of the period were embarking on state
control of industry and other measures that would change the nature of
society. But at the time what was more obvious was how much society was
not moving forward to secure the advances that had been made during the
war, how in some respects it even moved back. In 1918 the Representation
of the People Act gave women the vote – but only women over thirty, and
not even all of them; it was ten years before women and men were placed on
equal terms. These were years of repressive interference with individual
liberty by illiberal politicians like Joynson Hicks.

Within the Conservative party these were times of strict control, when
any exercise of individual freedom of thought or of action was discouraged.
Many MPs had served in the forces during the War, and a regimental ethos
permeated the party. Hierarchy was important in a way that is difficult to
imagine today. There was a premium on conformity. Particularly in
Chamberlain's time, the Whips exercised a powerful control over members.
Dirty tricks and smear tactics were used. But overt interference was rarely
needed. Party disloyalty was equated to a lack of patriotism. It was for this
reason that in the early months of the Second World War, those rebels who
believed that Chamberlain's approach would mean defeat for their country

repeatedly held back from striking a blow. In the Norway debate, which brought him down, Chamberlain thought it was enough to say that he had his friends in the House. He was wrong, but all the same, many of the Tories who voted against him, men who had faced the horrors of the earlier war without flinching, went in to the lobby with tears coursing down their faces.

It was against this political background and in this sort of House of Commons that the issue of Indian Home Rule was debated. It is hardly surprising that it did not receive a favourable wind. The debate centred round three interwoven issues in an historical passage that dominated political life for the next eight years and that focused and defined positions – particularly within the Conservative party – as only a few others, Free Trade and Imperial Preference, later Suez and later still Europe, have done. They were the Simon Report, the Irwin Declaration and finally the Government of India Act, 1935. Before studying these political developments we shall have a look at some of the personages with whom they are associated.

IO

LORD IRWIN

With the appointment of Edward Wood, Lord Irwin, as viceroy, we start on the run of viceroys who held office from 1925 until Independence in 1947. Apart from Goschen, who was only a temporary appointment, there were five: Irwin, Willingdon, Linlithgow, Wavell and Mountbatten. Some were more able than others, and two weren't particularly able at all, but because of the press of events they were all important in the history of the subcontinent, and their attitudes and prejudices mattered.

Irwin confuses newcomers to Indian history because he has so many names. He started out as Edward Wood, and in time he inherited his father's title and became Lord Halifax. Before then, because of the convention that the viceroy should be a peer, he was created Baron Irwin of Kirby Underdale, and it is as Irwin that he is generally known in relation to Indian history. When his father died, at the age of ninety-four, in January 1934, Irwin duly became Viscount Halifax, and in May 1944 he was created 1st Earl of Halifax.

Even if his father was only a viscount, Wood or Irwin or Halifax came from an emphatically aristocratic background. His maternal grandfather was the 11th Earl of Devon and his great-grandfather was Earl Grey of the 1832 Reform Bill. He had a family connection with India: his paternal grandfather, Sir Charles Wood, was the second Secretary of State for the subcontinent.

At a personal level, as well as a nominal one, Irwin was confusing too. His nickname, 'the Holy Fox', was a pun on his title, but it alludes to the dominating importance in his life of religion, and his affection for hunting. He hunted in India; when he was Ambassador to the United States he hunted there; and in England he was master of the Middleton Hunt. In 1937 he even accepted an invitation from Göring to attend a hunting exhibition in Berlin and, appallingly, to *shoot* foxes in Pomerania.

His piety was very real. His father was President of the English Church Union for a total of fifty-eight years and worked all his life for the Union of the Christian Churches. Irwin and his father were very fond of each other. Of four sons, only he survived childhood. The two men became very close and Edward inherited his father's Christian commitment in full measure. At Oxford he gained a first in Modern History and was elected to a fellowship of All Souls'. His first book was a biography of John Keble.

The 'Holy Fox' nickname also hints at his political acumen. Despite his high principles, and without ever compromising them, he had occupied important ministerial offices before he was appointed viceroy in October 1925, and on his return from India, as well as helping Samuel Hoare with the drafting of the India Bill, he returned to high office, becoming, finally, Foreign Secretary on Eden's resignation in 1938. His name has always been associated with appeasement, but he was in reality more realistic and less committed to the policy than Chamberlain.

This was the enigmatic figure who could have been prime minister in 1940 if he had chosen even to hint that he wanted the job. The king and the royal family wanted Halifax; Chamberlain wanted Halifax; the overwhelming majority of the Tory party wanted him. At the decisive meeting with Churchill and Chamberlain he put the critical question, 'Can you see any reason, Winston, why in these days a peer should not be prime minister?' Churchill turned his back, looked out on Horse Guards Parade and maintained that silence which he subsequently described as seeming 'longer than the two minutes which one observes in the commemoration of Armistice Day'. It was Halifax himself who broke the silence, not to say that he thought himself the better qualified, but to declare that as a peer, he could not carry out the responsibilities of prime minister. Earlier in the day he had told Rab Butler, his parliamentary Under-Secretary, that he felt he could do the job, but when it came to the bit he did not have the stomach to push his claim: literally – he felt sick at the prospect and that morning, when the chief whip had been unable to decide between him and Churchill, 'my stomach ache continued'.

The most filial of sons, Edward Wood initially refused the appointment as viceroy, knowing that if he left England for five years he would be unlikely to see again his father, a frail eighty-six-year-old. His selection was endorsed by the king himself, although at first he had suggested his own friend, Douglas Haig, a totally unsuitable man for an essentially political role. Two weeks after he declined the appointment Wood was invited by Baldwin to come to Chequers with his wife. This time he felt that his duty and destiny could not be avoided, and his father had already made his views clear. In October 1925 Wood accepted the appointment, and his father wrote to him most touchingly: 'My dearest, dearest Edward, you have been all your life, and now more than ever, the pride and joy of my life'.³³ Wood was raised to the peerage and went to India as Lord Irwin. He was seen off from London by the prime minister, representing the king, the Archbishop of Canterbury, Winston Churchill and old Lord Halifax.

Irwin was an impressive figure, very suitable viceroy material. He was six feet five inches tall (exactly the same height as Lord Linlithgow, his successor (if we ignore Goschen)). Although he had been born with an atrophied left arm (like the Kaiser) and no left hand, he did not allow that to bother him. He enjoyed the pomp of the office but he was not a stuffy man and did not depend on it. He had the confidence of his aristocratic, Whiggish background, and he and his wife (Lady Dorothy Evelyn Augusta Onslow, the daughter of the 4th Earl of Onslow) were amused that Lady Reading, the wife of his predecessor, was saddened to be abandoning the trappings of viceregal life.

Like Reading, he came to India with great goodwill towards the native population. Indeed, he probably had more genuine sympathy for Indian aspirations than any of his successors until Wavell. This conciliatory approach was criticised as 'Irwinism' by fellow Tories who opposed his policies. Yet, coupled with that goodwill and sympathy there was a determination that India should remain within the imperial fold.

Irwin saw his mission as being to humanise the government of India after Reading's inflexibility. His first remark to his military secretary was, 'We are in India to keep our tempers'. The Irwins were less pompous than the Readings – to the extent, that is, that they expected only three curtsies from ladies in the course of an evening, rather than seven. All the same, during the cold season of 1930 Lady Irwin noted that they never dined with fewer than forty-two people at the table. When tennis was played there were fifteen men to pick up the balls.³⁴ Despite the seriousness of his purpose, his routine at Delhi was not burdensome. He started work at 9.30 after an early ride once or twice a week with the Delhi hounds. He worked till lunchtime and did not resume work thereafter until he'd played tennis or gone for a further ride.

Irwin had a degree of respect for Motilal Nehru, father of the future prime minister, Jawaharlal Nehru, and the Congress *éminence grise*. He considered the old man to be subtle and resourceful, not unreasonable, yet as committed to Independence as Gandhi. Like Gandhi, Motilal Nehru gave up elegant English clothes in favour of flowing robes of white home-spun, but he wore his robes with style and majesty, and his Gandhi cap was made by Scott of London.

The viceroy had much less time for Nehru *fils*, Jawaharlal. Despite the latter's background (Harrow, Cambridge and the Inner Temple), and despite the reputation he was much later to have as a statesmanlike leader of his country and of the uncommitted nations, at this time he seemed to Irwin irresponsible, loving trouble for its own sake, a revolutionary rather than a politician, a disastrous influence on the youth of India.[35] Even those who later worked closely with Jawaharlal Nehru, like Cripps and Mountbatten, had to overlook the outbursts of an excitable man who was always ready to focus on trivialities and to take offence.

The Times pointed out that Irwin had no experience of oriental problems and as far as the public were aware had never displayed any special interest in Indian affairs. That may be true, but it was perhaps no disadvantage to him: he approached the problem of the subcontinent with a fresh mind. He rejected the notion of an essentially long-term trust which was to be redeemed at some day in the distant future. Irwin said that Birkenhead, the Secretary of State, had in mind a timetable of 600 years.[36] Irwin himself concluded after studying the problem on the ground for about three years that the timescale should be a short to medium one. Birkenhead of course was politically as remote from Irwin as two men in the same party could be. Most newspapers reacted very favourably to Irwin's appointment. Birkenhead's comment on this to his friend Reading, the outgoing viceroy was fairly typical: 'How much better in life and how much more paying it is to be blameless rather than brilliant . . . '[37]

What Irwin was saying about Birkenhead's timescale was that the prejudiced forces of darkness wanted to postpone change for as long as possible – ideally for ever – rather than see Britain's standing diminished. But even informed and liberal men were thinking in terms of perhaps two generations. In 1933, for instance, Sir Malcolm Hailey, with the experience of having governed two provinces, envisaged that Britain would still be in India in fifty years – and at no great cost: 'an increasing measure of Indianisation of the Army'.[38] But such assumptions weren't shared with the Indians.

As Irwin's views evolved, he had found himself increasingly at odds with his first Secretary of State and political master, Birkenhead – Churchill's best friend, but with even more die-hard views. Unlike Churchill and Birkenhead, Irwin did not see the conflict between Hindus and Muslims either as a justification for continuing British rule or a device for sustaining it. We shall see how he reacted to – and indeed directed – the important political developments of the following years. But first I want to look a little more closely at Birkenhead.

II

F.E. SMITH AND THE SIMON COMMISSION

In the rapid political changes of the time, two secretaries of state followed Montagu between March 1922 and November 1924, when Baldwin formed his second government and appointed the Earl of Birkenhead, the former F.E. Smith.

In the 1920s Smith soared across the political sky, a dazzling comet, finally and sadly falling to earth, burnt out, broken by drink, financing his elevated lifestyle by second-rate journalism. He had vices in abundance and was quite without morality. At the same time, he was intellectually prodigious, capable of working very hard and effectively, and not without a redeeming loyalty. When Churchill was asked in the darkest days of the Second World War whom he would have liked to have in an ideal Cabinet at that time, he included 'F.E. in his prime'.

In relation to India he was an unashamed spokesman for the Tory diehards. As usual with Birkenhead, however, there are surprises. In the House of Lords he spoke out to condemn those who supported General Dyer, the man who ordered his troops to fire at the crowds in Amritsar, a villain in the Commons but a hero in the Upper House.

He regarded the Congress party with contempt. He saw its representatives as self-serving, ambitious politicians who had no true identity with the illiterate Indian masses. He could have been looking in a mirror. He 'felt a profound mistrust of the Montagu–Chelmsford policy and a belief that India would not be capable of supporting dominion status for centuries'. He told Reading that he, alone in the Cabinet, distrusted and opposed the report. 'To me it is frankly inconceivable that India will ever be fit for dominion self-government'. His views were shared by many. His danger lay in the fact that he could express his anachronistic opinions with elegance, and defend them with a wit which was amongst the most dazzling of the time.

The Indian Councils Act provided that its effectiveness was to be reviewed after ten years. Initially Smith did not think that the review would lead to any extension in political liberties to the Indians.[39] At this stage he intended to let the full statutory period of ten years run before the reforms were reconsidered. But as time passed he became concerned by the prospect of a change of government in advance of the review. He wrote to Reading in 1925:

> I always had it plainly in mind that we could not run the slightest risk that the nomination of the 1928 Commission should be in the hands of our successors. You can readily imagine what kind of Commission would have been appointed by Colonel Wedgwood and his friends. I have, therefore, throughout been of the opinion that it would be necessary for us, as a matter of elementary prudence, to appoint the Commission not later than the summer of 1927 . . . Having a regard to the political contingencies in this country, we must keep the nomination of the personnel of this Commission in our own hands. In this matter we cannot run the slightest risk. My present view, therefore, is . . . that we shall in any event, playing for safety, be driven to nominate the Commission in the middle of 1927 . . . [Ante-dating the Commission would please the Indians and] would deprive us of nothing valuable. We can play with the time as we want.[40]

He dismissed the need to wait the full ten years with typical flippancy: 'Wise men are not the slaves of dates'.[41] His decision put an end to the period of relative quiet which Reading's policies had created.

Birkenhead took care in appointing the Commission which was to carry out the review. He decreed that there should be no Indians on it; indeed he restricted the membership to members of parliament. He wanted to avoid a mixed-race Commission on which Indians and Labour party members might coalesce. He went on to pack the Commission with his own nominees.

The chairman who gave his name to the Commission was Sir John Simon. From the start of his time in politics Simon seemed marked out for a brilliant career, after a first in Greats (Classics, Ancient History and Philosophy) at Oxford, Presidency of the Union and a Fellowship of All Souls'. Indeed, he went on to occupy three of what could in his day still be referred to as great offices of state (Foreign Secretary, Home Secretary, Chancellor of the Exchequer) without the hint of oxymoron which is attached to the use of the phrase today. He went on to add the Lord Chancellorship to his collection. Yet despite having the most powerful of intellects and, according to Hore-Belisha, 'the most remarkable head in London', he moved through political life without leaving a trace of his progress either on events or on his contemporaries. He was acutely shy – all the more so after the death of his first wife, from which, despite a second marriage, he never truly recovered – and sought to ingratiate and insinuate himself where he could not achieve true friendship.

In his politics he was firmly on the Right of the Liberal party and would finally have been a Conservative except that Churchill kept him out. His legacy as a lawyer, as Lord Chancellor and as editor of *Simon's Income Tax*, is greater than his political legacy. That is not what he would have wanted. His report has been said to constitute a brilliant analysis of the problems of Indian administration. That may be so, but before it was even published Irwin superseded it (with the Declaration which I shall describe later), and very few have ever read it.

Irwin, now viceroy, agreed that Indians should be excluded from the Commission. Birkenhead's reasons for not having any Indians on the Commission were self-evident. Irwin's were of course more complicated. He thought the whole problem fraught with difficulties: Indians on the Commission might vote with British Labour MPs; Muslims and Hindus would fight; the appointment of some Indians would irritate others. He could also see the argument that a parliamentary commission should consist solely of members of the houses of parliament. In the event, the Commission was described even by *The Times*, edited by Irwin's friend, Geoffrey Dawson, as 'a terribly weak team'.* Irwin had little time for Simon, and delighted F.E. by reporting that Sir John spent half an hour looking for each ball he lost on the golf course.

The decision to have no Indians on the Commission, to have an enquiry by foreigners into India's capacity for self-government, was made against the advice of many. It should have been no surprise that Indian parties boycotted the Commission. Congress called upon Indians not to cooperate with the Commission and organised demonstrations against it. The Commissioners were met with banners reading 'Simon go back'. Initially

---

* The members included Attlee (a reluctant member, who realised why the Commission had been appointed early), Lord Burnham, a Tory diehard and proprietor of the *Daily Telegraph*, Lord Strathcona, a close friend of Baldwin, and George Lane-Fox, a Tory who rode to hounds and was Irwin's brother-in-law.

the Muslim League had said that it would cooperate, and the assumption was that Congress would therefore do so too. In an attempt to bring Congress to heel, Birkenhead ordered that any meetings between Simon and 'representative Moslems' should be publicised in order to 'terrify the immense Hindu population by the apprehension that the Commission is being got hold of by the Moslems and may present a report altogether destructive of the Hindu position'. In the event, even the Muslim League divided, a part joining in the Congress boycott.

For a time Irwin said that even with hindsight he continued to feel that a parliamentary commission was less dangerous than a mixed commission would have been. He had failed to see how unacceptable it was to even moderate Indians in the late 1920s that their destiny should be decided by the group of foreign tourists who arrived in Bombay on 3 February 1928. Eventually he, unlike Birkenhead, realised that a mistake had been made. It was one which he continued to regret and which he attempted to repair by issuing the Declaration which bears his name and which overshadowed Simon so effectively.

After the Commission got home, Birkenhead wrote to Irwin, reporting that Simon had 'conceived a deep resentment at the antics and demeanour of the *Swarajists*, and an absolute contempt for their political capacities'. (The Swaraj party was a hard-line breakaway from Congress, let by Motilal Nehru, which flourished briefly following Gandhi's temporary abandonment of civil disobedience in 1922.)

The report, largely written by Simon himself, but with a lot of help from Attlee and Findlater Stewart, the Permanent Under-Secretary for India, was published in two instalments on 10 and 24 June 1930. It rather quaintly said that 'the British parliamentary system . . . has been fitted like a well-worn garment to the figure of the wearer, but it does not follow that it will suit everybody . . . British parliamentarianism in India is a translation, and in even the best translations the essential meaning is apt to be lost'. From the perspective of Indian politicians, the report was negative rather than positive. Rather than offering responsible central government, it proposed a limited extension of control to the Provinces. It recommended the abolition of diarchy. It did not envisage the transfer of power to Indians, and the emergency powers to be retained by governors limited the significance of even provincial autonomy. To Irwin's great regret, it did not mention dominion status at all, even as a desired but distant possibility. Baldwin thought this would keep India happy, and within the Commonwealth.[42]

12

EMPIRE, DOMINIONS AND COMMONWEALTH

The Irwin Declaration was much more important than the unread Simon Report. It was all to do with the promise of 'dominion' status which Irwin offered. What was dominion status?

Dominion status was not favoured by the men with whom Birkenhead had packed the Simon Commission. He had decreed that 'the phrase "dominion status" should not be used to describe the ultimate goal' of British policy. It had 'been laid down that dominion status means "the right to decide their own destinies", and this right we are not prepared to accord India at present, or in any way pre-judge the question of whether it should ever be accorded'.[43] But Irwin was soon to be free to enunciate views that were more in keeping with his liberal outlook.

Many of the promises that were made to India were based on an imprecise, almost metaphysical concept, the idea of moving from being part of the Empire to becoming a dominion or a member of the Commonwealth. An analysis of the three institutions reveals how indistinct each one was in theory and how different they were in practice. It was impossible for two people to be sure that they meant the same thing by the same words. Misunderstandings arose even when both parties acted in good faith. This chapter will briefly trace the development in these institutions, and show how confused the development was, how amorphous the institutions.

Birth of Dominion

There is no precise moment which can be marked as the birth of the dominions – or indeed the death of the Empire. The Durham Report in relation to Canada in 1839 is a possible starting point. Or again, in 1887 the first colonial conference took place in London. It was attended by the prime ministers of all of the self-governing colonies together with United Kingdom ministers. It was the first of a series of conferences that finally morphed into stately family gatherings, the Commonwealth prime ministers' conferences that started after the Second World War and continue to this day, commemorated by a picture of the queen surrounded by her smiling prime ministers.

And 1907 also has its claims. In that year the word 'dominion' came to be adopted to describe the self-governing colonies. The demeaning implication of *colonial* conferences was replaced by *imperial* conferences. Dominions weren't to be thought mere colonies. But the distinction between dominions and Crown colonies was pretty flimsy: the dominions were still under something very like a colonial yoke. The Acts which set up the constitutions of Canada, Australia and South Africa reserved legislation for the consideration of the British Government, and the British Government had an overriding power to disallow legislation, whether it was reserved or not.

Lewis 'Loulou' Harcourt, who was Colonial Secretary in 1911, may have been franker than most when he said that it would 'never do to *say* we [the British] are too good for them, and that they are not good enough for us', but there is no doubt that the British representatives were conscious of the gap between *their* sophistication and the down-to-earth manners of the horny-handed sons of toil from the wastes of Canada or the outback of Australia. Dick Sedden of New Zealand was said never to have read a book – common enough amongst British prime ministers a hundred years later, but at that time a stark contrast with a particularly intellectual generation of politicians such as Arthur Balfour, John Morley, Haldane. Morley was particularly irritated by the rambling, homespun speeches of the Australian Alfred Deacon: he feared that they were in danger of turning the 1907 conference into 'the greatest bore that was ever known'.[44] The dominions, and the self-governing colonies before them, were alienated by the condescension of the British, and at every conference there was a tacit alliance between all or some of the former against the latter.

How Independent Were the Dominions?

It is important to remember that although the dominions were regarded and certainly regarded themselves as self-governing, their independence was limited in two respects. First, in terms of the Colonial Laws Validity

Act of 1865, the British parliament could set aside any colonial legislation which was incompatible with British constitutional practice or English common law. This provision was rarely invoked, but its existence reduced the imperial legislatives to the status of county councils. More importantly, Britain paid for almost all of the costs of the Royal Navy, which defended the dominions. The dominions themselves had tiny and insignificant fleets until only just before the First World War. The consequence was that they couldn't claim to be in charge of their own defence policies or their foreign policies.

Foreign affairs were reserved to the grown-up parliament, the imperial parliament, as Westminster was often called. In 1895 the Colonial Secretary sent a despatch to the overseas governments: 'To give the colonies the power of negotiating treaties themselves . . . would be equivalent to breaking up the Empire into a number of independent states'.[45] In what was called the 'imperial sphere' the Crown acted on the advice of British ministers. Gradual evolution took place. Canada took a large part in shaping this movement – to the extent that the Canadian prime minister, St Laurent, declared in Ottawa in 1950, 'Canadians have virtually shaped the Commonwealth as it exists today'. But the process was *very* gradual. It was pretty demeaning to be a dominion before the Second World War.

An important imperial conference was held in 1917, but it left behind it unfinished business: the clarification of the constitutional position of the dominions after the war. The dominions did not even have the power to sign the Peace Treaties. In 1921 Lloyd George declared in the House of Commons that the British Foreign Office was 'the instrument of the policy of the Empire'. When war with Turkey over Chanak appeared likely in the following year, he sent a telegram to Commonwealth governments asking for troops in the expected war. He even allowed news of his request to appear in the press. This time, unlike 1914, the Commonwealth premiers were of independent mind. Mackenzie King of Canada said that he couldn't think of sending troops without consulting his parliament and indeed he didn't really think that the situation justified summoning parliament. Smuts took the same line in South Africa and the Australian Prime Minister said that 'we cannot blindly submit to any policy which may involve us in the war'.

At the 1923 Imperial Conference it was accordingly agreed that each Commonwealth country had the right to negotiate and sign treaties. Britain would only ratify treaties at the request of the country concerned. The need for definition of the nature of the Empire was addressed tentatively in the Balfour Report of 1926, and more comprehensively in the Statute of Westminster of 1931. The Balfour Report set out the conclusions of a Committee on Inter-Imperial Relations. Balfour presided over the Committee 'with a smile like moonlight on a tombstone', according to Hankey, the creator of modern British Cabinet government and Cabinet Secretary under five prime ministers, 'somewhat deaf, occasionally somnolent' but 'with intellectual powers unimpaired by the years'. (He had been described in much the same terms twenty years earlier.) The report concluded that there was no point in attempting an imperial constitution but that the components of the Empire could be described as 'autonomous communities within the British Empire, equal in status, in no way subordinate one to another in any respect of their domestic or external affairs, though united by a common allegiance to the Crown, and freely associated as members of the British Commonwealth of Nations'. This statement leaves a number of questions unanswered. Did 'free association' mean that dominions could withdraw if they wanted? Was there a common Crown, or a Crown for each dominion?

The Balfour report was important, because its definition of the relationship between the dominions was carried forward into the legislative structure of the Statute of Westminster in 1931. The Statute remains the basis of the relationship between Britain and the dominions: the British parliament has no authority to legislate for a dominion unless with its consent, and no law passed by a dominion parliament can be invalidated by reference to English law or British practice. The changes were welcomed by Ireland, South Africa and Canada. New Zealand and Australia were less enthusiastic. R.G. Casey, for Australia, said 'We've torn down a castle to build a row of villas'. This nostalgic view was of course echoed by Churchill. The Statute of Westminster was 'pedantic, painful and, to some extent, almost repellent'.

And while the Statute of Westminster might be thought to have inaugurated an entirely new phase in imperial relations, its effect was qualified by the fact that several dominions explicitly requested that it should not affect them unless or until their parliaments chose to apply the Statute. The Statute was not adopted in Australia and New Zealand until 1942 and 1947 respectively. Some dominions, like South Africa and the Irish Free State, were anxious to throw off the shackles of imperial control without delay – and indeed rather resented the fact that it required an Act of the British parliament to achieve their object. Others were in no hurry to distance themselves from Westminster.

Was the 'dominion status' offered to India in the Irwin Declaration the pre- or post-Westminster status? The two were very different. No one knew and Britain was careful to leave the answer well wrapped in obscurity.

Commonwealth: the End of Empire?

As we shall see later, towards the end of British rule in India there was much thought given to the question of whether an independent India would remain in the Commonwealth. In reality in 1947 that institution was nebulous and metaphysical. Although the word 'commonwealth' had been bandied about for centuries, the legal Commonwealth was not created until 1949, three years before Queen Elizabeth II's accession. All the same, it is largely her creature. It was launched as the Empire was dismantled, but there was no clear vision about what it was for. The queen, in her capacity as Head of the Commonwealth, and not as Queen of the United Kingdom, has had her own vision, a familial concept with a distinctly liberal bias, in which the Commonwealth countries are seen as individuals and not as clones of Great Britain.

That view has given shape to something shapeless, a vague searching for a means of continuing the Empire under a different name. We shall see that it was briefly envisaged as a means of maintaining Britain's spheres of influence, securing her defence interests and promoting her economy as the imperial nexus came adrift. Within Britain, the queen's policy in relation to the Commonwealth is not noticeably appreciated by politicians. The queen as Head of the Commonwealth is entitled to take a broader view than she can as Queen of Great Britain. Thus, she was against Eden's policy over Suez. Three years later she unusually sent a telegram to Harold Macmillan, congratulating him on his 'winds of change' speech in South Africa: 'the Queen was very interested and much impressed'. She was against Heath over the resumption of arms sales to South Africa, and against Mrs Thatcher when she opposed sanctions against South Africa. The queen's non-participatory role in British politics is a reflection of British constitutional theory; she has a different role in Commonwealth constitutional theory. British politicians don't like that.

The far Left regard the Commonwealth as an imperial fossil and some on the Right take a slightly similar view. Enoch Powell regarded the Commonwealth as a 'relic of a bygone system, . . . [a] gigantic farce'. The Foreign and Commonwealth Office is not particularly concerned about the Commonwealth, even though William Hague promised to 'put the C back into the FCO'. It is reported that the Foreign and Commonwealth Office has tried to dissuade newly emerging African nations from taking the queen as their Head of State and has urged them to become republics. Visiting ministers from Commonwealth countries are neglected by the Foreign and Commonwealth Office, which concentrates on the greater powers and European states.

13

THE IRWIN DECLARATION

The idealistic Irwin and the amoral F.E. Smith had made strange bedfellows. But Birkenhead's fears for the outcome of the 1929 election were well founded. The Conservatives were replaced by a minority Labour Government under Ramsay MacDonald. Before then Birkenhead had already been succeeded briefly by Lord Peel, and the latter was now replaced by William Wedgwood Benn.

Benn was a brave man. He started out in the Yeomanry in the First World War and fought at Gallipoli, where he was awarded the DSO. Then he moved to the Royal Naval Air Service and was awarded the DFC. Although sixty at the outbreak of the Second World War, he volunteered for the RAF as a Pilot Officer, ending as an Air Commodore. He was the father of Tony Benn. He started his political career as a Liberal, but changed to Labour in 1928. As Secretary of State for India he had the advantage of bipartisan support from the Conservatives under Baldwin.

Benn was then a very different man from F.E. Smith. The Irwin Declaration was the combined effort of a Labour Government (always more favourable to Indian aspirations than the Conservatives) co-habiting with a high-minded Conservative viceroy. The purpose of the Declaration was 'to restore faith in the ultimate purpose of British policy'. It was confirmation that the progress of India's constitutional development, starting from the Montagu Declaration of 1917, would be the achievement of dominion status, whatever that meant. There was no indication of timescale, but in the meantime, at any rate, it was planned that the provinces would be autonomous in domestic affairs.

The motive behind the Declaration was Irwin's divergence from Birkenhead and his wrecking policy. Irwin saw through the Simon Commission. He could see clearly enough, as Rab Butler did, that '[Birkenhead] appointed a small parliamentary commission, composed exclusively of the conventional and the then obscure, and chaired by the highly legalistic Liberal Sir John Simon'.[46] Irwin realised it was designed to impede rather than promote the movement to responsible government. At the cost of humiliating Sir John Simon and strangling the outcome of his Commission's labours at the moment of parturition, he moved the debate forward.

The Simon Report represented Conservative thinking and Irwin thought that Baldwin had ducked responsibility by taking advice from Austen Chamberlain: 'His contact with India is distant and his mind is always that of a log of wood.' When Irwin had received a telegram from his Conservative colleagues discouraging him from setting out his own views, he could see that party policy reflected the views of Austen Chamberlain, Peel, Birkenhead and Eddie Winterton. He complained that the Simon Commission had not understood anything of India's problems and was concerned that its conclusion should now be taken so seriously by members of his own party. Fortunately his own party was in opposition, and he told Benn that if he were in Britain he would not want to see the Conservative party returned to power.

The initiative for the Declaration came, then, from Irwin. But in Benn he had a sympathetic political master. The viceroy returned to London in the summer of 1929 for his mid-term leave to argue his case. He had welcomed the arrival of the Labour Government and the prospect of a more liberal policy in India: 'I am not much afraid of any policy they are likely to produce as long as the direction remains in the same hands as at present. I think Wedgwood Benn ought to be rather good for the India Office. He is a nice fellow, keen, with lots of ideas, and a gentleman, which is worth a good deal. He was always rather a friend of mine in the House of Commons, and I have no doubt I shall get on with him'.[47] He found that Benn wanted, as he did, to make a gesture which would restore confidence amongst the political classes in India. He discussed matters in London with Geoffrey Dawson, editor of *The Times*. Motilal Nehru had already told Dawson that a commitment to dominion status was the sort of gesture that was needed. As well as canvassing this idea, Irwin suggested a tripartite meeting of representatives of the UK parliament, the princes and British India. A Round-table conference was planned for October 1930 and in the meantime political detainees would be released.

All this was going on before the Simon Commission issued its report. Indeed, a series of discussions took place between Irwin, Simon and MacDonald, when it was agreed that the Commission's terms of reference would be adjusted to allow them to deal with the Round-table conference. Though in reality the Simon Commission was now an irrelevancy, that was not to appear to be the case.

Simon was initially cautiously in favour of the statement about dominion status, but then decided to oppose it. The Liberals were against it. Lloyd George, who had presided over the 1917 Declaration, was only interested in India as a means of political mischief. Reading, Irwin's predecessor as viceroy, was against the Declaration unless Simon was in favour of it. Baldwin, on the other hand, at this stage more liberal than the Liberals, was ready to accept Irwin's advice.

Baldwin greatly respected Irwin. He was perhaps closer to him than to any of his other colleagues. The two men shared values and a High Church faith. Baldwin wrote to Irwin in 1927, 'Profound reflection has convinced me that the one unselfish action of my life was persuading you to go to India. I have missed you every day'.[48] Baldwin had started out without any great interest in India, certainly not looking beyond the 1919 settlement, but Irwin liberalised him, and he came to see the achieving of a more progressive settlement as a crusade for which he was prepared to fight – facing Churchill and elements of the Conservative party, at the cost, if need be, of his political career. 'The speeches of 1930, chiefly that of 12 March, were a vivid signal that he was prepared to fight his own party rather than wait for their conversion.' But it was for a practical objective that he was prepared to fight, not the ideal of the nationalists, not Independence. It was, he said, 'to keep India within the Commonwealth'.[49]

As Leader of the Opposition, Baldwin was briefed personally by Irwin about the Declaration and subsequently received a letter from Downing Street when he was on holiday. The letter said that the viceroy and Secretary of State wanted to take steps that would have 'a sedative effect on the Indian situation'. Baldwin was never averse to sedation: 'I am prepared to concur in what is proposed and you may rely on my doing all that is in my power to secure the unanimous support of my party,' he said, without knowing what it was in which he was concurring.[50] He was however concerned that the authority of the Simon Commission should not be eroded. He wrote to Snowdon, acting as prime minister in MacDonald's absence abroad, and asked him not to allow the authority of the Commission to be impaired. The message was sent on to Irwin, who said that it was too late to back down as Indians were aware that the Declaration was coming.

On 13 October 1929, when the *Sunday Times* leaked the news of the Declaration, Baldwin realised how far he had become detached from his party's position. He had made the mistake of not keeping in touch with his colleagues. Now, ahead of the Declaration, the Conservative Shadow Cabinet met in an uncomfortable room in the party offices in Palace Chambers on 23 October. At this meeting Baldwin was formally told what he must have known already: that Simon had been against the Declaration for the past month. He backtracked and said that he had only approved of the Declaration in his personal capacity and not as party leader, whatever that meant.

The hostility he faced was led by Birkenhead and Austen Chamberlain. In a letter to Irwin in 1928, before the Statute of Westminster had been passed, but when the theory behind it was already accepted, Birkenhead had said (as had been noted in relation to the Simon Commission) that 'it has been laid down that dominion status means "the right to decide their own destinies", and this right we [are] not prepared to accord to India at present, *or in any way to prejudge the question whether it should ever be accorded*'. (I stress the last section.) How could men with such views approve the Declaration? Baldwin had not applied himself to its detail. He had not even seen the words in their final form. When the prime minister sent them to him, he was on the way to his prolonged annual cure at Aix and he didn't trouble to peruse the documents. He had simply told MacDonald that he was happy if Simon was happy. MacDonald and Wedgwood Benn authorised the viceroy to make his statement without obtaining Simon's agreement. Simon was annoyed, but little troubled Baldwin when he was taking the waters, or indeed on his leisurely way to and from Aix, when his travels proceeded at a slower pace even than would have been possible in the pre-railway days of the post-chaise.

At their meeting in Palace Chambers the Conservative Shadow Cabinet rejected the Declaration, and according to a number of important members of the Shadow Cabinet, Simon himself had by now decided that he'd resign if it were made. After the Shadow Cabinet meeting, Lord Salisbury wrote to Baldwin, 'I need not say what a shock it was to learn that the Declaration was to be made before anything had been laid before the Country, though we had appointed a Commission for this very purpose . . . [I]t is cold comfort to me to be told that you – most honourably – were careful not to commit any of us. What a dislocation! Poor Conservative party!'

Belatedly Baldwin tried to pull Irwin back. He told him that the Conservative party disapproved of the phrase 'dominion status' because it was bound to be interpreted in India in a manner that neither Irwin nor the government had intended. He wanted the Round-table conferences deliber-ations to be confined within the framework of Simon's recommendations.

Inevitably this prince of gradualism said that gradualness was fundamental to Simon's proposals and to the support of the Conservative party. Irwin, to his credit, said that he would resign if there were any suggestion of withdrawing or modifying his Declaration in regard to dominion status. He had difficulty not only with the leader of his party, but also with the leader of his country. George V told him that the Simon Report had to be taken seriously and that Irwin should apologise to Simon. Irwin stuck to his guns and, taking his political life in his hands, Baldwin decided that he would personally continue to support MacDonald's policy and Irwin's Declaration.

The Declaration was made in the form of an official communiqué in the Indian *Gazette* on 31 October 1929:

> In view of the doubts which have been expressed both in Great Britain and in India regarding the interpretation to be placed on the intentions of the British government in enacting the Statute of 1919, I am authorised on behalf of His Majesty's Government to state clearly that in their judgement it is implicit in the Declaration of 1917 that the natural issue of India's constitutional progress as there contemplated is the attainment of Dominion status.

The Declaration might have seemed straightforward enough but every word was subjected to analysis and exegesis. The significance of Curzon's drafting change in Montagu's 1917 Declaration from 'self-government' to 'responsible government' was re-examined. Above all, what did dominion status mean? The importance of the Declaration lay entirely in its recommitment to that status. The diehards bitterly opposed the Declaration purely because of the recommitment. In reality Irwin's promises were pitched so far in the future that they meant nothing.

One of the viceroy's advisors conceded that there was a lot of fuss over nothing at all when he referred in the Legislative Assembly to different *degrees* of dominion status. Southern Rhodesia, for instance, was given as an example of a limited dominion. Similarly it is interesting and important that Irwin did not bear to be enunciating a new policy, simply restating what had been said in 1917. In 1917 nothing had been said about self-government. The only reason that the Declaration *looked* innovative was because of the change in the significance of dominion status as a result of the Balfour Declaration, soon to crystallise into the Statute of Westminster. That change was why there was a swift reaction to the Declaration in Britain.

The Indian nationalists knew what they wanted. As far back as 1906, Congress had declared that its object was 'the attainment of a system of government for India similar to that enjoyed by the self-governing dominions of the British Empire'. This aim was jointly adopted ten years later by Congress and the Muslim League. An All-Parties Conference in 1928 under Motilal Nehru recommended that India should have the same constitutional status within the British Empire as the white dominions, 'with a parliament having powers to make laws for the peace, order and good government of India, and an Executive responsible to that parliament, and should be styled and known as the Commonwealth of India'. If the Declaration had meant that the nationalists were getting something of this sort, with the new right to secede, the implications would indeed have been serious. India provided defence for the Suez Canal and for the connection of the Middle East with the Far East. In a BBC broadcast in January 1935, Churchill was to point to this and to the threat from the Japanese. Both the Liberal and Conservative parties immediately criticised the reference to a goal of dominion status. *The Times* attempted to take the sting out of the Declaration: 'A three-cornered conference had long been mooted and was approved by all parties at Westminster. The viceroy was primarily speaking on procedure and only incidentally restating the ultimate end; there was ample precedent for using the phrase "dominion status" while details were vague.'

But the Declaration implied no early threat to Empire: the viceroy had been presented with a memorandum by the Indian Home Department in Delhi which concluded that dominion status and responsible government were so inseparably intertwined that one couldn't have one without the other. The obstacles in the path of full responsible government were 'immense' and consequently a commitment to dominion status meant nothing. The memorandum is so important in showing how little Irwin's assurance meant that it is worth quoting from it at some length:

> Are the implications of dominion status now so wide that the imperial government could not feel itself able honestly to assert that dominion status is the goal of its policy equally with responsible government? The answer might seem to be in the negative, since the implications of dominion status need to be considered conjointly with the implications of responsible government. In each case whether the goal of parliament be responsible government or whether it be dominion status, the problem is essentially the same, namely the extent to which government in India can

be released from external control. In neither case can the consummation of the policy be reached by a stroke of the pen. The reality of dominion status cannot be obtained until the goal of responsible government has first been reached. If we assume for the moment that the immense obstacles in the path of full responsible government have been successfully removed, that the entire executive and legislative authority in India has been made to accord with the will of Indian electorates, and the Parliament has ceased to be responsible even that there shall be a government in India, it would seem to follow that the imperial government, even if it so wished, might then be unable to deny to India a status equal to that of the other autonomous units of the Empire, which also reached dominion status through the same channel of responsible government. If there be anything in this argument, the difficulty of accepting dominion status as the goal of British policy may be little, if at all, greater than the difficulty involved when responsible government was adopted as the declared policy of Parliament; and the connection between the two may be found to be so intimate that the final consummation of full responsible government may automatically involve the realisation of dominion status. [51]

So the dominion status which Irwin promised wouldn't be available for a very long time. That was important. The Balfour Report, before the Declaration, and the Statute of Westminster after it didn't really matter a great deal, in view of 'the immense obstacles in the path of full responsible government'. These practical obstacles were real enough. From the fact that they were never removed, simply finally ignored, flowed the tragedies of 1947. But for the moment, from Irwin's point of view, there was no immediate problem. Whether the words 'dominion status' retained their old, uncommitting, woolly insignificance or the new and precise import conferred by the Statute of Westminster was not important, since nothing would happen until the goal of responsible government had been reached. Irwin stressed to the Right wing of the Conservative party that the status, whatever it was, was a long way off, but he did not say what it meant or make any reference to the significance of the Statute of Westminster. Andrew Roberts says that Irwin 'took full advantage' of the constitutional change in relation to dominion status,[52] but it seems much more likely that he didn't agonise about it. His use of the words 'dominion status' in describing the natural issue of India's constitutional progress was informed by the memorandum he had received from his officials. Moreover there is no evidence to suggest that the words weren't used loosely, without a lawyer's concerns over the precise meaning they were in the course of acquiring. Birkenhead and Reading were lawyers. They found it inconceivable that India could ever attain the status or attributes of a dominion – not least because of its inability to defend itself. They were appalled. 'How,' they asked, 'could India, with its communal differences, its many languages and religions, its Indian states and British Indian provinces, and last but not least, its inability to defend itself, become a dominion after the manner of Canada, Australia and South Africa?'[53]

When Irwin met Gandhi in December 1930 and was told that Congress would not participate in the Round-table conference unless assurances were given that its purpose was to draft a dominion constitution, he did not give that undertaking: that wasn't at all what his Declaration meant. Baldwin had asked MacDonald what the statement, which he had already undertaken to support, actually meant. MacDonald replied that it meant no change to British policy. Samuel Hoare equally 'failed to see anything either new or revolutionary in the statement'.[54]

So here was the usual duplicity. Those who framed policy in London were well aware that Indians thought that there was something new and revolutionary about the statement, and encouraged them in that belief.

14

SIMON AND IRWIN COLLIDE: THE POLITICAL REACTION

The Conservative reaction to the Declaration is very revealing. It lays bare the nature of the party's attitude to India. To understand it, it's worth drawing back a little to the point just before the Declaration was issued.

To some extent, Simon collaborated in the supersession of his own work by joining in the discussions with Irwin and others. His Commission considered the proposals on 24 September 1929. They agreed to the Round-table conference idea but didn't want to be involved in the negotiations over dominion status. To save face, the initiative for the Round-table conference was presented as coming directly from the Simon Commission, rather from being injected after their deliberations were pretty well complete.

Simon had been intimately involved in all of Irwin's activities, but he proved to be extremely touchy about the episode. He thought the Round-table conference proposal downgraded the significance of his Commission's report. Although he unhappily gave way on this point, he remained against the dominion status Declaration. Irwin didn't understand Simon's attitude. He had known that Simon's Commission did not like the idea of dominion status but didn't know how strongly they were against it. But whatever Simon had said when Irwin was with him in London, as time went by he certainly became increasingly peeved. He had thought the Round Table discussions would simply debate his report, and he was increasingly unhappy as he gradually became aware that the discussions were to be free and not limited to a pre-determined agenda.

On 24 September, his Commission formally objected to the fact that the agenda for the conference was to be 'open' and not based on their recommendations, and on 25 September he and Reading announced their opposition to the Declaration. On the same day, Baldwin got home from his continental sojourn and on 29 September stayed with Lord and Lady Irwin.

Andrew Roberts is surely correct in saying that during his stay Baldwin cannot have been unaware, as has been alleged, of Simon's opposition. He did not, however, withdraw his support for the Declaration and seems to have thought that he could carry his party with him.

All the same, Irwin toned down the draft of his Declaration somewhat. He also told Baldwin, either in ignorance or in disingenuousness, that there was nothing very novel about 'proclaiming dominion status . . . to which we look through the constitutional developments foreshadowed in 1917'.[55]

I have suggested that if looked at dispassionately the Declaration didn't mean a great deal. Irwin said frankly enough that so far as dominion status was concerned, the 'realisation of the aspiration is not in sight'.[56] But in parliament and the country the Declaration was said to undermine British policy, the Simon Report and thus parliamentary authority. Irwin couldn't understand what it was all about. He knew that Birkenhead would have liked to have seen the 1917 Declaration torn up, but he didn't understand why 'Simon and Co.' were so hot under their collars. Birkenhead was briefing members of the Simon Commission – his stooges – 'to treat that which the government have instructed and authorised the viceroy to do as irrelevance'.[57] Lloyd George attacked the Declaration mischievously but effectively. The Lords in particular were hostile. So was the press. Rothermere's *Daily Mail* wanted the promise of dominion status cancelled: 'British rule in India is irreplaceable. Our duty there is not to argue with base agitators BUT TO GOVERN.'

Churchill wrote an article for the *Daily Mail* in November 1929. He looked at what Britain had done for India. He thought that the Raj had rescued India from barbarism and was preparing it for 'civilisation'. Against the beneficial influence of the Raj, he contrasted the horrors of the Hindu attitude to the Untouchables, sixty million Dalits who would be forever trodden down if a Hindu majority took power. Churchill saw the world divided between good and evil. The Empire deserved to be preserved because it was a force for good. The will to govern and thus to fight for what was good had been eroded. The Labour party he regarded as by definition hostile to the Empire, but even Conservatives under the 'business man' Baldwin, were no longer prepared for a 'robust assertion of British imperial greatness'.[58] For what was a 'robust assertion of British imperial greatness' a euphemism?

The Tory uproar was enormous. The ostensible cause of the uproar was the impropriety of sidelining Simon's Parliamentary Commission. Its true root was the horror aroused in Conservative circles by the idea of conferring the same status on India and Indians as that of Canada and Canadians. Lord Salisbury wrote to Baldwin telling him to remind Irwin that he was a Tory, to 'convince Edward that the Party will be shaken to its centre'.[59]

Edward had no intention of being shaken. He was now back in India and leaking the news of the forthcoming Declaration whenever he thought that this would generate political good will. There is a suggestion that the whole procedure of promoting the Declaration when the prime minister was in America and Baldwin was taking the waters had been a deliberate attempt by Irwin and Benn not just to hijack the Simon Commission, but quite deliberately and substantively to reverse its decision to reject dominion status. Certainly Irwin refused point blank to delay issuing the Declaration. He made quite certain that it was too late to row back. He even rejected a telegraphic appeal from Baldwin, his party leader and political sponsor. And so the Declaration was issued on 31 October.

Irwin was far too grand an aristocrat to be bothered by the storm. The *Daily Mail* said that he was part of the section of the Conservative party 'which manifested dangerous leanings towards platonic flirtations with Socialism', an interesting concept. He affected surprise: 'My statement . . . seems to have precipitated something of a political storm at home. I can't myself conceive the justification for this, as our purpose has always been proclaimed to be that of representative government . . . . Lloyd George . . . is, as always, being thoroughly dishonest . . . . Diehards both in England and in India combine to make the task of sensible people as difficult as possible'.[60]

On 8 November the government's policy on India was debated in parliament. In the House of Lords, Reading and Birkenhead, with the respective authority of a former viceroy and a former Secretary of State, spoke against the policy. Birkenhead had described the Declaration as 'this foolish and deceiving declaration'.[61] Reading proposed a motion objecting to the use of the words 'dominion status', which he claimed imported a change of policy at the very time when the Simon Commission was considering policy. Birkenhead said that the Simon Commission should treat the Declaration as impertinent. He wrote in the *Daily Telegraph* that 'the appetite of the Indians would merely be whetted by the Declaration, which would lead them to further and more extravagant demands'. He said that there was no prospect of any government's conceding dominion status to India in the present generation. Lord Peel, twice Secretary of State for India and an opponent of Baldwin's policy, complained that the Declaration blurred the distinction 'between ultimate issues and ideals and immediate practical issues'. He argued that the phrase, 'dominion status' was too indefinite to mean anything.

Baldwin, by now aware that he had only precarious support from the Shadow Cabinet – and even less from his intransigent and rebarbative back-benchers – told the Commons that the Conservative party supported the Labour Government and the Declaration. Churchill, who had been absent from the Shadow Cabinet meeting, was described by J.C.C. Davidson, at that time chairman of the Conservative party, as having 'sat through S.B.'s [Baldwin's] speech glowering and unhappy; he had sat forward during the "Goat's" [Lloyd George's] speech cheering every mischievous passage in it'. According to Davidson, about a third of the Conservative MPs, plus some Liberals, were prepared to vote against government policy and the Irwin Declaration, despite Baldwin's support for it. Geoffrey Dawson, editor of *The Times*, wrote to Irwin on 13 November, saying that Baldwin's speech had been heard in 'almost icy silence by the House'.

Some of those who listened to Baldwin in icy silence were reminded of their duty and repented of their independence of mind. George Lane-Fox, MP, a member of the Simon Commission, wrote to Irwin on 13 November, saying that in the bare six days since the debate 'the vast majority of the Conservatives have returned to their loyalty to S.B.' Loyalty was the heart of the matter. Criticism of the bi-partisan Indian policy was disloyal. Baldwin committed himself emotionally to Irwin and Irwinism: 'If the day ever comes when the Party which I lead ceases to attract men of the calibre of [Irwin], then I have finished with my Party'.

Churchill was prepared to face accusations of disloyalty. On 16 November he wrote in the *Daily Mail* speaking of British rule in India with conde-scending approval: 'The rescue of India from ages of barbarism, tyranny and internecine war, and its slow but ceaseless forward march to civilisation constitute upon the whole the finest achievement of our history. This work has been done in four or five generations by the willing sacrifices of the best of our race.' The achievement was a British achievement and not an Indian one: 'Progress would have been more swift, health and prosperity more abounding, if the British Civil and Technical Services in India had not been hampered by the forbearance we promised to observe towards Indian reli-gious and social customs.' Thus, although he purported to approve of the post-war policy of helping India to be involved in her own advance, there were limits to the assumption by Indians of full responsible government, 'limits – hard, physical, obvious and moral – arising from Time and Facts'. So it had been an enormous mistake for the Labour Government, 'amid all

the Utopian dreams and predatory appetites and subversive movements'
which the presence of the Simon Commission in India had excited, to make
the new Declaration of eventual dominion status, a premature Declaration:

> Dominion status can certainly not be attained by a community which
> brands and treats 60 millions of its Members, fellow human beings, toil-
> ing at their side, as 'untouchables', whose approach is an affront and
> whose very presence is pollution.
>
> Dominion status can certainly not be obtained while India is a prey to
> fierce racial and religious dissentions and when the withdrawal of British
> protection would mean the immediate resumption of mediaeval wars.
>
> It cannot be attained while the political classes in India represent only
> an insignificant fraction of the 350 millions for whose welfare we are
> responsible.

The battle within the Conservative party was not yet over, and Baldwin's
position as leader was insecure. As he looked at how the Declaration was
received in India he could not but wonder whether he had chosen a worth-
while issue to champion at such cost.

15

REACTION TO THE DECLARATION IN INDIA

On 23 December 1929 Irwin was on his way to Delhi on his private train to take up residence for the first time in Lutyens' new Viceregal Lodge, when a bomb blew a hole four feet wide in the rails.

The detonation was slightly mistimed and the engine and four coaches had passed the bomb before it exploded. A few hours later an unperturbed Irwin met Gandhi, Motilal Nehru and other political leaders. Gandhi was concerned about the assassination attempt but was unimpressed by the dominion status promise. Despite congratulations on Irwin's narrow escape, the meeting went badly. The viceroy was asked for assurance that the purpose of the Round-table conference was to draft a scheme for dominion status. Irwin had to explain that that was not the purpose of the conference. At midnight on 31 December 1929 the Indian National Congress unfurled the flag of Independence, called upon its members to resign their seats in provincial legislatures and authorised the launch of a campaign of civil disobedience. Gandhi did ask that a resolution be passed condemning the attempt on Irwin's life. The motion was carried by a majority of just 38 votes out of 1,832. Churchill telegraphed Irwin with his congratulations on the failure of the assassination attempt.[62] Irwin told Lady Harlech that he wasn't disturbed by the bomb as he was used to his Cona coffee machine blowing up.

The Declaration was enough to worry Baldwin's colleagues, but not enough to impress Congress. Jawaharlal Nehru and Subhas Chandra Bose (who would abandon Congress and in the Second World War become the puppet of Germany and Japan as leader of the so-called Indian National Army) had rejected gradualism and demanded immediate Independence. Nehru's position was consolidated when Gandhi acknowledged him as the spokesman for Congress. Nehru had a flair for publicity. At the party meeting in Lahore in 1929, he arrived on a white horse like the bridegroom at a Hindu wedding and told the assembly, 'I am a socialist and a republican, and no believer in kings and princes, or in the order that produces the modern kings of industry, who have greater powers over the lives and fortunes of men than even the kings of old.'[63] This was fairly rich, coming from the barrister son of a barrister, whose house had electric lights, a tennis court, a swimming pool and swarms of servants. Young 'Joe' Nehru had an English tutor and had been sent off to Harrow, followed by Trinity College, Cambridge.

Many of India's political leadership were in Delhi for the announcement of the Declaration, amongst them Gandhi, Mrs Annie Besant, the Nehrus, Motilal and Jawaharlal. Only Jawaharlal Nehru opposed the idea of a Round-table conference. He was against political advance by means of negotiation. After just two days of debate, Congress issued the Delhi Manifesto agreeing to attend the Conference, but only on conditions: the release of political prisoners, the largest representation at the conference for Congress, the understanding that the purpose of the conference was not to determine whether or when dominion status was to be reached but to draft a constitution for the dominion. The conditions were not met: Congress boycotted the conference.

So in India the Declaration persuaded no one. Congress could see that dominion status was still a chimera. In March 1930 Gandhi began his new civil disobedience campaign, which concluded with the salt march. Nehru and his radical supporters thought that even the new Balfour-type dominion status was not true Independence. So Irwin was under attack both in India and also in London – particularly by Churchill, whose accusations were described by Birkenhead's son as 'superb in eloquence, biting in scorn and containing charges of the viceroy's weakness and irresolution, which indeed skirted the frontiers of his honour'.[64]

Reports of the civil disobedience campaign sustained Churchill's allegation that Britain was losing the will to govern. The Home Member of the Viceroy's Executive Council complained that the 'government may not be retaining that essential moral superiority which is perhaps the most important factor in this struggle'.[65] It's interesting that he uses the word 'struggle'. Irwin was disappointed by the Indian reaction and told Wedgwood Benn: 'Though I am, as you know, a pacifist by nature, I am not disposed to go all lengths to meet people who seem to be behaving with utter unreason'.

Gandhi reached the sea on 6 April 1930 and by August Irwin was being pressed to crack down on the disobedience campaign. Because of the fluidity of the situation the king's brother, the Duke of Gloucester, was not allowed to re-join his regiment in India. Wedgwood Benn told the Cabinet that they would have to consider putting four provinces, with a total population of about 100 million, under martial law. Irwin continued to resist demands for repression in order not to compromise the chances of success for the Round-table conference. Dawson, of *The Times*, warned Irwin that 'The tide here is running very strongly against your ideas, and you cannot hope to carry them out by depending on the Labour Party alone.' Churchill told Baldwin not to be affected by his friendship with Irwin.[66]

Irwin remained quite unmoved. He was aware of the criticisms he faced. He was a big enough man to ignore them. He did not believe, 'as George Lloyd* would say, that we are lacking in fibre and morale . . . Only that we do seek faithfully to face facts which are, whether you like it or not, altering very fast.'[67] His handling of the unrest was sometimes described as laziness or incompetence, but rather than meddle officiously, he did what was much more difficult and stood back, letting the men on the spot exercise their judgement. He dismissed Churchill's increasing agitation as 'mad-dogging'. But he could take decisive action when he needed to. On 4 May Gandhi was arrested under his mango tree. In his absence, one of his supporters, Mrs Naidu, plus 2,500 volunteers, raided the Dharsana Salt Depots as he had planned to do. Between now and December 1930 the viceroy issued no fewer than ten ordinances. Jawaharlal Nehru was arrested and those regarded as troublemakers were thrown into jails throughout India. The press was muzzled. The Working Committee of Congress was declared an unlawful association and it and the All-India Congress Committee were outlawed. Even Motilal Nehru, the venerable President of the All-India Congress Committee, went to prison.

----

*   See Chapter 16.

16

The Gandhi–Irwin Pact

So Gandhi hadn't responded to the Declaration as Irwin had hoped. He had demanded complete self-government and dominion status. He had refused to attend the Round-table conference, launched a new campaign of disobedience and been sent to prison.

When the first Round-table conference opened on 12 November 1930 Gandhi was still in jail in Yeravda and the two Nehrus in Allahabad. Attempts were made to persuade them to allow Congress to attend the Conference. Gandhi was entirely negative and the Nehrus were not prepared to discuss anything other than the complete Independence of India. The three were allowed to meet. The Nehrus were brought to Gandhi's prison for what was called the Conference of Convicts. Nothing came of it.

After the failure of the first Round-table conference, which I shall describe in the next chapter, Irwin decided in January 1931 to release Gandhi and his supporters. The gesture was unpopular in India amongst provincial officers and local district officers and the army. It was badly received in London too. The political Right saw it as another contemptible example of Irwin's liberal weakness, an initiative, moreover, which did not even receive a conciliatory response from Gandhi, whose first act on his release was to call for an enquiry into police excesses during the emergency.

But after a pause, in which Motilal Nehru died, Gandhi wrote a letter to the viceroy in tones which suggested that he was prepared to confer on the representative of the king-emperor the privilege of an audience. Irwin agreed to meet. He told the Secretary of State that Sastri, a moderate nationalist and a close associate of Gandhi, had said to his friend: 'If you see the Viceroy I guarantee you will come out a conquered man and you will be his man henceforth', to which Gandhi had replied: 'I wish to be conquered'.[68]

It was this meeting which led to Gandhi's being photographed between two soldiers of the viceroy's bodyguard climbing the steps of Lutyens' palace. That photograph resulted in Churchill's famous speech in which he said how painful it was to 'see Mr Gandhi, a seditious Middle Temple lawyer, now posing as a fakir of a type well known in the East, striding half-naked up the steps of the Viceregal Palace, while he is still organising and conducting a defiant campaign of civil disobedience, to parley on equal terms with the representative of the King-Emperor'. The memory of this striking phrase has been corrupted in Indian myth, and Churchill is very widely believed to have written Gandhi off as 'a half-naked fakir'.

Churchill was not alone in his views. He was supported by the *Daily Mail*, Lord Lloyd, Michael O'Dwyer, Sir Henry Page Croft and others. Churchill talked of Irwin 'doing obeisance before Gandhi' and said that it was 'like feeding cats' meat to a tiger'.* That was extreme, but Irwin was unrealistic: he believed that the essential fairness of the Declaration would be enough to convince Indians that Britain meant well.

Of the three men who supported Churchill, we have already met O'Dwyer, the governor of the Punjab at the time of Amritsar. A word about the other two is appropriate. Lord Lloyd is the George Lloyd who, Irwin thought, was likely to accuse supporters of the Declaration of lacking moral fibre.† Lloyd had been a member of the Arab Bureau in Cairo in the First World War, stiff and pompous, not much liked by his colleagues. He went on to be High Commissioner of Egypt and the Sudan, where his imperious style and rejection of what he saw as the government's liberal policies resulted in his recall. Thereafter his energies were devoted to a die-hard defence of the status quo in India. He led the opposition to the India Bill in the Lords, and in the Chamber and elsewhere made between thirty and forty speeches a year, frequently recalling what had happened to Rome when the legions were brought home. He approved of Mussolini and Franco. Irwin's reference to lack of moral fibre alludes to Lloyd's belief that national morale had been

---

* Someone who, perhaps surprisingly, did not disapprove of Irwin's contacts with Gandhi was George V. On 27 March 1931, following an earlier Irwin–Gandhi meeting, the king's private secretary, Sir Clive Wigram, wrote, 'The King deprecates as much as you do the attitude which the Conservatives, egged on by the retired die-hards from India, are adopting . . . The King is full of admiration for the patience and forbearance you have shown in dealing with Mr Gandhi. Indeed, His Majesty feels that you deserve the very greatest credit for bringing about this temporary truce with Gandhi and the Congress, which, in the King's opinion, no one but you could have achieved.' (Nicolson, *King George V*, p. 507.)

† Referred to in Chapter 15.

eroded by female suffrage, Baldwin and the National Government. He held it to be axiomatic that Western institutions were superior to oriental ones.

The name of Henry Page Croft, later Lord Croft, will also reappear in the course of the narrative. His position is worth considering as he is an example of another, and less atavistic, strand of opposition to Indian political reform. He acquitted himself very well in the First World War, fighting on the Somme and spending twenty-two months on the Western Front – longer than any other MP. The experience stimulated an idealistic patriotism. Politically he was inspired by Joe Chamberlain's Tariff Reform programme and was vastly impressed by Chamberlain personally and by the strength of his vision. Having spent, as he said, thirty years fighting for the unity of the British Empire, he was appalled by the thoughts that any part of it, the white dominions or the Indian subcontinent, would drop out. He saw the Empire as a force for good. He thought that India's interests would be served by economic advance, not divisive political activity. The Empire was a providential mission with which God had entrusted Britain, 'the greatest instrument for the advancement of Christian ideals in the world . . . To exchange that for government which may lean towards the precepts of the Hindu worship of Shiva or Kali is, in my view, "a spiritual abdication" '.[69] He spoke against the India Bill nearly 300 times.

The meeting which resulted in the Pact was not the first meeting between Gandhi and Irwin, but it was the first time that they had been in a position to talk freely. Irwin described Gandhi to the king as 'small, wizened, rather emaciated, no front teeth . . . [A] personality very poorly adorned with this world's trimmings. And yet you cannot help feeling the force of character behind the sharp little eyes and immensely active and acutely working mind'. Gandhi wore only a loincloth and dhoti. His grin was as naked as his body: he only inserted his teeth in order to eat. What he ate was unusual. He extracted mixtures of dates and goat's milk from the folds of his garment. On one occasion a British representative, Sir Francis Humphrys, was present. He said, 'I remember Gandhi squatting on the floor and after a while a girl coming in with some filthy yellow stuff which he started eating without so much as by-your-leave'. Humphrys amused himself by imagining what would have happened if this had taken place during the days of Curzon.[70] The 'girl' was a Miss Slade, a daughter of an English admiral and one of Gandhi's devoted followers.

After Gandhi's release from prison Irwin met him on no fewer than eight occasions. He wrote to his father, saying that, 'It was rather like talking to someone who had stepped off another planet onto this for a short visit of a fortnight and whose whole mental outlook was quite other to that which was regulating most of the affairs on the planet to which he had descended'.[71] Despite the difference between the outlook of the two men, a difference which meant that Irwin never really understood the element of unpredictability and mysticism in which Gandhi was suffused, enough agreement was reached at their meeting in what was called the Delhi Pact to allow Gandhi to attend the second Round-table conference.

One of the members of Congress who worked with Gandhi at this time wrote thirty years later to the second Earl of Birkenhead, son of the former Secretary of State for India and author of Lord Halifax's official biography, 'My colleagues and myself in the Indian National campaign have dealt with many viceroys in India in our campaign for freedom lasting over many decades. I can testify to the general feeling among us all that Lord Irwin, as he was then called, was both as a man and as a viceroy the most Christian and the most gentlemanly representative of Great Britain among them all. I can testify to the fact that Mahatma Gandhi certainly was of this opinion. Faith in a higher Power and sincere allegiance to moral principles bound Lord Irwin and Mahatma Gandhi together from the first time when they met and it lasted right through. They became friends in a common cause though they began as consecrated knights in opposing camps. The Gandhi–Irwin Pact over the Salt *Satyagraha* was a historic memorial of what two God-fearing men could achieve though history placed them in opposite camps'.[72]

Gandhi agreed to end the boycott, to call off the civil disobedience campaign and to attend the second Round-table conference. In return, the government agreed to withdraw the measures taken in response to the civil disobedience movement. Making and selling salt was allowed in limited circumstances. Thousands of political detainees were released. The deal was at the time treated as of enormous significance, but Irwin was realistic and never saw it as more than a temporary device to get the conference going.

The Pact was debated in the House of Commons on 12 March 1931 (the debate brought forward by agreement between the parties to pre-empt a huge anti-pact rally over which Churchill was to preside in the Albert Hall on 18 March). The *Daily Mail* had called Irwin 'a second Kerensky'.* It was in this debate that Baldwin made the famous speech in which he used the line from his cousin, Rudyard Kipling, about the press having 'power without responsibility . . . the prerogative of the harlot throughout the ages'. The phrase was said to have lost him 'the tarts' vote'.

---

* Kerensky was the Russian prime minister who preceded the Bolshevik Revolution.

A few weeks later, Irwin's viceroyalty ended and the *Viceroy of India* carried him away forever from the subcontinent. When he arrived at Victoria Station there was a huge reception party. His old father was not in it, but only to avoid the tiring formalities. Happily he was still alive and waiting to welcome his son in quieter surroundings. When Irwin reached his home village of Hickleton, young men from the estate stopped his car, attached ropes and hauled it to the door of his family home where his father was standing to welcome him. Despite his age, old Lord Halifax declared in a ringing voice, 'I think that with God's help, my son has been able to do a good work in India for his king and country, and for that other great country that has so many claims on his affection and interest'.[73] Irwin deserved that.

17

THE ROUND-TABLE CONFERENCES

Irwin had come up with two Big Ideas after his initial period of viceregal reflection. The first was the Declaration, which was intended to win hearts and minds and failed to do so. The other was designed to provide a practical way forward, and consisted of the Round-table conferences, three in number, collectively the Conference on India. The Conference proved entirely unproductive, barren of ideas other than an evanescent proposal for federation. It opened the door to the 1935 India Act: in the absence of other ideas, the government was left to improvise for itself, and based its improvisations on a federal solution which proved as impractical as any impartial observer would have expected, diverting energies for a decade down a policy *cul-de-sac*.

The Conference on India was convened by the Labour Government but Baldwin, to Churchill's disappointment, gave it Conservative approval and selected four men to represent the party. Churchill was not one of them. He was the principal speaker on 12 December 1930 at the first public meeting of the Indian Empire Society at the Cannon Street Hotel, London, when he sought to appeal to those interest groups which might not welcome the replacement of the British Raj by the 'Gandhi Raj': the rule of the native states and the Muslims. In a leading article on 13 December, *The Times* said that Churchill was 'no more representative of the Conservative party [than] the assassins of Calcutta' represented the Indians who were present at the Round Table.[74]

The first Round-table conference was attended by eighty-nine delegates, fifty-seven from British India, sixteen from the princely states and sixteen representatives of the government and opposition. Congress had boycotted the conference. Many of its members were in prison. It was opened in St James's Palace by the king, George V, in November 1930.

The idea of federation was brought to the conference by the princes. On their way by ship to London they had discussed the establishment of a federation in which their states could participate, free from the 'irritating interference' of the political department which managed their relationship with the Indian government. The idea of federation wasn't entirely new. It had been mentioned in the Simon Report and in a document known as the 'Government of India's Despatch on Proposals for Constitutional Reform' in 1930. It had also been suggested in vague terms in earlier documents. It had never been very seriously canvassed. The princes argued, rather improbably, that federation would create a stabilising factor and encourage national unity.

As soon then as the Conservative delegation (Peel, Zetland, Oliver Stanley and Hoare), met the princes, they found themselves faced by a much more radical demand than they had expected. Hoare realised it was the result of deliberation in the course of the voyage to England: a sea change. As far as the Simon Report was concerned, not one Indian delegate was prepared to accept the proposals for provincial autonomy without a parallel transfer of responsibility at the centre.

Sir Samuel Hoare became Secretary of State in August 1931. Churchill speedily became his most outspoken opponent. Hoare allied intelligence (he achieved a double first at Oxford) to industry (he was an extraordinarily hard-working and efficient administrator). He wrote well but spoke badly. He was stiff, cold and had few friends. He didn't like the abbreviation of his Christian name to 'Sam', but tolerated it because he realised it made him sound approachable. He was a talented figure skater, and this almost ended his political career. On his way to a skating holiday in Switzerland in 1935, when he was Foreign Secretary, he stopped off in Paris to talk to the French prime minister, Pierre Laval, with whom he made an agreement to conciliate Mussolini, 'the Hoare–Laval Pact'. The reaction to the agreement was so strong that it was disavowed by the British Government (although they had already approved it) and Hoare was obliged to resign. To make matters worse, when he reached Switzerland he was injured as he skated. George V's reaction to the pact was unusually witty: 'Well that's it. No more coals to Newcastle and no more Hoares to Paris.'

When the conference began, Hoare was still in opposition. Even in opposition he was an important element in the development of Indian policy and soon he was in government, to preside over that policy. He became convinced that an All-India Federation was the only way forward. This obsession with federation, which required consensus among princes, Hindus and Muslims, put a stop to any constructive debate for the next ten years.

On the whole the Indians made a favourable impression at the conference, and public opinion warmed to them. But not Churchill: it was now that he made the 'jewel in the crown' speech, in which perhaps he cast his mind back to similar words his father had once used, and said that Britain had no intention of giving up her mission in India, 'no intention of casting away that most truly bright and precious jewel in the Crown of the King, which . . . constitutes the glory and strength of the British Empire'.

As a result of his pact with Irwin, Gandhi attended the second conference from September to December 1931. Gandhi claimed that Congress represented over 85 per cent of the population of India. He blithely brushed aside communal differences, which were the consequence of British interfering. When Britain steps aside, 'you will find that Hindus, Mussulmans, Sikhs, Europeans, Anglo-Indians, Untouchables will all live together as one man'.

Jan Morris provides some charming vignettes of Gandhi's time in London for the Round-table conference, receiving cat-calls from London children: 'Hey, Gandhi, where's your trousers?', chatting with Charlie Chaplin and Bernard Shaw, receiving two woolly dogs and three pink candles from children on his birthday, exasperating Oxford dons, one of whom exclaimed, 'Now I understand why they made Socrates drink the hemlock.'

There was to be an afternoon party at Buckingham Palace for all the Round Table delegates. Hoare, now Secretary of State, asked King George V what his views were about receiving Gandhi. 'What! Have this rebel fakir in the palace after he has been behind all these attacks on my loyal officers?' Finally the king relented, although towards the end of the audience with Hoare he had misgivings about having 'the little man' in his palace with 'no proper clothes on, and bare knees'.

The knees continued to be a problem. Gandhi attended the party and was in due course presented to the king. Although the conversation went reasonably well, Hoare was alarmed to see the king more than once looking resentfully at the knees. As Gandhi was about to leave, the king, failing dismally to rise to the level of events, tried to impart a warning to Gandhi: 'Remember, Mr Gandhi, I won't have any attacks on my empire!' Gandhi's manners were better than the monarch's: 'I must not be drawn into a political argument in your Majesty's palace after receiving your Majesty's hospitality.'

When Gandhi left the palace he was asked if he had felt underdressed in his dhoti and sandals. 'It was quite all right. The king had enough on for both of us.' The king's secretary, Lord Stamfordham, subsequently wrote to Irwin, who had undergone many long conversations with Gandhi in the viceregal palace and had conceded that Gandhi was 'not a very practical person to deal with'. Stamfordham reported that 'His Majesty was only troubled by the comical situation of the religious fanatic with his very restricted covering being admitted to your beautiful new house for what, his Majesty feels, must be rather interminable and irksome conversations'.[75] George V was only a constitutional monarch, and a pretty dim one at that, but Lord Stamfordham ought to have known that 'irksome conversations', was a rather inadequate description of the momentous dialogue between mother country and subcontinent of which these exchanges were the expression.* 'The religious fanatic' scarcely captures the admittedly complex essence of Gandhi and what he was doing.

When Gandhi met Hoare at the India Office, he shivered in his flimsy *khaddar*. He was pleased to warm the knees in front of a huge coal fire. It might have been simpler to keep them warm in a costume more adapted to the London climate, but he didn't break with his routines at the Round-table conference, including his habit of holding a day of silence once a week. He attended the conference on the silent days, but communicated by way of scribbled notes. Despite Gandhi's assurances about the different communities living together in harmony, the conference failed to find a way of protecting those who would be a permanent minority in the context of Hindu majority rule. Churchill was delighted to see progress blocked by the division between Hindus and Muslims of which he made so much.

The Conservative-dominated National Government which was in power by the time the second conference opened was impatient with negotiation and bargaining. Irwin had been succeeded by Lord Willingdon, who had little time for Gandhi. He said that he knew that his predecessor had seen something in Gandhi, but that for his part he regarded him as really dangerous and opportunist. The government issued an Indian White Paper at the end of the second conference. The second Round-table conference had failed. The campaign of resistance and disobedience started again.

---

* Maybe 'dim' is unfair. George V did have a useful fund of common sense. He was, however, no intellectual. When it was suggested that he should send a telegram of congratulations to Hardy on his eightieth birthday, a telegram was sent not to the poet and novelist Thomas Hardy, OM, but to the king's rod-maker in Alnwick. The king's official biographer, Harold Nicolson, complained privately that for eighteen years as heir apparent George did nothing but stick stamps in his album. He also did a prodigious amount of killing. At Hall Barn, Buckinghamshire, in a single day in December 1913 his party killed 3,937 pheasants, the largest pheasant bag recorded in Britain at that time. The king accounted for more than 1,000 of the birds himself. 'Perhaps we went a little too far today, David,' he said to his son.

A third and unproductive conference followed, again without Gandhi. Irwin was a parliamentary delegate at this brief session. It would have been interesting if he and Gandhi had both been representatives, but Gandhi's chair was empty and its occupant was concentrating on non-cooperation in India.

There were no more Anglo–Indian conferences before the outbreak of war. Before we look at what Britain unilaterally settled on, it's time to meet another viceroy, Irwin's successor, and a much less imaginative man.

18

WILLINGDON

Freeman Thomas, who adopted the additional surname of Freeman by deed poll to become Freeman Freeman-Thomas and who was created Earl of Willingdon on his appointment as viceroy of India and raised to the rank of marquess when he returned home, was the viceroy who ruled India between Irwin and Linlithgow. Prior to his appointment, he had governed various parts of the Empire. He was Governor of Bombay in 1913, Governor of Madras in 1919 and Governor-General of Canada in 1926. His qualifications for all this governing are not self-evident. His first experience of the life was as ADC to his father-in-law, Lord Brassey, when he was Governor of Victoria, and it must have appealed to him. He was briefly a Liberal Member of Parliament and a very junior minister. He was an outstanding sportsman. He played in the Eton Cricket Eleven for three years and in the Cambridge First Eleven for four years and he also played for Sussex and I Zingari. He was a Master of Foxhounds. Although his political career was not distinguished, he was close to the centre of power and worked as Asquith's secretary. He was George V's favourite tennis partner and a lord-in-waiting to the king.

In Bombay he tried to advance the integration of Indians into Western society and took an interest in the welfare of the Indian Army units fighting in Mesopotamia. He met Gandhi, just returned to India from South Africa: 'Honest, but a Bolshevik and for that reason very dangerous.' In 1917 there was a famine in the Kheda region of the Bombay presidency. Gandhi organised his first *Satyagraha*. Willingdon refused a request to waive taxes and thus precipitated Gandhi's first, and eventually successful, campaign of non-violence. Willingdon had launched Gandhi on his Indian career.

When Willingdon became Governor of Madras, he tried to keep Gandhi out of the province, but was over-ruled by the Government of India. In Madras he had to address the recently enacted Montagu–Chelmsford reforms. Although he didn't greatly like diarchy, he worked constructively with the reforms and created a unified government in which the elected representatives exercised their new powers alongside the officials working on the reserve powers. He was impressed by the result and pressed – unsuccessfully – for Madras to be given full responsible government.

So when he returned to India in 1931 as viceroy after seven years away, he arrived with a reasonable reputation for constructive liberalism. He continued to work for social integration. When, for example, he was refused entry to the Royal Bombay Yacht Club despite being viceroy because he was with Indian friends, he established the Willingdon Sports Club, which was open to all races.

At the political level he was not particularly progressive. Gandhi's influence continued to haunt him. He sought to balance 'the due observance of the laws' with implementation of reform.[76] While he was in India, the Round-table conferences and the preparation for the India Act were going on in London. The consequence was great confusion in India. Gandhi revived his civil disobedience campaign and Willingdon introduced the first all-India emergency powers legislation in 1932. Over 30,000 Congress politicians were arrested, as was Gandhi, 'one of the most astute, politically-minded and bargaining little men I ever came across'.[77]

There were many threats on Willingdon's life and his Military Secretary, Hastings Ismay, whom we shall meet again, devoted much time to safe-guarding his person. Willingdon continued to be well-meaning and charming, but he was increasingly at the mercy of events. Moreover, the Conservative party in London was bitterly divided over India. The White Paper would eventually translate into a new India Bill, but for the moment the government could not give clear directions to the viceroy.

19

Confusion Within the Conservative Party

Baldwin and the St George's Election

In the Commons debate on the result of the first Round-table conference on 26 January 1931, Sir Samuel Hoare expressed general satisfaction from the front bench. But in his speech to the Indian Empire Society at the Manchester Free Trade Hall at the end of January Churchill revealed that he was prepared to rock the boat. He said that India was something 'one cares about far more than office, or party or friendships'. Churchill maintained that the Simon Report, cautious and negative as it was, should be the basis of any legislation that was contemplated rather than the 'weak and foolish' Irwin Declaration. Baldwin kindly and elegantly described Churchill's speech as something that George III might have said had he had the tongue of Edmund Burke. But Baldwin's speech was received with more applause from the Labour benches than from the Conservative side.

These were bad days for the Conservative leadership not only because of India, though Baldwin's perceived liberalism over India added to his problems. He was attacked by the press, both Rothermere and Beaverbrook. He was thought to be too weak to hold on for long. Churchill was seen as his successor (the better bet would have been Neville Chamberlain). A memorandum from the Conservative party's chief agent, Robert Topping, to Neville Chamberlain of 25 February 1931 suggested that the party would not win a general election under its present leader. On India Topping said, 'Many of our supporters are worried about the question of India. They lean much more towards the views of Mr Churchill than to those expressed by Mr Baldwin in the House of Commons . . .'[78] On 1 March 1931, the Topping memorandum was shown to Baldwin. He had no need of further bad news. He was about ready to throw it in. The *Times* leader had already been set up:

'Mr Baldwin withdraws'. In the event the headline was reset, but Baldwin's reprieve was only temporary. There was an upcoming by-election in the St George's division of London, the safest Conservative seat in the country. What would have been the most routine of change-overs suddenly became the focal point for Conservative mutiny when the party's candidate, J.T.C. Moore-Brabazon, stood down, saying that he could not support Baldwin. Baldwin's future now rested on the outcome of the election.

There was a bizarre suggestion (emanating from Mrs Baldwin as well as others) that Baldwin should himself stand against the independent Conservative candidate promoted by the press barons. Wisely he did not take their advice and, in the event, Duff Cooper, a Baldwin supporter, stood as official Conservative candidate.

Then Irwin and Gandhi reached their agreement. Gandhi accepted the outcome of the first Round-table conference and was ready to attend the second. This strengthened Baldwin's position to an extent. He rallied and set to defending his policy with the sort of speeches which he made so much his own, direct and sincere, very effective with the party and the country. His setbacks rarely occurred at meetings at which he spoke.

He made an important speech of great frankness to the Commons on 12 March 1931 which went down very well: 'He might lose his party and his place, but would go down with the great mass of the country on his side.' From this basis he went forward on the offensive. On 14 March, again he spoke to the Commons in fighting mood and sold his policy on India more effectively than Churchill, speaking in the same debate, sold his opposition. Three days later, on 17 March, he made the 'prerogative of the harlots' speech.

The conflict over India was personalised as a conflict between Baldwin and Churchill, the darling of the press barons, 'the harlots'. The *Daily Mail* described the disagreements over India as the 'Baldwin–Churchill India duel'. Rothermere announced, 'GANDHI IS WATCHING ST GEORGE'S'.

On 19 March Duff Cooper won the seat with a majority of 5,110. Baldwin was safe and his stock in the party and the country rose steadily. Churchill's support began to leach away. In any case, he was very busy now on literary pursuits, working on *Marlborough* and the last volume of *The World Crisis*, as well as going off on a lecture tour of America which earned him £10,000. When he came back he found his standing in the House had been weakened by his position on India. In December 1931 the House was debating the Statute of Westminster and Churchill hoped to use the fact that the new legislation would allow an Indian dominion to withdraw from the Empire as the means of rallying support against government policy. He forced an amendment but lost by 43 votes to 369. Hoare saluted this as the 'collapse of the Churchill movement'.[79]

Pressure Groups

Perhaps the most noticeable of the various bodies that were set up in an attempt to sabotage what the Right saw as the government's abandonment of the subcontinent was the India Empire Society. We noted that Churchill addressed it at the Cannon Street Hotel on 12 December 1930. It had been founded just two months earlier. The society's six-man executive committee was made up entirely of ex-governors of Indian provinces. Its manifesto declared adherence to the provisions of the Government of India Act of 1919: 'India should remain an integral part of the British Empire'. It also emphasised Britain's responsibility for the tens of millions of peasants, industrial workers, minorities, untouchables and tribesmen 'who are incapable of protecting their own interests under any elective system'.[80]

Another die-hard pressure group, the India Defence League, was launched in June 1933. It had ten privy councillors, twenty-eight peers, fifty-seven MPs, two former governors and three former lieutenant-governors of Indian provinces and a mass of other grandees as vice-presidents and members.[81] The Indian Empire Society and the India Defence League were supported by groups such as the Junior Imperial League, the Grand Council of the Primrose League and the League of Conservative Women.

The government did its best to smear Churchill and his supporters. Conservative Central Office, covertly and while denying it, supported an opponent organisation called The Union of Britain and India. Through it, J.C.C. Davidson, the creator of the modern Conservative party, simultaneously Baldwin's *protégé* and his *eminence grise*, 'could spread his anti-Churchill poison. Even sixty years later the sour grapes of his propaganda pollute the stream of history, by encouraging doubt over Churchill's motives', says John Charmley.[82] All sorts of claims and rumours were circulated. Churchill's association with dodgy men like Lloyd George and Beaverbrook was emphasised. It was said that his Indian campaign was just a device to gain the leadership of his party, that he had even prepared for victory by drawing up a list of his Cabinet.

The Union was launched on 17 May 1933. One of those involved in establishing it was Rab Butler, Under-Secretary at the India Office. Like J.C.C. Davidson, he was a member of the Joint Select Committee appointed to consider the India Bill* and thus supposed to avoid partisan activities (which is why Churchill chose not to join the committee); they had no business to be doing what they were doing. The Union had none of the robust vitality of the die-hard organisations and Butler admitted later that it had been very difficult to find anyone to join it. The Union was subsidised by Conservative party funds, although this fact was hushed up. Edward Villiers, a former president of the European Association in India, had a knighthood dangled in front of him if he were prepared to help set up the Union. He did and was duly rewarded.

Despite considerable government pressure, some fairly neutral organisations, such as the Conservative Womens' Conference and the Junior Imperial League (an early format of the Young Conservatives), voted against the government's White Paper. But when the Conservative Central Council met on 4 December 1934 the Joint Select Committee had published its report, and its members could now take part in public debate. This was therefore a pretty serious and definitive test of party views. A motion from Lord Salisbury, condemning federation, was defeated by 1,102 votes to 390 votes. The result was achieved at the cost of much effort by the government, but it was still a very substantial victory for Baldwin, who spoke well at the meeting. Churchill spoke badly. His supporters, of course, also put as much pressure as they could on the delegates, but at the end of the day the threats and promises available to the whips would be more persuasive.

The activities of the various pressure groups, for and against reform, never cut much ice with the electorate generally, but the controversy over India poisoned relations within the Conservative party and created divisions within it. These fault-lines weakened the position of those who would depart from government policy over appeasement. There was little room for honourable dissent and discussion.

Churchill's main argument was the presentable one that a government dominated by Congress, of whose members 97 per cent were Hindu, would result in oppression of the Muslim minority and a perpetuation of the misery of the Untouchables. His views in truth proceeded at least in part from a deeply felt conviction that white men, the English-speaking peoples in particular, were inherently more 'civilised' and able than black men. He was steeped in the nineteenth-century view of history which saw gallant whites pitted against vicious savages, history which recalled with lingering horror the Black Hole of Calcutta and the Indian Mutiny. On the other

---

* Dealt with in Chapter 21.

hand, when Churchill became convinced that Gandhi genuinely wanted to secure humane treatment for the Untouchables, his view of the man who had been 'a malevolent fanatic' began to alter (though not dramatically). And in August 1935, just two months after the India Bill became law, when the Indian industrialist Ghanshyam Birla visited him at Chartwell, Churchill, who was building a brick wall, greeted him warmly and told Birla that he hoped that the new governments would try to create a prosperous India: 'I do not mind about education, but give the masses more butter. I stand for butter.' He asked Birla to 'tell Mr Gandhi to use the powers that are offered and make the thing a success'.[83] This acquiescent goodwill did not persist, yet Churchill's humanity constantly emerges and disarms. I shall examine his thinking in more detail in the next chapter.

20

LOOKING BEHIND CHURCHILL'S WORDS

Churchill plays such an important part in this story – first in his opposition to the India Bill and indeed any attempt to advance India's progress in the 1930s, and then as prime minister, when he presided over (if that's the correct way to describe his obstructive and negative role) the series of initiatives that included the Cripps Mission and its post-dated cheque – that his standpoint deserves some analysis. He was more complicated than most of the diehards, but understanding his position helps to understand what motivated some of his simpler supporters.

Churchill's faults were few and his virtues were abundant. The former, alas, were more evident than the latter in relation to India. I yield to no one in my admiration for Churchill, and my admiration is not confined to his role in the Second World War. I have summarised his qualities elsewhere. I said, 'The scale and range of his abilities was matched by a profound sense of humanity and magnanimity'.[84]

I stand by that evaluation of his career taken as a whole. But that is not to say that he never faltered, and India was not his finest hour. It is all the more delicious to reflect that Baldwin, apparently genuinely, toyed with the idea of making him Secretary of State. The prime minister wrote to Irwin in February 1929: 'I have had an idea (among many!) of putting Winston at the India Office. He was very good all through the Irish troubles: he has imagination, courage: he is an imperialist: he is a Liberal. BUT – we do know the risk'.[85]

He was ambitious and aggressive in his self-promotion. Lloyd George said of him in 1934: 'He would make a drum out of the skin of his own mother in order to sound his own praises'.[86] He was for most of the 1930s a potential leader of his party, and an element of his Indian campaign was certainly informed by selfish ambition. Paradoxically, the campaign threw him into such 'a politically ruinous stance'[87] that it, more even than his defence of Edward VIII, so endangered his political career that only war rescued him. Harold Macmillan, from the Left of the Conservative party said, 'The majority of the party regarded [Churchill's] attitude as reactionary and unrealistic'.[88] Other critics described him as unbalanced, scheming and dishonest.

In his exuberance he expressed himself in words and attitudes that were extreme, indeed downright silly. For instance in 1942 he said to Leo Amery, then Secretary of State for India: 'I hate Indians. They are a beastly people with a beastly religion.' His positions in opposition were always less judicious than when they were tempered by the responsibility of office. All responsibility tended to refine his judgment and absolute responsibility tended to refine it absolutely. But only tended to: in the case of India he was so far committed before he became prime minister that the beneficial restraint of authority had only a limited effect.

He was in part simply a product of his time. In his autobiography, *My Early Life*, Churchill described himself as 'a friend of the Victorian era'. Much later in his life, in 1952, he reflected to his doctor, Charles Wilson, 'When you learn to think of a race as inferior beings it is difficult to get rid of that way of thinking; when I was a subaltern in India the Indians did not seem to me equal to the white man'.[89] Irwin recognised the influence of Churchill's youth. He suggested that his views on India were like those of 'a subaltern a generation ago', and that therefore he might like to bring himself up to date by meeting some Indian activists who were in London at the time. 'I'm quite satisfied with my views on India. I don't want them disturbed by any bloody Indian.'[90]

Paul Addison has concluded that Churchill's fundamental views were settled in the period between 1895, when he decided to make his career in politics, and 1900 when he became a Member of Parliament.[91] Addison is of the view that of all the books which Churchill read so voraciously at this time in order to prepare himself for public life, the one which made most impact on him was Winwood Reade's *The Martyrdom of Man*. This book was published in 1872 and was based on the implications of the then popular notion of Social Darwinism. The nub of Reade's version of the theory was that advance took place by a process of struggle and striving, of which warfare was the epitome. Suffering was a price worth paying. When a nation lost the appetite for conflict it was doomed to decay.

Churchill saw the collapse of *anciens régimes* in and after 1918 as a symptom of decay and decline, evidence of a lack of the desire to strive. He did not wish to see Britain entering a similar phase. This was the philosophy which, in part, animated him in his campaign against the India Bill. In the course of that campaign he said that if Britain lost India she would sink within two generations to the level of minor powers like Portugal. So she did, though the loss of India was not the cause.

Even before the First World War he had concluded that Britain derived no financial benefit from India, and his desire to hang on to the jewel in the crown was not motivated by commercial considerations. In February 1922 he told a conference of ministers:

> An idea was prevalent among many people, both in India and at home, that we were fighting a rear-guard action in India, that the British *Raj* was doomed, and that India would gradually be handed over to the Indians. He was strongly opposed to that view of the situation. On the contrary, we must strengthen our position in India . . . He believed that opinion would change soon as to the expediency of granting democratic institutions to backward races which had no capacity for self-government.[92]

His approach was not entirely uninformed. Remember that Churchill's first government office was as Under-Secretary of State for the Colonies under Campbell-Bannerman. He was appointed in December 1905. He had then had recent experience of the Empire not only in the South African War, but also in India as a subaltern. He had more authority as Under-Secretary of State than might have been expected, as the Colonial Secretary, the Earl of Elgin, was in the House of Lords and more interested in his estates than in the minutiae of his responsibilities. At the Colonial Office, of course, neither Elgin nor Churchill had responsibility for India. Churchill did, however, have to deal with Gandhi, at this stage in his career in South Africa promoting the case of the Indian community, there subject to numerous indignities and constraints. Gandhi came to London in November 1906, to complain that Indians were now being fingerprinted as part of their official registration in South Africa. He went back to South Africa to launch a campaign of passive resistance. Churchill and Gandhi were never going to be friends.

Churchill understood the economics of Empire reasonably well, though he studied it from a partial viewpoint and a perspective which directed his gaze particularly towards India. He was initially MP for Oldham. His speeches at that time made many references to Britain's role in relation to India. Their tone is vastly condescending; contrasting the benefits of Britain's civilising influence with the unqualified deprivations of native existence. He was next MP for North-West Manchester, and then Dundee. All these seats had important trading links with India.

On 31 May 1904 he crossed the floor, leaving the Conservative benches to sit on the Liberal side of the House, in his father's old seat. He became one of the foremost opponents of the Protectionist campaign which Joe Chamberlain had just opened. On 8 March in the following year he spoke in the Commons to his own motion, 'that, in the opinion of this House, the permanent unity of the British Empire will not be secured through a system of preferential duties based on the protective taxation of food'. He complained that Chamberlain had forgotten India, which he described, using the words of his father which prefigured the words he would himself later use about the jewel in the crown, as 'that most truly bright and precious gem of the Crown'.[93]

When he stood for North-west Manchester at the 1906 General Election he was standing as a Liberal in what was traditionally a Tory city. But as Randolph Churchill, junior, put it, '[A]lthough Manchester had for nearly fifty years been a Tory stronghold it was, after all, the city of Cobden and Bright (John Bright was for ten years its MP) and the Free Trade Hall stood – still stands for that matter – as a witness and reminder in the North-West division of Manchester to the enthusiasm that their anti-corn law league, anti-tariff policies aroused there'.[94] Churchill received a great deal of traditional Tory support. The Manchester Guardian Society for the Protection of Trade, the British Cotton Growing Association and the Free Trade League all endorsed his candidacy.

As a man of his time, he used the language of his time. He could talk of 'baboos', describing them as gross, dirty and corrupt, or of 'Hottentots' likely to throw white people into the sea. He said 'I hate people with slit eyes and pigtails'. But he also argued that 'there should be no barrier of race, colour or creed' and he would deprecate Kitchener's triumphalist conduct after his victory at Omdurman[95] and what Dyer did at Amritsar. He could make extremely offensive remarks which on the face of them appeared to be anti-Jewish, although in reality he was strongly biased in favour of the Jewish community, had a predilection for Jewish friends, was a committed Zionist and is listed as one of the Righteous Among the Nations on the Wall of Honour in the Garden of the Righteous at Yad Vashem in Jerusalem.

Such dichotomies may be difficult for us to understand today but were not unusual in Churchill's time. He was not a racist except to the substantial extent that he unalterably believed that the British race was superior to the races in the black colonies, that Britain had a civilising duty and that it was neither in the interests of Britain or of the subject races that there should be any transfer of power.

As between the Hindu and Muslim communities in India, Churchill was distinctly disposed towards the Muslims. He started from a preference for the monotheistic religion. To that was added an admiration for the martial qualities which he perceived amongst the Muslims. He encountered these qualities himself when he served on the North-West Frontier and recorded them in his autobiographical volume, *My Early Life*. In 1889, in *The River War*, there are critical references to Islam, expunged from the second edition. The First World War reinforced his views: 'During the Great War the Moslems of India confounded the hopes of their disloyalty entertained by the Germans and their Turkish ally and readily went to the colours. The Punjab alone furnished 180,000 Moslem recruits'.[96]

Churchill certainly saw Hindu–Muslim antagonism as a tool for prolonging British rule, as he told the War Cabinet in 1940, but his predilection for Muslims was genuine. His father, from whom he said he took his politics 'almost unquestionably' (did he mean unquestioningly?) had been pressed in this direction by Wilfrid S. Blunt, and Churchill himself was friendly with numerous prominent Muslims from the Aga Khan to Jinnah.[97]

21

THE BACKGROUND TO THE INDIA BILL:
CIVIL WAR IN THE CONSERVATIVE PARTY

The outcome of the government's deliberations was the Bill which would become the 1935 Government of India Act. The classical view that Independence was the outcome of well-meaning and consistent policy depends very much on what the 1935 Act was about. Its apologists hailed it at the time as a progressive measure, and some of them even defended it in retrospect. Some of its provisions were subsequently embodied by independent India in the country's constitution. Rab Butler, much involved in the legislation, defended it long after Independence.

It is, however, incontrovertible that the Act was meant to preserve British India for at least another generation – perhaps even permanently. The content of the legislation as it was finally enacted in June 1935 is examined in some detail in Chapter 23. For the moment its essence can be said to be that it envisaged an all-India Federation of which the princely states would be part. The communities (princes, Muslims, Hindus) were balanced in an equipoise that their relative numbers did not justify. This formalisation of divide-and-rule led to the claim that the Act was 'deliberately framed so as to exclude as far as possible the Congress Party from effective powers'.[98] When Sir Samuel Hoare said in debate that the Act would lead to dominion status (not something that the Bill itself said) he was attacked by the Labour party, who saw the Act resulting simply in power-sharing with the princes. If the India Act had been implemented in full measure it would have led to an India no more independent than the Egypt or Iraq of the 1930s.

This federal approach appealed to Hoare, Baldwin, Chamberlain and their colleagues. The denial of a Congress majority guaranteed an ongoing role for Britain. The princes' enthusiasm for federation didn't last. They soon changed their minds and decided that they didn't want it after all. In that knowledge the Cabinet simply sat tight. The Muslims didn't like the

Bill because they had no reserved seats in the provinces where they were in a minority. Jawaharlal Nehru was little more enthusiastic than the Muslims. He demanded unqualified Independence. The Act had become an obstacle and not a means to Constitutional progress.

Churchill described it as 'A gigantic quilt of jumbled crochet work.' This was his metaphor for a complex scheme that sought to intertwine Muslims, Hindus and the princely states in a federal web. The Act was not an end in itself. Even its supporters thought that it would be no more than the beginning of a movement towards self-government which would take many generations.

The legislation was enacted in part because no alternative could be found. Back when the Simon Commission was still under way, Birkenhead had made a much-criticised speech which caused offence, although what he said was true enough. He said that the Indians could not get together to agree on anything and pretty well challenged them to produce their own constitution. The response was the All-Parties Conference mentioned earlier, set up by Congress in February 1928 and dominated by Motilal Nehru and Sapru, which produced the Nehru Report. Its recommendations can be ignored now, as they were in their own time.

It took a huge effort to get the Bill through parliament. The Government of India Act, 1935, was in its time the longest piece of legislation the United Kingdom parliament had passed. At its second reading, the Bill was debated for forty-three days in the House of Commons and for thirteen days in the House of Lords.

When the government published the Bill, Lloyd George's response was 'Who in India wants it?' He could also have asked who in the Conservative party wanted it. Certainly not the whole of the party. The Bill divided the party and thus informed its character for a generation.

Before the 1931 general election and after it Conservative die-hard opposition to Indian reform was pretty much the same – about fifty rebels. But as a result of that year's landslide (the biggest in British parliamentary history) the rebels were now 50 out of 473 rather than 50 out of 261. Allies in other parties brought in another eighty-one votes to confront the rebels. Opposition members who opposed the government's Indian policy did so because they felt it did not go far enough, rather than that it went too far. The government could play off its rebels against its opponents. On the other hand, in the House of Lords there was a consistent and significant body of die-hard opinion. Lord Lloyd commanded substantial forces. Lloyd won 58 votes against the government's 106 in a division on 3 December

1931. When Lloyd and others formed the India Defence Committee, their plausibility was compromised by the fact that they committed themselves in advance to reject the government's policy, whatever the White Paper revealed it to be. It was easy to characterise them as dinosaurs.

Hoare sought to disarm the Indian rebels by bringing them into the legislative process. He established the Joint Select Committee of both Houses which has already been mentioned. Diehards would be brought in to membership of the Committee. In this way he thought that he could derail 'Winston's most damaging line of attack, namely that parliament was going to be edged out of the final settlement'. Having the whole question in the hands of the Joint Select Committee would stop 'the extreme Right [from] mobilising an extensive attack'.[99] Churchill rather welcomed this approach, which he thought would give his followers and the Indian Empire Society the opportunity to improve the legislation. A vote of the Conservative Central Council on 28 February 1933 justified Churchill in asking the Chief Whip for eight out of twenty Conservative seats on the Joint Select Committee. He didn't want to be a member himself. He told Hoare that he would not join the Joint Select Committee. He wanted 'neither part nor lot in the deed you seek to do'.[100] He thought that participation would gag him and that he would do best to conduct his campaign publicly. His enemies – there were a lot – said that he'd declared a Tory civil war.[101]

On 22 February 1933 Sir Henry Page Croft proposed a motion which would have effectively limited the remit of the Joint Select Committee, and therefore the scope of the subsequent legislation, to consideration of the Simon Report rather than the government's white paper. In the debate on this motion, which came top of a private members' ballot, the usual rebels mustered only a typical vote of 42; but no fewer than 245 Tories abstained or absented themselves – and that despite a three-line whip. Although the motion failed, the Government was concerned. Rab Butler found more waverers than supporters on the Government benches and Hoare deprecated the activities of what he called 'the Winston crowd'. At this stage, the diehards were doing quite well. Hoare was afraid of 'a breakaway of three-quarters of the Conservative party'.[102]

Before he spoke in the debate, Churchill hubristically announced that his speech would have an enormous impact. He was inclined to say this sort of thing in advance of speeches, and the result was usually what would have been expected. Hoare wrote to the viceroy, Willingdon, telling him that Churchill's 'much advertised speech was one of the greatest failures of his life'.[103] The build-up to the speech meant that pretty well whatever he said was going to be disappointing. Austen Chamberlain wrote to his sister that Churchill had become hysterical and that it was impossible to have a rational debate on India with him even in private. Many members considered Churchill to be mercurial and unrealistic, probably motivated very greatly by personal ambition. He might be witty but he lacked authority and judgement.

As the India Bill went through its parliamentary stages, it faced opposition from loyal Conservatives quite separately from the opposition it faced from Churchill's supporters. The credibility of the latter group was affected by the fact that many saw Churchill's campaign as not so much reasoned opposition to the legislation as a self-interested campaign to bring down the National Government. Lord Lloyd was particularly hurt by the idea that he was being disloyal. He asked Baldwin to 'indicate to me what Conservative cause I have ever abandoned since I entered public life'.[104]

Lord Linlithgow, chairman of the Joint Select Committee which Churchill had chosen not to join, a future viceroy and no enemy of Churchill, wrote to him, 'The Indian problem does *not* interest the mass of voters in this country.' Churchill responded ponderously, 'I do not think I should remain in politics, certainly I should take no active part in them, were it not for India . . . You are greatly mistaken that India does not interest the mass of voters. It interests profoundly all those loyal, strong, faithful forces upon which the might of Britain depends'.[105]

The use of the phrase 'the might of Britain' is interesting. Churchill saw Britain's strength as declining while that of Fascist Europe was increasing. He thought it was no time for Britain to be surrendering resources. Duff Cooper, though he did not agree with Churchill on India, spent part of a summer holiday in Germany and wrote to tell him how horrified he had been by seeing the enthusiastic steps the Germans were taking to prepare for war.

Baldwin had no interest in the Nazi threat. He saw Churchill simply as dangerously atavistic. He spoke at Worcester, saying that the diehards would destroy national unity as they conducted their campaign across the country. Churchill wasn't upset. He entertained Austen Chamberlain at Chartwell and told him that although the India Bill would be carried, the fight would leave such bitter memories that the Government would have to be reconstructed. He continued to court the press. He was supported by the *Morning Post*, to an extent by Beaverbrook's *Daily Express*, but above all by the titles owned by his friend Lord Rothermere. In 1934 he wrote eleven articles for the *Daily Mail* and in 1935, thirteen. His son, Randolph, wrote for the Rothermere *Sunday Despatch*. Lord Camrose, the proprietor of the *Daily Telegraph* and a friend of Churchill's, refrained from support but equally from personal attacks. *The Times*, strongly supportive of the Government, was of course against him.

22

CHURCHILL AND THE PRIVILEGES COMMITTEE

Churchill's opposition to the Bill was compromised by the view that he was unprincipled, ambitious, capricious and above all lacked judgement. Any credibility which remained was destroyed by his incautious resort to the Privileges Committee of the House of Commons.

On 15 April 1934 he and Hoare had lunch with Philip Sassoon, a marvellous aesthete, a society darling noted for his wit and love of gossip. Kenneth Clark described his 'idiosyncratic and infectious *style*', and said that 'he moved quickly and always seemed to be in profile, like an Egyptian relief'. Over lunch there was no hint of what Churchill was about to do; but later that same day he wrote a letter to Hoare. He said that he believed Hoare had breached the privileges of the House of Commons and that he had asked the Speaker to rule on the matter. Hoare and his advisers had to give over weeks to refreshing their memory about the events to which Churchill's allegations related. Hoare spent two days giving evidence and never forgot the resentment he felt as he waited outside the House of Commons Committee Room to be summoned for his cross-examination, 'as if I were a prisoner outside the courtroom in the Old Bailey'.[106]

The *Daily Mail* had given Churchill information that suggested that pressure had been put upon the Manchester Chamber of Commerce Committee by Lord Derby with Hoare's acquiescence to alter its evidence to the Joint Select Committee. Churchill went to Sir Robert Horne[*] and Lloyd George for advice. Frances Stevenson, Lloyd George's secretary and mistress, reported that Churchill was 'working extremely hard to

---

[*] A remarkable, now forgotten, politician, Chancellor of the Exchequer, but ultimately more interested in money, and thus, said Baldwin, 'that rare thing – a Scotch cad'.

undermine the gov and appeared to be gaining ground'. Derby wrote to Churchill telling him that he had not pressed for a change in the Chamber's evidence. This was untrue but could not be proved to be so: the Government concealed incriminating correspondence between Derby and the Secretary at the India Office, Sir Louis Kershaw. The evidence available to Churchill was very slender, and in hindsight his move was wildly misguided, but if it had succeeded, in Hoare's view the Bill would have been dead and possibly the Government with it.[107]

The Speaker referred the matter to the Committee of Privileges. The enquiry was hardly a model of open justice. The diehards were not represented on the committee, and Churchill was denied the opportunity of cross-examining and questioning witnesses. The committee found that the Joint Select Committee had not been a judicial body and was therefore not bound by the rules which Churchill alleged it had broken. The complaint was dismissed. Churchill should have accepted the situation graciously. He did not. He argued the case and appeared bitter, obsessed and unbalanced.

After Churchill spoke in the House, Amery spoke. In the course of his speech he used the Latin saying, *'Fiat justitia ruat caelum'*.* It's a convention in the Commons that speeches should be in English. Amery knew that and had prepared a trap. Churchill fell into it. He asked for a translation. Amery had it ready: he said that it meant 'If I can trip up Sam [Hoare], the government's bust.' It was a wonderfully effective ruse. It touched on the prevalent conviction that Churchill's primary interest was to seize the leadership of the party. It also made him look silly. The House broke down in laughter at Churchill's expense, the most damaging treatment a Member of Parliament can face.

Hoare described the whole thing as one of Winston's 'mare's nests', part of the campaign to hold the clock back and obstruct development: 'The splendid memories gathered round the Indian Empire blinded him to the changes that had come about since the days of Clive, Wellington, Lawrence and Kipling. The India that he had served in the Fourth Lancers was the India of polo and pig-sticking, of dashing frontier expeditions, of paternal government freely accepted, and the Great White Empress revered as a mysterious goddess. "Settle the country, make the people happy and take care there are no rows", the words of Henry Lawrence to his band of brothers, still seemed to him sufficient for maintaining the British Raj.'[108]

---

* 'Let justice be done, even if the heavens fall.'

Many years later, Hoare looked back on the opposition which Churchill led:

As I was one of the principal participants in the battle over India that raged from the day on which [Churchill] left the Business Committee [of the Parliamentary Conservative party, because it accepted Hoare's support of federation] in 1931 to the final passage of the India Act in 1935, I am not an impartial judge of his action. Nonetheless, I may perhaps make two comments. From the point of view of India, the consequences were altogether bad. His formidable opposition embittered a constitutional discussion that should have been kept free of recrimination. It delayed by many months and perhaps years the passing of the Act . . . If the Act had reached the Statute Book in 1933 instead of 1935, I am convinced that it would have been in effective operation before the war started. Even more serious than delay was the atmosphere created by years of parliamentary wrangle . . . with the inevitable result that Indians came to believe that instead of giving them the fullest possible opportunity for obtaining responsible government, we were intent upon tying them up in a straitjacket.[109]

23

THE LEGISLATION

On the second reading of the India Bill, on 11 February 1935, eighty-four Conservatives voted against their Government. The Government carried the day, but at the cost of a bigger rebellion against a three-line whip than on any other second reading in the twentieth century.[110] Shortly afterwards, the princes, meeting in Bombay, declared that they rejected federation outright. Churchill was delighted. He saw that as the end of federation, which it was, and possibly the end of the Bill, which it was not. The report stage was completed on 30 May and the third reading on 5 June.

When the India Act finally passed, in June 1935, it did so by 382 votes to 122, eighty-four Conservatives voting against the Government. The parliamentary debates preceding the passage of the Bill made up a total of some 2,000 speeches and 15,500,000 words.

After the third reading, Churchill conceded defeat. By then he was becoming increasingly preoccupied by events in Germany. In any event, he said to his wife before the report stage, 'Of course the government will get their beastly Bill through, but as the princes will not come in, all the parts I've objected to will remain a dead letter.'[111] He wrote on behalf of the diehards to the new viceroy, Linlithgow, on 8 August 1935, 'As long as the princes are not nagged and bullied to come into federation, you need not expect anything but silence or help from us. We shall count more in the new parliament than in this fat thing'.[112] That was the nub of the matter: federation would never work. Given the reserve powers, the Bill itself would never be acceptable to Congress, and the princes' attitude to federation was the *coup de grâce*.

In his 1974 Ford Lectures Professor J.A.Gallagher argued that the Act was designed to revise British India, but not to weaken British control: the 'keys of the political kingdom', control over foreign policy, defence and internal security, with an ongoing territorial presence, were to continue.[113]

A more recent analysis of the views of the Conservative majority of these years and of its powers, particularly when organised under Chamberlain, concluded that:

> Hoare, Baldwin and Neville Chamberlain and their hard-headed Cabinet colleagues consciously chose a federal plan which would act primarily to protect Britain's interests rather than hand over control in vital areas, and that in this intention were the seeds of the policy's failure. The scheme was structured first and foremost as a means of stopping any chance of a Congress majority at the centre. This policy reached its most cynical, and foolish, point in 1938–39, when the Conservative-dominated Cabinet decided, despite almost universal opposition in India, to sit pat on the Act, knowing full well that the Princes would never agree to federate; thus the Act itself, and not the federation it was designed to create, became a bar to constitutional progress.[114]

In the provinces, the Act replaced diarchy with responsible government. Defence and foreign affairs were excluded from the competence of the federal executive and were administered by the viceroy and his nominees. The Act provided that federation would not be established until rulers of states representing at least half of the aggregate population and entitled to not less than half the seats allocated to the states in the federal legislature had agreed to accede. The effect of an Instrument of Accession was to limit sovereignty to the extent to which a ruler had acceded. The anomaly was thus that the federation would consist of different constituent elements, the power of the central government varying according to its relationship with each constituent.[115] As long as the princes retained their wealth and privileges, they didn't hugely mind whether they were part of a federation or part of the Raj.

They could afford to watch and wait; but the positions of the Hindus and the Muslims hardened. Till now, surprisingly, most Muslims had supported Congress rather than the Muslim League; but in 1937 the first provincial elections held under the 1935 Act vividly demonstrated the power of Congress, with absolute majorities in six of the eleven provinces and the larger share of the vote in three others. Now the Muslims were truly concerned by the prospect of a Hindu-dominated Raj. During the election campaign, Congress had rejected any question of power-sharing with the Muslim League. The League's leader, Mohamed Ali Jinnah, previously a Congress supporter, increasingly mobilised the League. Nehru said that the forces of communalism had been vanquished. He knew this was nonsense, but he didn't know just how far wrong he was.

Attlee, the Labour party's chief spokesman on India by now, had criticised the legislation from the start. He said it failed to 'provide a medium through which the living forces of India can operate'. It relied upon 'the dead India of the past'.[116] Attlee had attended Haileybury. The school's full name, 'Haileybury and Imperial Service College' emphasises that it had specialised in preparing high-minded boys for work in the Imperial Service. Indeed in its earlier incarnation, it was the East India College, founded in 1806 to train recruits for the East India Company.[*] Attlee, like many Labour Members of Parliament, was a friend of Congress. He saw that the Bill was framed to exclude the Congress party from effective power and from the rewards to which the 1937 election results demonstrated the Party was entitled. The Bill gave undue weight to the princes and minority communities. He said that he aim was to exclude 'the Congress party from effective power in the new Constitution. On many occasions provisions have been deliberately put forward with that end in view'. For him, the Act encouraged separatism and dissension between the communities.[117] And yet, Congress members, his favourites, were not bent on making concessions to minorities.

Attlee's analysis was right. The Federal Legislature was to consist of two chambers, a Council of State and a Federal Assembly. In both Houses the princes were given disproportionate representation, 104 seats out of 260 in the Council of State, and 125 out of 275 in the Federal Assembly. Moreover 'weighting' reduced the number of 'general' seats open to direct election. In the Council of State, after the princes' seats were taken, further seats were given to different groups: forty-nine to Muslims, four to Sikhs, six to Scheduled Castes, six to women, seven to Europeans, one to Anglo-Indians, two to Indian-Christians. The 'general' seats amounted to only seventy-five. In the Federal Assembly only eighty-six were 'general'. The arithmetic meant that even if Congress won all the general seats and those other seats for which it could stand, such as labour groups and women, it could never attain overall power.

---

* 'To the student at Haileybury the abiding subject of interest was the expansion and maintenance of British rule in India . . . Many a Haileyburian had been dandled as a child in arms which had helped to bind a province together or bring savage tribes into subjection'. Thus the College was described in 1893 (Haileybury Archives 10/2). Attlee went to the school in 1896 at the age of thirteen.

The powers of the Federal Legislature were seriously circumscribed. In relation to financial matters, 'non-votable' items made up something between three-quarters and four-fifths of total expenditure, and it was left to the viceroy's discretion to decide what fell into the 'non-votable' category. In regard to the remaining expenditure, the legislature could express an opinion but had no control. There were other detailed provisions which further limited the legislature's control over financial matters. It was for this reason that Harold Laski said that the Act 'seems to me the supreme example of economic imperialism in action'.[118]

Defence was not within the legislature's competence. The civil service and police were protected. Even in the spheres of legislation in which the legislature was allowed to dabble, the viceroy could withhold his consent to legislation that had been passed, and legislate for himself where no legislation had been passed. Ninety-four sections of the Act conferred 'special discretionary powers' on the viceroy.

All this meant that Congress had to take the view that given the provisions retained for the viceroy it would be dangerous to go ahead in reliance, as they were asked to do, on assurances that the viceroy would be far too generous-spirited to use any of his reserved powers. It is hardly surprising then that at the Faizpur Congress in December 1936 Nehru declared that 'utterly bad as the Act is, there is nothing so bad in it as this federation and so we must exert ourselves to the utmost to break this'. Congress rejected an Act which was aimed at the 'further exploitation of the Indian masses', and a year later the All-India Congress Committee passed a resolution expressing their 'emphatic condemnation and complete opposition to the scheme'.[119]

One of the intriguing minor features of the India Act was that it contained no preamble. This would not have been surprising in the case of a run-of-the-mill piece of legislation, but it *was* unusual in landmark legislation such as this. It was strange that there was none of the indication of broad policy or long-term objectives which a preamble would set out. Montagu's Act of 1917 had contained the memorable preamble that referred to 'the gradual development of self-governing institutions, with a view to the progressive realisation of responsible government in India as an integral part of the British Empire'.* The 1935 Act repealed the 1919 Act – with

---

* In a long speech in the House of Lords in 1925 Birkenhead had referred to the preamble to the 1919 Act. He said with fine insincerity that the preamble was an excellent aspiration, but that 'I should be guilty of disingenuousness if I painted at this

the exception of its preamble, which was left floating in the legislative air. The 1935 Act contained no reference to dominion status. It was not on all fours with the legislation that had paved the way for dominion status for the white dominions.

In the course of the debates Hoare referred to the absence of reference to dominion status, either in the Bill or in the White Paper. He did say that there was no intention of going back on the preamble to the 1919 Act or of repudiating the Irwin Declaration. That is disingenuous: what is significant is what he did not do. He did not make a specific promise of dominion status in the Bill. It was argued that the words were deliberately excluded to avoid stirring up opposition.[120] In India, the lack of reference to dominion status was perceived to be indicative of a lack of commitment.

Having been drafted with the strength of Conservative opposition in mind, the India Act was guarded and mean. The 'safeguards' in the Bill inevitably gave Indians the impression that the legislation was designed to limit, not facilitate, Independence. 'The British hoped to be able by their superior political knowledge and experience to modify and limit the independence which they knew that India would ultimately acquire.'[121] Sir Robert Horne said, 'In view of the enormous powers and responsibilities which the Governor-General [the viceroy] must exercise in his discretion or according to his individual judgement, it is obvious that he is expected to be a kind of superman.' The concern in India was that the safeguards undermined anything that the Act promised. Jinnah felt that too much power was invested in the viceroy and the provincial governors, and Muslims could not be enthusiastic about the idea of federation. Their experience of Congress majorities at provincial level made sure of that. He was unhappy. The princes were unhappy and Congress was unhappy. The princes were not going to allow their authority to be subsumed in a federal government. The arithmetic of the Act would deny Congress the extent of representation that reflected their popularity: the electoral machinery envisaged by the Bill meant that Congress would be unlikely to have more than 100 seats in the Lower House of 346 seats. Hoare said, as well he might, that the arithmetic was 'not unduly alarming'.

---

moment the prospects in colours too vivid or too sanguine. I am not able, in any foreseeable future, to discern a moment when we may safely, either to ourselves or to India, abandon our trust.'

24

AFTER THE ACT

After the passage of the India Act Hoare looked back on the efforts which had been needed to bring the Act on to the Statute Book. He had seen 473 clauses and sixteen schedules through all the critical stages and although he had left the India Office and become Foreign Secretary before the Third Reading, he had delivered the largest share of the speeches that filled 4,000 pages of Hansard.* 'There had never been a better example of government by parliamentary discussion.'

It's difficult to know how he could write that. The Government's huge majority, backed by intimidation, smear and threats, could not have failed to get the legislation through, and the legislation never served any useful purpose. The constitution it contained never came into operation; Hoare's objective, an All-India Federation, never came into existence; and the unity of India was destroyed. Churchill was severed from the Conservative party by a gap which took four years and a war to bridge.

Churchill described the India Act as a 'monstrous monument of sham built by the pygmies'. His words have sometimes been misquoted as a monument of 'shame'. This is an erroneous report of the radio speech in which the phrase was first used. Churchill certainly thought that the Act was shameful, but he used words with precision, and he said and meant that the Act was a sham, a piece of legislation designed to placate opinion, at home and in America as much as in India, but ultimately something that would never work or lead anywhere. The Act was flawed not by mistake, but deliberately, and the sham was to offer the prospect

---

* In Committee, Hoare gave evidence for six weeks, going through the White Paper section by section. In the course of the first week he wrote, 'I shall be dead soon.' (Bridge, *Holding India to the Empire. The British Conservative Party and the 1935 Constitution*, p. 108.)

of a move towards collective Independence when this could never happen.

The most intensive periods of public protests in India between the wars were probably in 1919 and between 1930 and 1934, but unrest continued at varying levels after the passage of the Act. On the whole, the message of Amritsar had been two-fold: first that British rule depended on power, and secondly that Britain could still deploy it at a requisite level. Britain possessed modern arms, armoured cars and aircraft that Indian protestors did not. Britain also had some 200,000 policemen and an army (in 1939) of 194,000. Morale in the police and army was high and until the outbreak of war, at any rate, both forces were loyal to the Raj.

In the early 1920s there had not been the hostility between the Hindus and Muslims which was later to develop. Most Muslims had supported Congress. The reason for this was in part that Britain had alienated the Muslims following the defeat of the Turks in the First World War, when she required the sultan to renounce his title of Khalifah, in which lay his authority to claim leadership of Muslims throughout the world. During that war, Britain had been sorely concerned by the risk that the Khalifah could suborn the loyalty of Muslims in the subcontinent by declaring a Jihad which would bring the Muslims of India into the war on the side of the Central Powers and against Britain. Strangely enough, while the sultan held the office of Khalifah, Indian Muslims remained loyal to Britain. It was depriving him of the title which threw them into the other camp and their uneasy alliance with Congress.

That alliance began to disintegrate after 1924, when Muslims started to direct their anger towards the Hindus who threatened to imprison them within a united India in which they would be a minority. Some of the worst clashes were in Calcutta in 1930. Muslim shopkeepers declined to join a *hartal* in February of that year, and in the resulting riots between 400 and 500 died. The hostility between Muslims and Hindus was not only based on the insecurity of the Muslims; they were the successors of the Mughals, Britain's predecessors as imperial masters, and there was a Hindu folk-memory of resentment against them which predated hostility towards the British. When Jinnah motored through Karachi in October 1938, he was followed by a three-mile-long procession of supporters in a parade which was reminiscent of those of the Mughal emperors.[122]

The Muslim League had existed before 1935 but it only really came to life in reaction to the 1936–37 elections. Jinnah, its president, remained in Britain after the second Round-table Conference, practising at the Bar. The

League was a patrician body, dominated by landed proprietors. The secretary was Liaquat Ali Khan, a substantial landlord. Jinnah returned to India in 1935 and revived the League to condemn particularly the federal aspects of the 1935 Act. The party's showing in the elections was extremely disappointing. Gandhi's popularity and the skill of the Congress leaders, Azad and Patel, made sure of that. Nehru travelled over 50,000 miles on the course of his campaign in the election. One hundred thousand people attended his meetings and millions more lined the route to see him.

25

RAB BUTLER

Before we leave the India Act, it is appropriate to look at a politician who was much involved in seeing it through parliament, and who continued to take a close interest in India until 1947. R.A. Butler was always referred to as 'Rab'. That gratified his father, who chose his son's names precisely so that his initials would create the nickname. He has made a few entrances already and will continue to come on stage from time to time. Rab Butler is worth looking at not just for himself but as an interesting example of the British establishment in its relations with India.

India was of enormous interest to him. In his autobiography he said that he had spent forty years of public life perched on a tripos. 'One of its legs has been planted in academic groves, another in the arena of politics, the third in what was once a great Raj and is still culturally a microcosm of the world'.[123] He was born in India, where his father was at the time Settlement Officer of Campbellpur District in the Central Provinces of India. To be precise, he was born in the rest house attached to the fort at Attock which had been built by the mogul Emperor Akbar. He never forgot travelling with his parents across India followed by a camel train. The greatest regret of his political life was not that he had failed so closely – twice – to become prime minister, but that he was never viceroy. That at least was what he said, even if it sounds like Butlerian sour grapes.

He was a singularly bloodless man and it's surprising how close he got to being prime minister; but he was an outstandingly intelligent and perceptive observer. He could see that Birkenhead's appointment of the Simon Commission was designed to stymie forward movement. He could see too that Irwin disliked his fellow-Conservative Birkenhead, and welcomed his replacement by the Labour Wedgwood Benn.

Butler entered the House of Commons just five months after Irwin outflanked Birkenhead and Simon with his Declaration. Initially he seemed disposed towards the forces of light, but in September 1932 he became Under-Secretary of State at the India Office and his intimate involvement in the formulation of policy soon caused him to go native, to use an inappropriate expression. He became mesmerised by process, as so many do when immersed in the administrative detail of a large department of state. He worked closely with Sam Hoare, who took most of the burden of the India Bill on himself (even though he didn't arrive in the Office till half past eleven and left shortly afterwards for lunch). 'I was amazed by his ambitions; I admired his imagination; I shared his ideals; I stood in awe of his intellectual capacity,' said Butler of his boss. 'But I was never touched by his humanity. He was the coldest fish with whom I have ever had to deal'.[124] He must have been pretty cold.

In his autobiography Butler refers to himself with apparent pride as part of the Conservative party establishment. He had no great time for Harold Macmillan (unsurprisingly, given that Macmillan not only beat him for leadership of the party in 1957 but also when he gave up that leadership took the extreme step of ensuring that Alec Douglas Home rather than Butler succeeded him); he writes off Macmillan at least in the 1930s as irresponsible and Left-wing. As a representative of the responsible Conservative establishment, Butler remained for the rest of his life of the view that the India Act, which did so little for India, was a boon and blessing for the subcontinent. He claimed that the bill was founded on Dicey and Anson, the nineteenth-century English constitutional writers, and thought that its adherence to constitutional orthodoxy imbued it with virtue.

Like a remarkable number of the personages who dominate the story of the last days of the Raj, he had a problem with a limb. In his case he had suffered a riding accident as a child which left him with a right hand that wasn't fully functioning. It has been suggested that his limp handshake, as much as Macmillan's interventions, may have cost him his party's leadership. Only Simon and he have served in three of those great offices of state (Chancellor, Home Secretary and Foreign Secretary) without becoming prime minister.

26

LINLITHGOW: A NEW VICEROY FOR THE NEW ACT

Victor Alexander John Hope, Lord Linlithgow, 'Hopie' after his family name, was appointed viceroy on 18 April 1936 in succession to Lord Willingdon. He was an agreeable aristocrat. He was highly principled, an elder of the Church of Scotland, kindly and well meaning, with a compendious knowledge of the music hall. He enjoyed popular songs and in particular singing them with his family. He howled 'like a dog' when a wrong note was sung. His sense of humour was not elevated: his favourite comedians were Bud Flanagan and 'Monsewer' Eddie Gray. Although an abstemious man, on an expedition to a remote part of India he claimed that he had seen a pink elephant and he subsequently proved himself correct. Even his son acknowledged that he was not a clever man. He was a Scots countryman who derived much simple and commendable enjoyment from the observation of nature. As he made his way to India to take up his appointment, the estate factor at Hopetoun tidied the path to the family mausoleum. He said that one never knew what might happen.

Linlithgow identified the obstacles to progress as Indian political stupidity and British political dishonesty, but he was himself a master of the ability to say something which meant very little, and to decorate it with qualifications like 'in the light of the then circumstances', and 'subject to such modifications as may seem desirable'.[125]

Linlithgow had polio as a boy and his neck muscles were damaged. He couldn't turn his head without turning his shoulders as well. Like Irwin, he was exceptionally tall – six feet and five inches. His other qualifications were exiguous. He had chaired a Royal Commission on Indian agriculture and the parliamentary committee on Indian constitutional reform. He spent seven years in the office of viceroy, longer than anyone else since Lord Dalhousie, ninety years earlier.

The 1935 Act had created all the requirements for stasis. It set the princes, Muslim League and Congress in architectural opposition to each other. Linlithgow was the ideal man to preside over stagnation. He did not have vision. He was an old-fashioned administrator. He and his family went into dinner each night as the viceroy's band played 'The Roast Beef of Old England'. He lacked flexibility and took minor and technical breaches of etiquette very seriously. He wrote a four-page letter to the Secretary of State complaining that a maharajah had arrived wearing the insignia of two obscure European Orders of Chivalry, and asked 'What punitive action was recommended?' He and his wife Doreen, at just under six feet almost as tall as he, chased butterflies in the Simla hills.[126] There is a rather good photograph of this very large viceroy with an equally large butterfly net, riding on a very small pony in Kashmir in pursuit of his quarry.

Baldwin had chosen him as viceroy in preference to the Marquess of Zetland, who had been appointed Secretary of State in 1937. Zetland called the Laird of Hopetoun the 'wise, cautious Hopie'. Rab Butler called him an honest but rigorous man. Wavell, his successor, described him as 'a wise, strong man and very human really'. Others referred to his 'cold exterior'. The editor of the Calcutta-based but then English-owned *Statesman* found this 'cold, cautious, self-assured aristocrat . . . outwardly . . . an inscrutable rather unpleasant figure: stiff, unsmiling; physically very large . . . and in some indefinable way uncouth'; though he later conceded that Linlithgow had been 'perhaps an over-criticised man'. Nehru accepted his 'integrity and honesty of purpose' although he was 'heavy of body and slow of mind, solid as a rock and with almost a rock's lack of awareness'.[127]

But he was an honourable man. He worked hard by his lights, though not nearly as hard as the viceroys who succeeded him, Wavell and Mountbatten. He had time to visit remote parts of the subcontinent, both for fact-finding and sightseeing, with a reasonable amount of hunting and sport thrown in.

His principal objectives were to see the 1935 Act and the constitution it contained operating efficiently, to bring the princes on board and to establish federation. In all of these he failed. He is particularly criticised for not putting enough effort into the case for federation. The outbreak of war put an end to the project, though one senses that he was relieved to have an excuse. His supporters (of whom there are few) point to the fact that by then nearly two-fifths of the states were ready to join, though some of them made accession conditional on the protection of their treaty rights. Linlithgow himself believed that he could have secured federation by July 1941 if war had not broken out. Whether getting together twenty states out of fifty-two with a population of 11 million out of 39 million is a commendable achievement or a disappointing failure is open to debate. To be fair, the *Statesman*, even in the aftermath of the outbreak of war, thought that with one last push federation could be achieved within a day or two.

After the 1937 Indian election which followed the implementation of the India Act, Congress refused to take the seats which they'd won. Linlithgow was frustrated but not prepared to buy Congress support by an undertaking about how the governors would use powers reserved to them in terms of the constitution. Now and ever afterwards he was unhelpfully inflexible wherever the constitution was concerned. From London, Irwin (now Halifax) and Zetland felt that concessions should be made and that at any rate there should be a conference with the Congress leaders.

Zetland has been said to have been cast in the mould of Curzon, whose biographer he was.* He was for good government rather than self-government. He approved of Morley–Minto diarchy. As Secretary of State he was responsible for getting the India Bill through the Lords. He was fascinated by India and well-disposed to the subcontinent, but his outlook was informed by an orientalist concept of the alien, non-Western nature of Hindu culture. Like others he saw the role of the princes and Muslims as an essential balance to the aspirations of Congress. When Sir Michael O'Dwyer was shot dead at the Caxton Hall meeting in March 1940, Zetland was also hit. But it was Churchill's appointment as prime minister two months later and not the bullet that ended his political career.

Linlithgow dug his heels in and told Zetland that things were not as they had been in Halifax's time. There was now 'a Constitution written in an Act the ink of which is hardly yet dry, and which is being satisfactorily worked in five provinces' and he did not want his powers and those of the governors limited at this early stage.[128] The response in the *Statesman* was a headline of 2 May 1937: 'Indian impasse deplored – unofficial anxiety – the viceroy's silence unhelpful'.

In debate in the House of Lords shortly after the appearance of the *Statesman* article, Lord Snell, leading the Labour opposition, asserted that the deadlock was due to a clash of temperaments rather than to substantial differences. He urged that the Government should give an assurance that

---

* He even looked as if he wore a steel corset, as Curzon had done, according the historians of the National Trust, whose president he was. He didn't wear one.

the reserved powers of the governors would not be used indiscriminately. No assurance was given.

Meanwhile Linlithgow pursued a persistent policy of not talking to Gandhi, which was characteristic of his lack of flexibility. He told Zetland, 'As you know, I am moved by conditions of prestige only where I think that of any political importance. But I cannot altogether eliminate the political importance of the prestige element and the risk of a rebuff, or an embarrassing breakdown, in this case'.[129] The claim that he was concerned not about damage to his prestige for its own sake, but for its political implications, is unconvincing. He rejected a meeting despite the fact that Gandhi had indicated in a speech in June 1937 that he was very anxious that Congress should take office, provided only that the Government showed a willingness to conciliate. Zetland thought that this justified going forward to a meeting. Linlithgow was aghast at the idea that the Secretary of State was against him and at once sent a telegram saying that he would resign rather than yield. Zetland was surprised by the reaction and said that he had merely been thinking aloud, not imposing policy on the viceroy – but the question was irrelevant, because before Zetland could have responded Congress had decided to accept office unconditionally. Some thought the outcome was a triumph for the viceroy, whose nerve had held. Others thought that Congress displayed statesmanship in contrast to the viceroy's obstinacy.

When Linlithgow arrived in India he had found that the Indian Civil Service (ICS) took the view that the India Office in London was half-hearted about the idea of federation which had been contained in the India Act. He tried to dispel that impression, but without any marked success.

By now the ICS was finding it difficult to obtain suitable officers. There had been a drop in recruitment and in the quality of candidates since the First World War. Linlithgow considered it incapable of dealing with the government of India post-federation. In administration as in politics, the absence of planning was evident. There had been no forward thinking. Vacancies had not been filled and there was no continuous supply of properly qualified officers. In 1936 there was a numerical shortfall of ninety recruits. The Service resisted Linlithgow's attempts to improve it. By 1938 he had made a further assessment of his civil service. He was concerned that senior officials were overworked and under strain. There were instances of resignations because of ill-health. There was also a shortage of 'really competent men of sufficient seniority and experience'. He was aware that there simply was not an adequate administrative machine in place for the demands of the future, and considered the matter to be one of gravity. But he got nowhere. Recruitment was not increased – he particularly wanted to see the European intake supplemented – and senior members threatened to resign rather than see their juniors promoted over their heads.[130]

The larger context, the world picture, was of a deteriorating political situation in which no one really doubted the inevitability of war in the near future. Linlithgow was particularly aware of the threat to India from Japan. In the winter of 1937–38, one of his sons found him lying on the floor of his study looking at a map. He said something which few others noted until the fact had been brought home with tragic clarity: 'I believe that our guns in Singapore are facing the wrong way'.[131]

27

INDIAN POLITICS

Linlithgow's son says that the viceroy saw self-government for a united India as 'the ultimate goal, but, like most of those who understood the complexity of the situation, he saw the final step as a good many years ahead'. He also goes on to say, and here is the indictment of Tory policy, '[N]o-one knew what complete self-government amounted to. What were Great Britain's exact ultimate intentions? Was there to be unrestricted self-government for the old dominions under [the Statute of] Westminster but a restricted sort for India with Britain bent on keeping the reserved powers of defence and external affairs as defined in the 1935 Act? Neither Indians nor British people in India were sure.'[132] These questions, the reflection of indecision, are rarely voiced, but they go to the heart of Britain's failure.

As late as January 1939, Linlithgow thought that dominion status was so remote as to be not worth thinking about: 'No one can, of course, say what, in some remote period of time, or in the event of international convulsions of a particular character, may be the ultimate relations of India and Great Britain . . . but that there should be any general impression . . . that public opinion at home, or His Majesty's Government, seriously contemplate evacuation in any measurable period of time, seems to me astonishing'.[133] Given such a view, it's hardly surprising that negotiations with Indian politicians were not fruitful.

Linlithgow was initially concerned to advance federation. Zetland was not, although he claimed in his memoirs to have been. His attention was diverted from India by other matters – the abdication crisis and foreign affairs. There is little mention of federation in Zetland's early correspondence with Linlithgow. The viceroy argued that time was limited, but Zetland did not even press ahead with the drafting of the Instruments of Accession. The princes were 'shy birds . . . and might easily take fright'. Any precipitation would 'frighten them off'.[134] Linlithgow has been blamed

Image of empire. The Highlanders recover Cawnpore in the aftermath of what Churchill's contemporaries always called the Mutiny and Indians know as the First War of Independence. (Courtesy of the author)

Two men about as different as they could be.
F.E. Smith (Lord Birkenhead), arrogant, brilliant,
entirely cynical. (© National Portrait Gallery,
London). Gandhi (here in London), elusive and
inspiring. (Copyright © Getty Images)

Gandhi on the Salt March, daring the British to imprison him. (Mary Evans Picture Library)

In Delhi in 1931 Gandhi dictates the terms of his Peace Treaty with Irwin. Churchill and others excoriated the Viceroy for 'doing obeisance' before Gandhi. (Copyright © Getty Images)

Edward Wood. Viceroy as Lord Irwin, finally Earl of Halifax. Burningly sincere and with a grandeur of spirit even more impressive than his physical height. (© National Portrait Gallery, London)

The National Government 1931. Left to right *sitting*, Philip Snowden, Stanley Baldwin, Ramsay MacDonald, Herbert Samuel (Lord Samuel), Lord Sankey; *standing* Sir Philip Cunliffe-Lister, Neville Chamberlain, J. H. Thomas, Rufus Isaacs (Lord Reading) and Sir Samuel Hoare. (Copyright © Mirrorpix)

Lord Linlithgow, Viceroy 1936–1943. Well-meaning but often, as perhaps here, not at the level of events. (Copyright © Getty Images)

Leo Amery. A potential prime minister if he had been half a foot taller and his speeches half-an-hour shorter. But as Powys Evans shows him here for the *Saturday Review*, raised on peaks above the horizon, a man of vision. (Mary Evans Picture Library)

Wavell. A thoroughly decent and very able Viceroy. He could have achieved much if his political masters had been equally decent. (Copyright © IWM TR 842)

Stafford Cripps. High-minded but practical, ultimately frustrated by the Nationalists' refusal to compromise. (© National Portrait Gallery, London)

Cripps on his 1942 Mission. A happy moment with Gandhi in the course of a Mission that ended unhappily. (Copyright © IWM IND 740)

Mountbatten at the Conference in the course of which he revealed his partition plans to Nehru (left) and Jinnah (right). 'Pug' Ismay, in the background, seems to be enjoying himself more than the principals. (Copyright © Getty Images)

Lady Mountbatten looks on as Nehru is sworn in as India's first prime minister by the last Viceroy. (Copyright © IWM GOV 1929)

Mountbatten and Lady Mountbatten flank Jinnah on Britain's last day of power in Pakistan. On the following day Jinnah was sworn in as Pakistan's first governor-general and president of the Constituent Assembly. He had been ill for many years, and died just thirteen months later. (Everett Collection/Mary Evans)

The reality of the aftermath. One of countless images of the savagery that followed partition. Here the bodies of Muslim men, women and children lie in the streets of a town in East Punjab after Sikh *jathas* have passed through. (Copyright © Illustrated London News/Mary Evans)

THE MALIGNED MATRON

There was an old woman who lived in a shoe
She had dozens of children—adopted ones too;
She nursed them and taught them and said they might go;
But did they say "Thank you"? Not all of them—no.

The aftermath as *Punch* saw it. Britannia's now independent children aren't sufficiently grateful for all she's done for them. (Copyright © Punch) for delay, but Hoare himself when Secretary of State had argued for delay because he feared that there would not be an adequate take-up from the princes.

When war broke out, Linlithgow and Zetland were coming to the view that the future of federation, and of progress generally, would be more assured if Muslim apprehensions about Hindu domination could be addressed. They decided that the Muslim League should be strengthened so as to be on an equal footing with Congress, despite the fact that at the 1936 elections the League had only 105 out of 489 *Muslim* seats and did not control a single government *in any of the Muslim majority provinces*. (My emphasis.) Jinnah saw that he was wanted. Formerly he had been distant and uncooperative. He frequently found it inconvenient to attend meetings with the viceroy and always turned up late, unlike Gandhi, who was most punctual. Now, by his standards, he became genial. On 5 October 1939 he thanked Linlithgow 'with much graciousness' for what the viceroy had done to assist in keeping his party together. V.P. Menon* wrote that 'The League grew rapidly in the sunshine of favour.'[135] The sun shone ostensibly because Linlithgow thought it unfair that Muslim opinion should not be adequately represented; but he and other important officials, including the Commander-in-Chief, Sir Robert Cassels, were delighted to 'hit [Congress] over the head while we are in a position to do so'. At Linlithgow's request, Zetland said in the House of Lords that the British Government regarded an agreement between the Hindus and Muslims to be a pre-condition for constitutional changes. As Gowher Rizvi puts it, 'The government would thus be left free to carry on the war unhindered.'[136]

Linlithgow pretty well admitted what he was up to: '[Jinnah] had given me very valuable help by standing against the Congress claims and I was duly grateful. It was clear that if he, Mr Jinnah, had supported the Congress demand . . . the strain upon me and His Majesty's Government would have been very great indeed. I thought therefore I could claim to have a vested interest in his position.' In private he said that it would have been difficult to resist joint demands for what was essentially Independence. In public, he said that he had begged the leaders 'spare no endeavour to reach agreement'.[137]

---

* V.P. Menon started out as a railway stoker. He became a civil servant and had a crucial role in advising the last three viceroys on constitutional matters. His part in resolving difficulties with the princes is dealt with in Chapter 47.

He urged the League to put forward proposals to counteract Congress demands, telling Jinnah that if he did not wish to let the Hindu case gain acceptance by default he should put forward his own plans. Until now Jinnah had made no reference to partition, but when Congress demanded complete Independence in March 1940, the League, meeting three days later at Lahore, declared for an independent Pakistan.

Until around 1935 British politicians held the initiative. They didn't do much with it, but they largely controlled events, and if they had chosen to be bold and unselfish they could have changed things for the better. After that time things changed. Politicians now struggled to deal with circumstances they could not control. The change was the result of the concurrence of events, among them the outbreak of war and the resolution at Lahore.

The 'Pakistan Resolution' created a new dimension. The *Manchester Guardian* on 2 April 1940 said that 'Mr Jinnah has re-established the reign of chaos in India.' As late as the time of Wavell, Linlithgow's successor, the official view was that Britain would benefit best from an association with a united India, the nearest thing available to a continuation of the Raj; but for Linlithgow, at least in the current military context, the 'Pakistan Resolution' meant that the conduct of the war would not be imperilled by premature Indian Independence. So, 'Silly as the Muslim League [scheme] for partition is,' said Linlithgow, 'it would be a pity to throw too much cold water on it at the moment.' Divide and rule. There was no need to discuss what would happen after British rule, because the possibility was 'very remote . . . I am not a bit fussed about the post-war period'.[138] If ever a peaceful transition to a unitary state had been possible, the outcome of Britain's encouragement to Jinnah to formulate his own policy had made certain that it never would be again.

The League's plan for partition, standing apart from the union, was not as novel as it sounds, nor purely reflective of the Indian situation. In Canada, some of the former colonies came in late, and delayed accession is another facet of their partition. The original dominion was created in 1867 but Manitoba did not come in until 1870, British Columbia in 1871, Prince Edward Island in 1873 and Newfoundland in 1949. Similarly in Australia, New South Wales and Western Australia came in late and New Zealand stayed apart and became a separate dominion – a precedent for partition.

28

POLICY AND THE WAR

Returning briefly to the outbreak of war, on 3 September 1939 Chamberlain delivered his solipsistic broadcast to the British people, telling them how disappointing it was for him that Britain was at war with Germany. Linlithgow now made the greatest mistake of his viceroyalty. On the same day as Chamberlain, Linlithgow also made a radio announcement, a very brief one. Without consultation, without any decision by their own leaders, Indians learned that they too were at war with Germany. This precipitate move was to focus the constitutional struggle by Congress leaders for the rest of British rule.

Linlithgow was technically entitled to do what he did. The Government of India Act had been amended just a few months earlier to allow him to do so. But it was a serious political mistake. The reaction against it turned out to be even more serious than he could have imagined; but even without the benefit of hindsight it can seem to have been silly and unnecessary.

Congress was probably more strongly against Fascism than Britain had been. Congress had criticised Britain's policy of appeasement and of neutrality during the Spanish Civil War. But the party had made it equally clear by various resolutions that acquiescence in a Declaration of War was not to be taken for granted. For instance, when Indian troops were sent to Aden, Egypt and Singapore in August 1939, before the outbreak of war, Congress reacted strongly. Ahead of the declaration, Zetland and Linlithgow considered the situation, and specifically what would happen if Congress members resigned from office. Linlithgow arranged for emergency legislation at Westminster, which conferred executive authority on the central government. So he had not been unaware of the dangers of what he did.

While, as a matter of law, Britain's declaration of war took India with her, Linlithgow was as usual more concerned with constitutional theory rather than political realities, legally correct but politically ill-advised. Congress pointed out that the dominions had been allowed to decide for themselves. They argued that India, though not a dominion, should have been treated similarly. While consultation with the political leaders would not have achieved much – Nehru, for example, would have withheld his consent – Linlithgow could have gone through some process of consultation with the Council of State.

Gandhi's position at the outset of the war demonstrates a good deal of other-worldliness. He thought that in the face of Hitler's aggression, German Jews and Czechs should simply resort to non-resistance and Britain should submit to German occupation. But then he thought that Hitler was a 'patriot . . . not a bad man'.[139] Nehru, always more realistic, saw what Nazism and Fascism amounted to, unlike his Congress colleague, Subhas Chandra Bose, the future Indian National Army leader.

Almost as soon as war broke out, the British Government was pressed to define its policy in relation to India. Attlee understood India's resentment over Linlithgow's tactless unilateral declaration of war. In the House of Commons he criticised Linlithgow for being out of touch with reality and lacking 'imaginative insight'. Labour pressed the Government to define its policy. Linlithgow's reaction to the war was to batten down the hatches and sit out the storm. On 11 September he ended negotiations over federation. Zetland concurred, without even taking the matter to Cabinet.

When Congress asked the viceroy for clarification of Britain's Indian policy, Linlithgow had no response: 'It is a tragedy in many ways that at a time such as this we should have in so important a position a doctrinaire like Nehru, with his amateur knowledge of foreign politics and of the international stage'.[140] He proposed to say that Britain's objective remained dominion status and go on to talk about returning to the federal scheme when the war was ended. On 14 October 1939 the Cabinet generally approved of that, but – interestingly – suppressed the dominion commitment, saying simply that India would take its 'due place amongst the dominions'. When Congress responded by telling its members in provincial ministries to resign their offices, Zetland told the Cabinet that while everyone had thought that the road to dominion status would be a very long one, the events of the war meant that Cabinet members 'must make up their minds how far they were now prepared to go to implement the promises contained in our earlier pledges'. It was a novel concept that the Cabinet might actually have to keep its promises.[141]

Churchill, now back in the Cabinet as First Lord of the Admiralty but not yet prime minister, was of course not for yielding to those who were taking advantage of Britain's plight. He convinced the Cabinet that the issue of federation was now dead and that Linlithgow should not try to resuscitate it. So all Congress provincial ministers withdrew from office and their powers reverted to the governors. The Muslim-dominated governments of Bengal and the Punjab, however, supported the war and thus it was that Jinnah was able to say at the Lahore Conference in March 1940 that in return he expected partition and the creation of a Pakistan after the war.

But the issue of dominion status couldn't be entirely ignored. The British 'by their very honesty of purpose' as Linlithgow's son endearingly puts it,[142] were obliged to recognise that the Statute of Westminster gave a new definition to dominion status. Dominion status now meant – in general – complete Independence, including freedom to leave the Commonwealth.

Linlithgow believed very strongly indeed that there should be no constitutional changes during the war. He argued against taking any initiative, and particularly against doing anything that would upset the princes or the Muslims. Zetland, on the other hand, felt that some promises had to be given about the future. In response, on 10 January 1940 Linlithgow said in a speech at the Orient Club that the Government did wish India to achieve 'full dominion status . . . of the Statute of Westminster variety' as soon as possible, although not until the war had ended: he said that the Government was ready to review the Government of India Act of 1935 with India immediately after the war. This was the first time that the Government had committed itself to Statute of Westminster dominion status for India – but of course it was only undertaking to do so if agreement were reached with the Indians, and not during the war or at any specified time thereafter. In any event, Britain had now separated the communities so far that a constitutional settlement was the remotest possibility.

While Linlithgow's speech, in which he also referred to an expansion of his Executive Council, was quite well received in India, it provoked angry reactions in London. There were many there who had no wish to see India obtain an 'independence' which amounted to the kind of independence that Canada and Australia had. Sir Henry Page-Croft, later a Parliamentary Under-Secretary under Churchill, wrote to Zetland, saying that he was 'astonished' that 'the Viceroy should have gone out of his way to stress that dominion status was of the same kind as that provided by the Statute of Westminster'. His reaction shows the gulf between those in office, even at a low level, and the expectations of Indian politicians.[143]

On 24 March 1940, Linlithgow had a meeting with G.D. Birla, a rich Congress supporter who traditionally acted as an intermediary for Gandhi. The viceroy warned Birla that although British Conservatives accepted the principle of self-rule, they did not accept that India would achieve the type of dominion status envisaged by the Statute of Westminster.

And there were British Conservatives and British Conservatives. Two months later Churchill succeeded Chamberlain as prime minister. Zetland, who had been a very slightly reformist influence on the viceroy, immediately resigned as Secretary of State for India and wrote to Linlithgow saying that he was not likely to be a member of the Government any longer, as Churchill's approach to India was so different from his. He was succeeded by Leo Amery.

29

AMERY

Churchill's appointment of Amery as Secretary of State was surprising. He had been prominent in opposing Churchill and the diehards in the debates on the India bill in 1934–35. He had even humiliated Churchill with his 'Fiat justitia' trick. He was now 'to renew, in the privacy of the Cabinet, the same fundamental divergence of outlook which had separated us on the floor of the House for many years'.[144] In his first statement in parliament as Secretary of State, Amery said that the Government's goal was the attainment by India of free and equal partnership in the British Commonwealth.

Leo Amery was seventeen inches shorter than the viceroy, Lord Linlithgow. It was said that if he had been six inches longer and his speeches thirty minutes shorter he might have been prime minister. He was a strange choice for Churchill to have as his Secretary of State for India. Not only had he opposed Churchill during the debates on the India Bill; he and Churchill were not particularly close on other issues. Their acquaintance went back to Harrow, when because of Amery's lack of stature Churchill, not realising that he was attacking his senior, threw him into a swimming pool. He attempted to mollify his victim: 'My father, who is also not tall, is a great man.'

I have mentioned the reach of Milner's influence.* Amery was just too young to be a member of the Kindergarten, but he was closely associated with it, and Milner regarded him with approval and promoted his career. Amery regarded Milner as the greatest statesman of the Empire. Like Milner, he used All Souls' as a resource for research and a platform for the dissemination of his views. Even if Amery was too short to become prime minister, for a generation his influence, mostly from the back benches, was pretty powerful. He was Acting Secretary of State at the Colonial Office for

---

* See Chapter 3.

four months in 1919, when Milner was in Egypt, and Colonial Secretary from 1924 to 1929. He 'became the theorist *par excellence* of British Imperialism'.[145] He sought to replace incoherent policy improvisations with a degree of theoretical consistency. But while the Empire was for him 'the final object of the patriotic emotion and action',[146] his imperial policy, like that of Milner and Chamberlain, was a forward one, not informed by nostalgia. Thus he saw Churchill as not a constructive Radical, like Joseph Chamberlain, Milner and himself, but essentially as 'a retrospective Whig of the period 1750–1850, with very little capacity for looking forward'.[147] In relation to India, Milner's position was finely nuanced. He was not illiberal, no diehard, but that is not to say that he was in favour of Independence. His imperial policy remained a foward one. And yet there is no saying where his intelligence and logical response might have taken him, had he been at the India Office after the war.

Churchill had pretty well acquiesced in the loss of India back in 1935, when the Act was passed, but in power he found himself again in a position to be obstructive. And Amery had to deal not only with Churchill, but Churchill's former colleague in opposition to the India Bill, Lord Lloyd, who was now Colonial Secretary. He didn't receive much help from Attlee, even though the latter had been a member of the Simon Commission and was favourably disposed to Indian aspirations. Amery described the Labour ministers in the Cabinet as 'Mice . . . incredibly feeble creatures'.[148]

He made his first statement as Secretary of State in the House of Commons on 23 May 1940. The tone of his remarks was not significantly different from that of his predecessor's utterances. The Government's aim was to see India as a member of the British Commonwealth. Some sort of shift from the position of the 1935 Act was envisaged and India was to have a part in formulating that shift, a part which was originally described as 'predominant', but which the Cabinet toned down to 'vital'. There was also a reference to communal problems. Congress objected to this on the traditional and sometimes reasonable grounds that Britain was playing the 'divide and rule' card.

Sir Stafford Cripps urged on Amery what was really the germ of the mission Cripps would take to India in 1942 – the idea of Independence post-dated to the end of the war. At the same time Linlithgow got to work on Amery. The viceroy had moved from concentrating on implementation of the 1935 Act to looking at the practical problem of governing India in the war. He wanted to expand his Council and to appoint a War Advisory Committee which would include representatives of the princes, whether or not he had the support of Congress or the Muslim League. He also wanted, in a more conciliatory sense, to announce that the Government would aim at dominion status within a year of the end of the war. Amery was entirely with Linlithgow in these proposals, but he had forgotten to get the prime minister's agreement. When Churchill found out what had been going on he was furious. Amery was taken aback by the vehemence of Churchill's opposition in Cabinet – and by the lack of support amongst other Cabinet members. Only the Labour members, Attlee and Greenwood, supported him. Churchill insisted in interfering and seeing all the telegrams that passed between Amery and Linlithgow. This was unprecedented and Amery regarded it as 'absurd that what are in effect private conversations' should be censored in this way. Churchill didn't like the tone of the correspondence and Amery only refrained from resigning because the country was at war. Churchill cabled the viceroy:

Secretary of State has shown me the telegrams which have been passed on secret and personal file and for the first time I realised what has been going on. I must ask in the public interest and in justice to you to show these telegrams to the War Cabinet and two or three other colleagues who have great Indian experience and whom I have consulted . . . The Cabinet, on Thursday July 25, considered your new draft statement [regarding the War Advisory Council]. We did not reach any conclusion going beyond the declaration made by the Secretary of State in the House of Commons on May 23 which defined the policy of the new government in broad accordance with the views expressed by the late administration in the full knowledge of your views and wishes on the subject. The Cabinet has left it to me to draft for your consideration an alternative statement in harmony with the only policies to which we are at present committed. I will send this to you as soon as I have completed it for your perfectly free consideration and suggestions.

You must remember that we are here facing the constant threat of invasion with many strange and novel features, and this is only held off and can only be mastered literally from day to day by the prowess of our airmen at heavy odds and by the vigilance of the Royal Navy. In these circumstances immense constitutional departures cannot be effectively discussed in Parliament and only by the Cabinet to the detriment of matters touching the final life and safety of the State. I am sure that I can count upon you to help us to the utmost of your power.[149]

Amery had been inept in springing a new policy departure on his colleagues – and on Churchill of all people. The result – having Churchill himself involved in drafting a declaration – was the least helpful approach that could have been achieved. Amery complained to Linlithgow: 'The whole terrific fuss which he made, culminating in my showing him every telegram that passed between us, was really irrelevant and unnecessary. The trouble is that he reacts instinctively and passionately against the whole idea of any government of India other than that which he knew forty years ago . . .'[150]

In the event, after all of Churchill's interventions, Amery and Linlithgow got more or less what they wanted in an offer that was made to India on 8 August 1940, usually known as the August Offer. But the scope of what was offered was limited. There was no definite commitment to dominion status, although that status remained the ultimate object. All that would be available immediately was an enlargement of the Viceroy's Council. There was no timetable for progress, and there would be no transfer of responsibilities.

There was a critical proviso to any promises the Offer held out. There would be no transfer 'to any system of government whose authority is directly denied by large and powerful elements in India's national life'. For some years afterwards, this proviso was pulled out whenever the nationalists seemed in the ascendant. The Offer ended with the promise that if India co-operated the result would be a new understanding which would lead the way to 'free and equal partnership in the British Commonwealth which remains the proclaimed and accepted goal of the imperial Crown and of the British parliament'.

With the proviso about the interests of minorities, the offer meant nothing. Gandhi was not impressed: 'It has been the traditional policy of Britain to prevent parties from uniting. "Divide and rule" has been Britain's proud motto. It is the British statesmen who are responsible for the divisions in India's ranks and the divisions will continue so long as the British sword holds India under bondage.'[151]

Congress rejected the August Offer outright and the Working Committee of the Muslim League in part. Linlithgow prepared to crush Congress if it launched civil disobedience. He asked London for powers to arrest Congress leaders whenever he wanted and declare the whole body an illegal representation. He didn't minimise the importance of what he was doing.

But despite occasional prime ministerial eruptions, Linlithgow and Churchill worked well together. The viceroy by now saw his role as solely defending the integrity of India as a strategic centre. Churchill liked that. Linlithgow was due to retire in April 1941, but in October 1940 Churchill asked him to stay on for a further year. The diehard in principle recognised a reactionary in practice. Attlee, on the other hand, thought that Linlithgow wasn't taking the political part of his brief seriously enough and suggested to Amery in January 1942 that a 'mission should be sent out to bring the political leaders together'.

But that suggestion lay in the future. For the moment, still in 1941, Linlithgow asked for the Cabinet's agreement, which he received, to put the expanded Council Plan into limbo. Gandhi proposed civil disobedience. The Indian Government prohibited the printing or publishing of any matter calculated to foment opposition to the prosecution of the war. Nehru was sentenced to four years' imprisonment.

Far from moving towards ever more democratic government, India was now largely under direct rule by the viceroy. This didn't sit well in the context of the battle for democracy, and the United States in particular was becoming increasingly critical. By May 1941, Linlithgow and Amery decided that they *would* enlarge the Executive Council, bypassing Congress, and taking in useful private individuals. But the prime minister didn't want any of this. He wrote to Amery: '[Y]ou say "Linlithgow's proposals are the least with which I can continue to hold the House of Commons". This ought not to be the criterion for governing India. I may add that I should find no difficulty in riddling these proposals in Debate to the satisfaction of the overwhelming majority of Members, whether of the Right or the Left.'[152] He was telling Amery that he would have to give up his job if he couldn't carry the House of Commons.

But Churchill had to face the fact that – on this narrow issue – Amery, with the support of Attlee, Anderson and Simon, could carry the Cabinet. The Viceroy's Executive was duly reconstructed. Reform of the Executive did not however represent any sort of political *démarche*. Linlithgow's policy was one of inaction and Churchill treated the rejection of the August Offer as proof that Britain had done its best, to no avail. Stasis ruled.

30

Military Developments

For the first two years of the war, Congress was really remarkably quiescent. Its intention was to use the war to squeeze concessions out of Britain. It made little practical progress. The situation became tenser after the Japanese entered the war in December 1941. On 21 January 1942 Linlithgow sent a telegram to Amery which greatly disturbed Attlee ('Crude imperialism . . . an astonishing statement to be made by a Viceroy'):

> India and Burma have no natural association with the Empire, from which they are alien by race, history and religion, and for which as such neither of them have any natural affection, and both are in the Empire because they are conquered countries which have been brought there by force, kept there by our controls, and which hitherto it has suited to remain under our protection.[153]

His conclusion was that since India was needed for the war, it was better to carry on with things as they were than to attempt any constitutional changes. To keep parliament and British popular opinion happy, the government should 'harp' on Indian differences and insist that it would not go back on its pledges to the Muslims, whose demands were incompatible with those of Congress.

This was, as Attlee said, a pretty remarkable statement. Linlithgow was certainly under a good deal of strain and he was conscious of the strategic imperative of keeping India in Britain's war. All the same, his attitudes to the alien nature of India (and Burma) as opposed to the white dominions, reveal views that can never have been far below the surface. He treated it as axiomatic that the peoples of India were alien, exotic, unloved and unloving, quite evidently not on a conveyor belt to imminent dominion status and the cousinly bonds of the Commonwealth. The blunt recourse to divide and rule is disappointing. Attlee questioned the viceroy's judgement. He thought that his attitude justified 'the action of every extremist in India'.

The military element of the equation was important. The army's intelligence department constantly tried to assess the strength of loyalty amongst Indian officers. In Malaya in 1941–42, 6 per cent of the Indian officers serving in that country for the British (though not admitted to their clubs) were strongly nationalist. There is much anecdotal evidence to suggest that such views were widespread throughout the Indian Army. It was, as Lawrence James puts it, because 'brown men had to be persuaded to die for a white man's empire' that Sir Stafford Cripps went to India with his mission in March 1942.[154] A great deal of anecdotal evidence suggests that the Indian soldiers who volunteered to fight for Britain did so in part because of the belief that they would thereby hasten Independence. Churchill saw things otherwise – though endearingly when he heard of the contribution of Indian troops in Eritrea in April 1941, he was reminded of his own times on the North-West Frontier, as 'one who had the honour to serve in the field with Indian soldiers from all parts of Hindustan'.[155]

Gandhi did not want the Japanese in India, but worse still was Britain remaining in India and being joined, as they were, by American troops: 'American rule added to British'. His other-worldliness was never more evident than when he proclaimed that 'Japan would not invade India but if they did they would simply be defeated by *Satyagraha*.' In the meantime, to help events along, he inaugurated the Quit India campaign in the second week of August 1942.

I shall examine Quit India in Chapter 35, in the political context of the aftermath of the 1942 Cripps Mission. For the moment all that need be said in the military context is that this was the most systematic effort yet to paralyse the country. Britain could suppress the Quit India disturbances, but the Japanese were unstoppable and the military situation was grave. They captured Singapore in February 1942 and advanced through Burma, with all the appearance of being ready to attack India itself. Burma had not been part of India since 1935, but it had its own nationalist movement, and many Burmese openly fought alongside the Japanese and without payment. Later, when the British fought back through Burma under Slim to recover the territory that was lost to the Japanese, at least equal numbers cooperated with the British. At this stage, however, Britain was being driven out of Burma and looked very like being driven out of India too.

On 16 February 1942, the day after the fall of Singapore, Linlithgow cabled to Amery, 'I am carrying here, almost single-handed, an immense responsibility. Indeed, I do not think I exaggerate to affirm that the key to success in this war is very largely in my hands'.[156] He may have exaggerated slightly (he was inclined to dramatisation at this period), but even if he could not deliver victory he could certainly have presided over defeat. Eight days later, Chiang Kai-Shek, the President of the Chinese Republic, visited India and recorded, 'I feel strongly that if the Indian political problem is not immediately solved, the danger will be daily increasing . . . If the Japanese should know of the real situation and attack India, they would be virtually unopposed.' He told Roosevelt that if the British Government did not fundamentally change their policy, 'it would be like presenting India to the enemy'.[157] His views prompted Roosevelt to the anti-imperialist rhetoric which so irritated Churchill.

Another effect of the war on the Indian situation was financial. Until the war, India had owed money to Britain. As the war went on she became a substantial creditor, supplying men and material. The Treasury was concerned that at the end of the war India would have hundreds of millions of pounds' credit which could ruin an already severely depleted Britain. Linlithgow was concerned that Britain would repudiate Indian debts. Churchill was furious to learn that Britain owed huge sums to India. In the following year, Amery reported to Linlithgow that 'Winston harangued us at great length about the monstrous idea that we should spend millions upon millions in the defence of India, then be told to clear out, and on top of all that owe India vast sums incurred on her behalf. I tried, without much effect, to make him understand that a great deal of this expenditure was for goods supplied to the Middle East . . .' Churchill eventually agreed to retention of the present system with the proviso that Britain 'reserved the right to reopen the whole question and to consider a counter-claim against India'.* Linlithgow refused to accept this or even to communicate it to his Council. Nonetheless, his viceroyalty was extended for a third and final time until October 1943.

Churchill had by now shed entirely his 1935 acquiescence in Indian events. He was aggressive and militant. In July 1940 he told Amery that 'he

---

*   In 1939 India owed Britain £356m; by 1945 Britain owed India £1,260m. Until the war, Britain's concern was that the Indian economy might not be up to meeting her obligations, but by the end of war the positions were reversed. At the Bretton Woods Conference in July 1945 the Indian government representatives tried again and again to get assurances that their money would be paid. Britain's team, under Keynes, had much bigger problems to face, and brushed these anxious enquiries away unanswered.

would sooner give up political life at once, or rather go out into the wilderness and fight, than admit to a revolution that meant the end of the imperial crown in India'.[158] He continued to take the view that Congress did not represent the Hindu population of India, let alone the rest of the population. He saw it as an elite political organisation that flourished by virtue of the financial support it enjoyed. In July 1942 intelligence reports suggested that Congress was preparing for a trial of strength, and Churchill claimed to welcome that as an opportunity for demonstrating the slender hold that the party had on the Indian masses. In September 1942 he said in the Commons that Congress was 'a political organisation built round the party machine and sustained by manufacturing and financial interests . . . opposed by all Muslims and the millions of interests who were the subjects of the princes'.[159] Aneurin Bevan, knowing how differently the Labour party regarded Congress, asked whether the prime minister's 'silly language' was endorsed by his Labour colleagues. Churchill said it was and that Bevan was 'a merchant of discourtesy'.

Churchill's distaste for Congress was exacerbated by the party's failure to exhibit the martial fervour he had admired amongst the warriors alongside whom he had fought on the North-West Frontier. Gandhi's approach was dangerously fatalistic. He conceded that the Japanese might well be harsher masters than the British had been, but he would not depart from non-violence to fight the Japanese. If he saw one man strangling another, 'my self-esteem will not allow me to help strangle the strangler'. The development of the war in favour of the Axis, and, from an Indian perspective, in favour particularly of the Japanese, weakened the imperial ties. 'With whom are we going to negotiate?' Nehru asked, 'With an empire which is crumbling to dust?' Japanese aircraft were already bombing targets on India's eastern coast.

Japanese propaganda made the most of this, claiming that Indian soldiers had mutinied. Indeed thousands had defected to the Japanese, who were attempting to recruit them into the Japanese-sponsored 'Indian National Army', the INA.*

---

* Statistics on defections to the INA will be read in different ways, depending on the perspective from which they are approached. The facts are that (1) about 40,500 Indian troops were captured in Malaya/Singapore, of which 16,000 joined the INA; (2) a second unit of the INA was set up in 1943 and perhaps 24,000 Indian POWs were recruited; (3) at the war's end there were thus about 40,000 men in the INA; (4) the strength of the Indian Army, a voluntary body, was throughout the war rather over 1 million men.

In April 1942, the Congress Working Committee concluded that Britain had forfeited any moral right to rule. Indeed, in practical terms, they could see that the British were now relying to an extent at least on American support to defend the subcontinent: American forces had been arriving in India from the beginning of the year and by the end of the war there were half a million American troops there.

America was not only intervening materially. Roosevelt continued to exercise moral suasion. In Cabinet and elsewhere Churchill expressed himself very forcefully indeed on the subject of retaining India. Harry Hopkins, the envoy Roosevelt sent to Britain to assess Churchill, reported that a 'string of cuss words . . . lasted for two hours in the middle of the night' on this subject. All the same, Churchill was brought to the conclusion that he would have to face the unfaceable. On 4 March 1942 Amery told King George VI that Churchill was prepared to make an overture to India in order to get American support and support also from China, though he hated doing so.

Amazingly, at this critical stage in the war, he considered going out himself to India – how would he have been received? But in the event the task was given to Sir Stafford Cripps. Churchill thought that Cripps and Gandhi, as fellow vegetarians, would get on well. That was typical Churchill in throw-away mood. He took Cripps much more seriously than his many jokes about him would suggest. I look at Cripps, the only man whose personal following threatened Churchill's position as prime minister during the war, in the next chapter.

31

STAFFORD CRIPPS

Sir Richard Stafford Cripps is inextricably associated with austerity, the austerity of Britain's economic distress under the post-war Labour Government. The whiff of astringency is inescapable. In truth he was not an austere man. Churchill, in his tribute in the Commons on Cripps' death in 1952, said, 'Stafford Cripps was a man of force and fire. He strode through life with a remarkable indifference to material satisfactions or worldly advantages . . . His friends – and they were many – among whom I am proud to take my place, were conscious, in addition to his public gifts, of the charm of his personality and of the wit and gaiety with which he enlivened not only the mellow hours but also the hard discharge of laborious business in anxious or perilous times. In all his complicated political career he was the soul of honour, and his courage was proof against every test which the terrible years through which we have passed could bring'.[160]

There were many swipes, some of them famous. 'Wherever Sir Stafford has tried to increase wealth and happiness, grass never grows again.' 'He has put the cold hand of death on everything he has attempted to reform.' But one of his colleagues could write more revealingly, 'He is the nearest to a saint I have ever met. He was a man of complete selflessness and devotion to humanity. I hope and believe that I am a better man for having known him'.[161]

He suffered from bad health throughout his life. He was unfit for war service in the First World War, but worked as an ambulance driver in France and latterly shovelled coal until he was recalled to work as a scientist in the Ministry of Munitions. Soon afterwards the colitis that would become chronic made further physical work temporarily impossible. When he was fit to resume work, it was not in science, which he'd studied at university, but at the Bar that he made his career, like his father and grandfather. His ailments rather than principle or asceticism necessitated his sparing vegetarian diet and although he was never physically strong, he worked prodigiously hard at the bar. He became a teetotaller in reaction to 'the alcoholism' of the Parliamentary Labour party. At the Bar he had a highly successful career, combining the discipline of hard work with the advantage of a prodigious memory. Throughout all he did, he was animated by his strong religious views, a practical Christianity.

He was surrounded by liberal forces. His aunt was Beatrice Webb, and he was much influenced by his step-mother, Marion Parmoor, one of the Quakers who supported the India Conciliation Group of which Agatha Harrison was secretary. Agatha Harrison, a welfare reformer, quietly forceful, combining great presence with a disarming sense of humour, latterly a Quaker, was a key English element in the Independence movement. As secretary of the group she was an effective lobbyist. She was a close friend of Gandhi, and his spokesman during the 1939 fast.

Cripps became a friend of Nehru before the war. In 1937 he described his friendship with Nehru as the greatest privilege of his life. Nehru and his daughter Indira stayed at Cripps' country home, Goodfellows. They wrote to each other as 'my dear Stafford' and 'my dear Jawaharlal'. But their friendship did not survive the stresses of the negotiations which took place when Cripps went with his mission to India in 1942.

That mission was flawed because it rested on an absence of agreed government policy. Its inevitable failure justified continued inaction for the rest of the war. But if its immediate effect was perhaps negative, in the longer term it altered the political weather of the British–Indian relationship for ever. It did so because of Cripps himself, and what he, and not the government, injected into the mission. Before we examine the mission, I want to go back a little from the point we have reached, to look at Cripps' two earlier overseas expeditions.

The 1942 trip to India, known to history as the Cripps Mission, was the second of three important visits that Cripps made to the subcontinent in pursuit of what was to some extent a personal commitment to achieve a just settlement of the Indian Question. Between Missions One and Two he had an important sojourn in Russia. The rest of this chapter deals with the first mission and the Russian interlude.

Mission One (1939)

Linlithgow's declaration of war on behalf of India had alienated Congress pretty comprehensively. Gandhi's traditional supporters were pacifists in any case. Younger politicians would not have opposed participation in the war if they had been satisfied with the prospects for India. Cripps, like Attlee, thought that there was room for an imaginative approach. He was disappointed that Linlithgow had gone no further than confirming dominion status as a remote objective. In response, on 26 October 1939 Cripps spoke in the Commons, saying that the 'test question' was whether Britain would commit herself to democracy and Indian self-government immediately after the war, with an initial and immediate step in that direction. This contrasted with what Linlithgow told Gandhi: the war effort was 'not a question of fighting for democracy' which was not 'in the slightest degree' the government's policy.

Cripps canvassed the idea of a wide-ranging excursion – to Russia, China and India. His plans were widely discussed – with Halifax, the former viceroy and now Foreign Secretary, and with Rab Butler. A lot of discussion took place on precisely where he should go. Plans finally focused on India alone. He also consulted on what he should say when he got there. He prepared a draft statement which proposed an offer of dominion status – with the right to secede from the Commonwealth, an important new departure – as an earnest of the British Government's commitment to 'the present war for freedom and democracy'. The extent to which Cripps worked with the Government is surprising. The Government was overwhelmingly Conservative, not yet a coalition, and Cripps had been and would again be Labour; he had been expelled from the party in 1939 and for the moment sat as an Independent. His role was *quasi*-official. He had interviews with Sir Findlater Stewart, the Permanent Under-Secretary at the India Office. But his send-off wasn't a warm one and he had only lukewarm support from the Cabinet. He had the backing of Zetland, still Secretary of State at this point, and Amery, but most of the Cabinet, notably Churchill, was hostile, as, in Delhi, was Linlithgow.

So when he went off to India on his first mission in December 1939 Cripps' trip was partly official and partly a frolic of his own. The official line was that his voyage was of an entirely personal character. Zetland made it a pretty official unofficial expedition. He told Cripps that it would not be misleading to tell Congress that the Government would be prepared to consider his scheme.[162] On the other hand, Cripps certainly didn't carry the whole-hearted backing of the Cabinet. Churchill, still First Lord of the Admiralty, said in Cabinet that he welcomed 'the Hindu–Muslim feud as the bulwark of British rule'.[163] Simon, unsurprisingly, also favoured 'not going any faster than we're obliged to'.

Cripps took with him as his secretary Geoffrey Wilson, a young man with a connection to the Indian Conciliation Group. Cripps did all he could to avoid Indian food, which would be a challenge to his notoriously suspect digestion, and concentrated on the salads, fruit and vegetables. On one occasion Wilson pretended to be upset that Cripps had eaten the only two chocolate cakes before Wilson could get his hands on them. 'He later gave the somewhat lame excuse that unless he got what he could while the going was good, he might have to eat some of the Indian food'.[164] Wilson rather resented the amount of feminine attention which Sir Stafford, a good-looking and companionable man, attracted.

Cripps found the communities separated by the 1935 legislation, and Congress more independent than before. His friend, Nehru, played down these inter-communal problems. On the other hand, Liaquat Ali Khan, Secretary of the Muslim League, took a more pessimistic view: he said too that Western democracy was not suitable for India. Cripps had already known Jinnah when the latter practised at the English Bar. He met him now for the first time as a politician, and was impressed by the real quandary faced by the Muslims, in their inevitable continuing minority. Before he met Gandhi, Wilson told Cripps that the Mahatma's local nickname was 'Mickey Mouse'. Cripps met him in a mud hut in his ashram. He was certainly taking more trouble to meet the Indian leaders than Linlithgow. Linlithgow did not encourage meetings with Gandhi, as Irwin had done, and during his viceroyalty he only met Nehru on two occasions.

Cripps was not impressed when he met Linlithgow on 24 December 1939. Linlithgow made no comment on the report which Cripps gave of his tour. Cripps described the viceroy's 'sphinx-like manner of receiving . . . arguments'.[165]

So this, the first Cripps Mission, was not productive. Cripps was armed only with a vague hint, and not on an official basis, that if India toed the line during the war she might expect to become a dominion after it. He had neither enough to offer nor enough authority with which to offer it. Nehru was increasingly of the view that the British policy was one of unreformed imperialism 'any profession to the contrary notwithstanding'. He told Cripps that his proposals had not helped. He told others that Cripps had completely failed to understand the nature of the Indian problem.[166]

After a stopover in America, when he imprudently told reporters that it was class interest that caused the Muslim League to wish to create a separate Muslim state, Cripps reached London in April 1940. He had spent just twenty days in India. The favourable wind which had conveyed him there had blown itself out. Zetland, who had been encouraging at the outset, was now distinctly subordinate to Linlithgow, whose policy was to avoid any initiative: 'It is no part of our policy, I take it, to expedite in India constitutional changes for their own sake'.[167] Churchill was strongly behind Linlithgow. Within a few weeks, Churchill was prime minister and Zetland had been replaced by Leo Amery, whose whole political career had been built on the imperialist project. Cripps was sure that Linlithgow would continue to obstruct advance, and his pessimism was well-founded.

Moscow (1940–42)

Cripps' second trip was to Moscow as British Ambassador from June 1940 to January 1942. For the first year Russia was Germany's ally, but for the second half of his time, after Barbarossa, when Hitler attacked Germany, Russia and Britain were both at war with Germany. He returned from Moscow with his reputation burnished and the statesmanlike stature that later enabled him to play a major part in Indian policy.

It's not easy to see why this happened or to assess Cripps' role in Moscow. He did not keep conventional records, and the story has to be reconstructed from his own extensive daily letter-diary. During the first twelve months of his time there, prior to Barbarossa, he had little to do. There is some doubt about whether he foresaw Barbarossa or warned Stalin adequately.

Unlike many Labour politicians, Cripps had not disavowed Stalin, but sought rather to reach an understanding with him. Initially he was asked to do very little as, like other Western diplomats, he was geographically isolated from the Russian leaders – indeed from almost all Russians. Banished from Moscow, the diplomatic community languished in remote surroundings in Kuybyshev (now Samara).

After Barbarossa, Stalin was ready to talk. A British Military Mission was sent out and on 12 July Cripps was authorised by London to sign an agreement on terms which Stalin had approved. It was his thirtieth wedding anniversary and in the circumstances the teetotal Cripps took a glass of champagne.

Whatever history may think, Cripps certainly felt he had done very well and he told Eden that he thought he should stay just one more month discussing with Stalin the plans for a post-war Europe and then move on to a different role. The Foreign Office didn't share his ambitious views. Eden took six weeks to reply, and when he did told him that he should stay where he was and that Churchill had no place for him in the Government in the foreseeable future.

Even in Russia he was now side-lined. Beaverbrook (with Harriman on Roosevelt's behalf) was sent out on a mission from which Cripps was excluded. 'The Beaver' was characteristically malicious, undermining Cripps' authority and describing him to Stalin as a bore. Cripps was frustrated, well aware that he wasn't being told what was going on. He considered resignation. He knew that somehow – and certainly not through his own actions – he had become a potential rival to Churchill, whose position at home was far from unassailable at this stage in the war. The *News Chronicle* was suggesting that he might form an alternative government. He began to see himself not at the head of a crucial mission, so much as a political exile

But he was always supremely buoyant. When at the beginning of 1942 he was allowed to return to the UK he did so feeling that the Russian regime had been triumphantly vindicated and had 'shown itself the triumphant saviour of all that we profess to uphold in our democracy'.[168]

Even if his mission to Moscow had not been a huge success, his prestige at home had become enormous. Russia was now Britain's heroic ally. Stafford Cripps was seen to be the man who had brought her into the war. He seemed almost to have defended Stalingrad single-handedly. He was frequently presented as a big man, a leader, 'a man without a party'. The obverse was that, precisely because he didn't have a constituency of support, he could be dumped when his stock fell. But for the moment he was a big 'buy'. In an opinion poll in April 1942, when asked who should succeed if anything should happen to Churchill, 37 per cent were for Eden with Cripps just three points behind at 34 per cent. When the same question had been asked in November 1941, just six months earlier, there had only been 1 per cent support for Cripps. Churchill appreciated the threat. He invited Cripps and Lady Cripps to lunch at Chequers on 25 January 1942 and greeted him, 'Well, Stafford, how have you returned? Friend or foe?' Cripps' reply was a good one: 'a friendly critic or a critical friend'. Cripps became Lord Privy Seal in succession to Attlee and Leader of the House.

32

PREPARATION FOR THE MISSION OF 1942

The seed of *the* Cripps Mission, the mission of 1942, had been sown at a country weekend in Cripps' country house, Goodfellows, in June 1938, when Attlee and Nehru were visitors. With Nehru was the Indian politician Krishna Menon.* With Cripps were, as well as Attlee, Aneurin Bevan, Richard Crossman, Leonard Barnes (a Labour politician who was particularly opposed to colonialism) and Harold Laski. The Labour politicians, as always, were sympathetic to Congress and felt that the India Act did not accord a sufficiently important role to the party. They were there to talk about the fact that the (Conservative-dominated) National Government was not inclined to regard Congress as entitled to speak for India.

Later Attlee thought back to that weekend and wondered why Churchill agreed to the mission. Attlee wrote, 'I had a good many stiff contests with Churchill on India. It was a great surprise when he embraced the idea of the Cripps Mission. The lines on which Cripps was empowered to go went beyond anything previously considered by any government. It embodied in

---

* Not to be confused with the civil servant, V.P. Menon. Krishna Menon was a key member of the nationalist movement, his influence almost as great as Nehru's. He was a Theosophist and Annie Besant sponsored his career. Before returning to India he spent many years in England, where he was active in Labour politics (though suspected of Communist sympathies, as he was again when he returned to Britain, post-Independence, as India's first High Commissioner). He worked in publishing in London, latterly at Penguin. He had a huge circle of friends, not only in politics but among the intellectual elite. As its secretary from 1929 to 1947, he fashioned the India League into an effective lobbying machine for nationalism. When asked whether he'd rather see India occupied by the Japanese or the British, he said, 'You might as well ask a fish whether it preferred being fried in butter or margarine.'

fact some of the main ideas discussed by Cripps, Nehru and myself one weekend at [Goodfellows] '.[169]

A number of factors combined to provide momentum for the Cripps initiative. The importance of the Far Eastern Theatre was critical, and was emphasised by the influence of the Americans and Chiang Kai-Shek's nationalist Chinese. Agatha Harrison and the chairman of the India League, R.W. Sorensen, together with Labour party notables, were specifically pressing for Cripps to go out to India.

At a political level, following the reverses in the East, Churchill had been obliged, on 19 February 1942, to reconstruct the War Cabinet. Attlee's position was strengthened. He became Deputy Prime Minister and Secretary of State for Dominion Affairs. It was now that Cripps, back from Moscow, joined the War Cabinet, taking over Attlee's former position as Lord Privy Seal and also becoming Leader of the House of Commons. For the moment, the initiative in Indian affairs had passed to Cripps and those around him. Amery was aware of this and tried to dig his heels in. On 2 March, he appealed to Churchill to support him against being rushed ahead by Cripps and Attlee. Although he acknowledged Linlithgow's failings, the viceroy was 'at least entitled to have his views carefully considered'.

On 11 February 1942 Amery sent a telegram to Linlithgow: 'Take the strongest *peg* you can before continuing.' Churchill had embarked out of the blue on an initiative very much his own. He was going to broadcast to India, announcing that an Indian Council of Defence was to be set up, its members elected by proportional representation on a provincial basis. The princes would also be represented. This body would send delegates to the Peace Conference after the war (which never took place) and would frame India's post-war constitution. Amery said that the prime minister didn't intend any slight to Linlithgow 'but you know his sudden ways'. Initially these sudden ways had even envisaged a prime ministerial visit to India to launch his scheme.

Linlithgow was horrified. He wrote to Amery, 'I do again beg of you to see to it that I should be in some measure cushioned by you and your Office from the full impact of these explosions in the Prime Minister's mind . . . Let me only tell you that in my careful judgement, the manner in which I have been used over these past ten days is not in tune with the treatment which anyone holding my charge is entitled to expect from His Majesty's Government'.[170]

The reason for Churchill's activity was Pearl Harbor. At the start of the war India had not been at the centre of British strategy. The situation changed on 7 December 1941 with the Japanese attack. India was strategically critical. Moreover, Labour members of the Cabinet pressed for action which would both advance the cause of Indian Independence and also give a degree of protection against the Japanese. Amery and Linlithgow acknowledged the imperative but opposed the political implications. Amery wanted to go no further than repeating the 1940 August Offer. Linlithgow did not want to take a 'leap in the dark from the solid platform of the Act of 1935'.[171] Attlee responded with a War Cabinet paper of 2 February 1942:

[N]ow is the time for an act of statesmanship. To mark time is to lose India. A renewed effort must be made to get the leaders of the Indian political parties to unite. It is quite obvious from his telegram that the Viceroy is not the man to do this. Indeed, his telegram goes far to explain his past failures. His mental attitude is expressed . . . when he talks of regaining lost ground after the war. He is obviously thinking in terms of making minor concessions while resting on the status quo . . . We need a man to do in India what Durham did in Canada . . . My conclusion therefore is that a representative with power to negotiate within wide limits should be sent to India now, either as a special envoy or in replacement of the present Viceroy, and that a Cabinet Committee should be appointed to draw up terms of reference and powers.[172]

Churchill did not proceed with his broadcast. Having abandoned it and the intriguing idea of going to India himself, he set up an Indian Committee of Cabinet on 26 February. This committee remained in existence for five and a half years. It prepared the promises which Cripps took to India. It consisted of Churchill, when he attended, Simon, Sir John Anderson, Lord President of the Council, and Sir James Grigg, Secretary of State for War, Cripps, Attlee and Amery. Attlee took the chair unless Churchill was present. It did not contain a diehard element – except when Churchill was present. When it first convened on 26 February 1942 he was there and took the chair. When he did attend, Amery noted 'Winston's complete inability to grasp even the most elementary points on discussion'. In a moment of savage reflection he recorded that someone who did not know who the prime minister was 'would have thought him a rather amusing but quite gaga old gentleman who could not understand what people were talking about'.[173] Churchill's mood at this stage was flavoured by a melancholy acceptance of America's requirements. He told the Canadian prime minister, 'We have resigned ourselves to fighting our utmost to defend India in order, if successful, to be turned out.' This mood of resignation did not last and, as the Cripps Mission met with increasing difficulties, he was reassured to think that it might be a very long time before Britain was indeed turned out of India.

Although the visit and the broadcast never took place, Amery and Linlithgow were horrified by the uninformed *démarche* that completely overlooked the intercommunal problems which had led them to resort to a nominated Executive Council. Linlithgow now made his own proposals, eight in number, conciliatory in tone and unremarkable in content. In consequence, on 1 March Churchill proposed to broadcast yet another declaration. It was not one he particularly wanted to make. This declaration, for the first time, would have proclaimed officially that an Indian dominion could secede from the Commonwealth. This was a crucial new departure. Secondly, any province could stand apart from the union and still achieve its own dominion status.

On 4 March Churchill told Roosevelt about the proposed declaration. The War Cabinet met on the following day and Churchill shared the proposal with Ministers. There is no official record of the meeting, but according to Sir Alexander Cadogan, Permanent Under-Secretary at the Foreign Office, and an uninhibited observer of his masters, Churchill was negative and the meeting was heated, with talk of resignations. Churchill's reluctant acceptance of what was essentially an American requirement was in the course of reversing itself. According to Rab Butler, 'We had a great meeting of all members of the government . . . The Conservative reaction, i.e. the view that some British interest must be retained in India, appears to be on top of any other influence. There will therefore not be a statement in the immediate future, and, when it comes, it should not sell everything away'.[174]

Linlithgow had been annoyed to be told to comment on the proposed declaration within twenty-four hours. It appeared that he would not even have the opportunity of discussing matters with the Commander-in-Chief, Wavell. In the event he did manage to consult, and both of them, together with the Governor of the Punjab, concluded that the Government's proposal would imply acceptance of Pakistan, with particularly serious repercussions in the Punjab. While he could see that separation might have to be resorted to after the war, it could not be talked of for the moment. The idea of opt-out upset traditionalists in London, as well as Linlithgow in India. The India Office, and those like Butler who had been brought up to regard the preservation of Indian unity as central to British policy, thought that allowing Muslim provinces to secede would lead to the disintegration of India. The Commonwealth High Commissioners were upset about the idea that India would have a constitutional right to secede from the Commonwealth. By 6 March, Amery was letting Linlithgow know that the fate of the declaration was in the balance.

Churchill was now intent on stifling his own plan. The succeeding days, between 6 and 9 March 1942, were critical, and full of drama. Cadogan thought that if Churchill did not give way, Cripps would resign. If the Declaration were made then Linlithgow might well resign. The India Committee convened in the course of the weekend. Cripps was at Chequers on the Sunday. The resignation of the viceroy – or indeed of Cripps – would have brought down a government already shaken by the greatest military catastrophe of the war. If Churchill had fallen, Cripps would almost certainly have succeeded him; but in the event Cripps saved Churchill. On that Sunday at Chequers he produced a draft statement which said that instead of persevering with the inflammatory declaration, a member of the War Cabinet would go out to India to discuss a scheme and see whether it would receive a generous measure of acceptance. He volunteered to be that minister.

Cripps' offer to go to India was accepted by the War Cabinet just one hour before a telegram arrived from Linlithgow, saying that he would resign if the declaration were issued. Churchill replied: 'Yesterday before I was shown your [cable] we decided not to publish any declaration now but to send a War Cabinet Minister out to see whether it could be put across on the spot.' Churchill thought poorly of Linlithgow's threat and accused him of a lack of patriotism. The viceroy must not think of going, 'precipitating collapse in India and disunity at home . . . Do not . . . think of quitting your post at this juncture.'[175] Amery did not put it quite that way: 'So, old friend, whatever else happens, you must see this thing through.' He confirmed that Linlithgow's resignation could well have broken up the Government. In place of the Cabinet Declaration came the Cripps Mission.

During these four days there had been a battle between the progressives, who were for making the declaration, and the diehards, Churchill, Linlithgow and Amery, who did not want the declaration made. The outcome is usually represented as a victory for Cripps and Attlee. But in truth the diehards had won. Linlithgow was still viceroy and Churchill was still prime minister. No broadcast and no new declaration.

The declaration would have been a radical departure from the traditional position of the India Office and the Conservatives. India would have been given the right to make its own constitution after the war, with the entitlement to complete Independence from British institutions. This would have been very far from the idea that India would remain indefinitely within the Empire, even if as a dominion. Secondly, the right of Muslim or princely provinces to secede involved the end of that long-term *desideratum*, the preservation of unity. When the policy was discussed by the full Cabinet, dominated by the Conservatives, on 5 March, it was clear that many members would not acquiesce in India's departure from the Empire or its fragmentation. Cripps could discuss his scheme as much as he wanted in India, but the diehards were not unduly concerned. They had not surrendered and they had Linlithgow to support them in Delhi and Churchill in London.

Linlithgow's revealing reaction to the mission was recorded by a member of his staff, the Reforms Commissioner, H.V. Hodson:

> I try not to form pictures in my mind. It's dangerous. But I'll tell you what I think. I think Cripps is coming here out of public spirit. No one would choose this way of becoming Viceroy if that were his ambition. And if he wants to be Prime Minister what sensible politician would take the immediate risks of failure over this just when his stock is very high? No, I think he realised that India might take things from him which they wouldn't take from anyone else, and he is coming out here in a genuine public-spirited attempt to solve the problem. And I think he will go off very quickly unless he is confident of succeeding. It would be fatal to his reputation to hang around here while opinion hardens more and more against his offer – like hawking rotten fish. Personally, I think he'll fail with H.M.G.'s policy, don't you? . . . Of course the Congress and the Hindus are jubilant. They think they've scored with the British Government and that Cripps is their man . . . I don't know how he will proceed, but I think he'll work with a pretty free hand. On our side we must avoid at all costs any suggestion that we are standing in his way or forcing evidence on him.[176]

Pearl Harbor created a quadrilateral matrix of tension, resting on Britain, India, the United States and Japan. India was an important base for attacks on the Japanese. It was also, conversely, vulnerable to attacks by the Japanese. When Churchill was in Washington over Christmas 1941, Roosevelt again 'raised the Indian problem in the usual lines'. And, said Churchill, 'I reacted so strongly and at such length that he never raised it again'. Whether or not

Roosevelt personally raised the matter with Churchill thereafter, he did not depart from his views to the slightest extent and Churchill knew that. After the fall of Singapore, Roosevelt drafted a telegram to Churchill which he did not in the event send. He said that the former 'master and servant' relationship in Asia was now a thing of the past and beyond revival.[177]

The United States had been disappointed by Nehru and Congress and their lack of enthusiasm for the war, but they still felt very strongly about Britain's hold over India. They resented the fact that American diplomatic representation in Delhi was banned by the Indian Government. Roosevelt had been raising the question of India as early as his meetings with Churchill on the *Augusta* in August 1941, when the Atlantic Charter was signed, according to his admittedly very unreliable son Eliot, who thought that Churchill was going to explode with anger: 'I thought for a minute he was going to bust, POP.' Article 3 of the Charter referred to 'the right of all peoples to choose the form of government under which they will live'. When Churchill spoke about the charter to parliament, he told the House that the article only applied to European countries under Nazi domination, not to 'the development of constitutional government in India, Burma or other parts of the Empire'. Roosevelt took a different view.

There was excited speculation about what was happening when it became known that Cripps was going back to India. Had he been authorised to offer post-war Independence to India by Churchill and Amery? Oliver Harvie said in his diary, 'The cabinet are about to take an immense step, an offer of complete Independence like a Dominion after the War. The idea originated with the PM himself, who cut across the obstructionism of the Viceroy and the India Office'.[178]

Had Churchill indeed turned his back on the policy to which he had so strongly and publicly held? It's theoretically possible: a desperate situation might have resulted in a desperate policy. Singapore had fallen in April, Rangoon in March and later in the same month the Andaman Islands, lying off India's eastern shore in the Indian Ocean and an ideal stepping-off point for an invasion of the subcontinent, fell to the Japanese. A pro-Japanese Indian army was already in existence. The more allied troops deployed to defend India, the less were available elsewhere. And if India fell to the Japanese, the British Empire was at an end.

Churchill might therefore have turned his pre-War policy on its head. Or he might just have been improvising as he so often did in the darkest days of the War. But in reality he and Amery knew that the mission would almost certainly fail to deliver any substantial result. Cripps carried with him at best a vague adumbration and was without plenipotentiary powers. The mission failed – not just because it involved, as Nehru famously put it (though the quotation is often attributed to Gandhi), a 'post-dated cheque drawn on a crashing bank' – but for the rather more complicated factors set out in chapters 33 and 34. Churchill and Amery knew the obstacles that lay in Cripps' way, and knew that Linlithgow could be relied on to add to them.

The mission meant a great deal less than peripheral observers imagined. It involved no more than discussion round a proposal that had never been fully formulated or authorised. It was a damp squib compared to the Declaration that Churchill had toyed with making. The mission was bound to founder when it engaged with Congress's habitual nit-picking obstructiveness and hair-splitting, and Churchill had no reason to agonise over it. For all the capriciousness of his policy on India, he knew as much about Indian politics, of which these complicated factors were the expression, as any. He certainly thought that an imprecise promise, if it even amounted to that, could safely be made and would be unlikely to be accepted. The promise that Cripps carried with him to India may have been as insincere as Churchill's reply to Cripps when he reported by telegram that his negotiations had broken down. Churchill's reply was, 'Even though your hopes have not been fulfilled, you have rendered a very important service to the common cause and the foundations have been laid for the future progress of the peoples of India'.

Amery said that what prompted Churchill to allow the mission was that 'the pressures outside upon Winston from Roosevelt, and upon Attlee & Co from their own party, plus the admission of Cripps to the War Cabinet suddenly opened the sluice gates'. The question of whether or not the mission was sent in good faith is perhaps answered in Amery's telegram to Linlithgow of 10 March 1942: 'It would be impossible owing to the unfortunate rumours and publicity, and the general American outlook, to stand on purely negative attitudes and the Cripps Mission is indispensable to prove our honesty of purpose and to gain time for necessary consultations'. The mission was a public relations exercise. Its outcome was never in serious doubt. Amery himself heaved a sigh of relief when he heard of the failure of the mission and told Linlithgow that its only point so far as Churchill had been concerned had been its good effect on America: 'For the rest he isn't interested, really disliking the whole problem as much as before'.[179] The reaction of the *New York Times* was very satisfactory: '[W]e can say to the Indian leaders that if they refuse this gift of freedom for petty, or personal, or spiteful reasons, they will lose the American comradeship that is now theirs for the asking'.[180]

The politicians were certainly not spurred on by any burning concern on the part of British public opinion. In November 1939, in answer to the question, 'Should India's demand for self-government be granted during the war or should it wait until after the war?', about 30 per cent said it should happen during the war, about 50 per cent after, and a huge 20 per cent didn't know. In January 1942 only some 2 per cent of respondents said India should not have Independence at all, but when the November 1939 question was put to them again at this time, their response was pretty much the same as before. Now, in March 1942, asked whether they were 'satisfied or dissatisfied with the Government's statement on our future relations with India', only 36 per cent were satisfied; 20 per cent were dissatisfied and 44 per cent didn't know.[181]

33

CRIPPS IN INDIA

Cripps went off to India on Saturday, 14 March 1942, without any precise instructions. He was an emissary with 'full power to discuss with the leaders of Indian opinion the scheme upon which the War Cabinet is agreed'. There *was* no agreed scheme – just a Declaration which had been effectively rejected. Cripps had a pretty free hand, though an empty one. What he *was* told to do was to make sure that defence and good government were not compromised and to bear in mind the crucial importance of the military situation. Churchill told Linlithgow that Cripps was limited to discussing the draft Declaration; but his role was both more extensive and much vaguer, and Amery sought to bring that home to Churchill. There was thus confusion between what Amery was saying to Churchill, what Churchill was saying to Linlithgow, what Cripps himself had in mind, what the War Cabinet had decided and what the India Committee had told Cripps to do. Subsequently Linlithgow claimed that he had never been told what instructions the War Cabinet had given to Cripps.

Cripps did carry a promise of dominion status, with an Indian Constitution to be prepared in India by a Constituent Assembly, but all after the war. There would be immediate additional participation on the Viceregal Council – but not on strategy. After the war Muslims would have the right to take the provinces in which they were a majority out of India, as would the princely states. The dominion of India would be equal to the other dominions in all ways, including domestic and external affairs. But Britain always remembered the qualification to the August Offer of 1940: there could be no transfer of power 'to any system of government whose authority is directly denied by large and powerful elements in India's national life'. It was that caveat, supremely fair but supremely negative, which meant that the diehards had nothing to fear from the Cripps Mission.

At a press conference in Delhi on his arrival, Cripps was asked the crucial question whether the new dominion would be free to secede from the Commonwealth. He said that it would. He was asked whether Canada, as an example of an existing dominion, was free to secede and he replied 'of course'. George VI was taken aback when he heard about this.[182]

The earnest and self-important but engaging Cripps had a sense of destiny. He certainly thought that his powers were extensive. He told his wife that he had a – presumably metaphorical – 'private cipher code straight to the Prime Minister' and 'powers if he sees fit to use them'.[183] In reality he was controlled by Churchill and Amery and opposed by Linlithgow. He was carrying only promises about the future, and (although Congress was unaware of it) Churchill said frankly that promises made against the exigencies of war would not be honoured. He told Amery that when the war was over he would consider himself to be under 'no obligation to honour promises made at a time of difficulty'. Instead, there would be 'a great regeneration of India'.*

Cripps and Linlithgow were pretty well incompatible. Cripps visited the viceroy every evening after dinner but after an initial stay at Viceroy's House, lived at 3 Queen Victoria Road, Delhi, and he and his entourage were able to operate independently of the viceroy. At their first meeting, Cripps showed Linlithgow a list of his proposals for the membership of the reformed Executive. Linlithgow simply returned it to Cripps saying, 'That's my affair.'

Linlithgow didn't like Cripps or his mission. He referred to Sir Stafford Cripps as 'Sir Stifford Crapps' (not very imaginative – Churchill thought of the same Spoonerism) and his entourage as 'the Crippery'. He was very critical of Cripps: 'Cripps was crooked when up against it.' Quite what the crookedness was isn't clear.

Cripps certainly did engage with Congress in extensive negotiations of which Linlithgow disapproved.[184] The detail and complexity of the negotiations was striking and Cripps coped well with an exhausting regime. As usual, Gandhi was difficult. He didn't like the idea of partition, or the fact that British promises were about the future. At one stage he claimed to have no notion of points that Cripps had already communicated to

---

* And of course he would have had huge support for reverting to the status quo. At Conservative party conferences as late as the 1950s there were regular expressions of regret over the passing of the Raj. (Bridge, *Holding India to the Empire. The British Conservative Party and the 1935 Constitution*, p. 163.)

him. Eventually he acquiesced, saying that he had dismissed the earlier meeting from his mind as merely having been with one of the 'globetrotters'.[185] He reported that when he had looked briefly at the Declaration he said to Cripps, 'Why did you come if this is what you have to offer? If this is your entire proposal to India, I would advise you to take the next plane home.'

Churchill was kept in the loop. By 2 April he felt that quite enough had been done by way of concession and personally drafted a cable, which the War Cabinet approved, saying that the mission had demonstrated Britain's good faith. 'We all reached an agreement on it before you [Cripps] started and it represents our final position.' He queried whether Congress was really genuine in its negotiations and stressed that there could be no compromise on defence (which must remain a viceregal responsibility) without Cabinet agreement.[186]

The issue of responsibility for the defence of India exercised Linlithgow and Wavell, and the viceroy declared his independence on this point, saying that he and Wavell would report direct to the War Cabinet if defence were to be Indianised. Churchill was very much in favour of this stand, and increasingly he and Linlithgow dealt directly with each other without reference to Cripps. Churchill: 'Of course telegraph personal to me or Secretary of State exactly what you think. It is my responsibility to decide to whom it is to be shown after I've read it.' Cripps had little time for Wavell. He told Agatha Harrison, 'Wavell is the most difficult man to talk to . . . When Nehru and Wavell met, the latter plainly understood little of what Nehru was driving at.'[187]

Deadlock

The close relationship Cripps and Nehru had enjoyed disintegrated. Hitherto they had cultivated each other as useful contacts and on that basis had found themselves in agreement. Now, in direct negotiation, they discovered more than they had formerly known about each other. Cripps had never accepted that Nehru was in many ways a radical and extreme spokesman of Congress. Equally, Nehru found that Cripps was constrained by imperatives which meant that there were many points on which he was unable to compromise. In all the perils of the Far Eastern War, the British Government could not surrender control of India's defence efforts.

But at many stages Linlithgow was a bigger problem for Cripps than were the leaders of the Indian political parties. Linlithgow was strongly opposed to the appointment to his Council of Indian members, whom he thought he knew a lot more about than did Cripps. He was delighted when he saw Cripps thwarted by Congress or indeed by the League. He wrote gloatingly that Cripps was learning about India the hard way.

Because Churchill and Amery sent their telegrams to Linlithgow without copies to Cripps, Cripps appeared in his communications with London to be out of touch. Briefed by Linlithgow, Churchill was able to bombard Cripps with 'What does this mean?' telegrams. Cabinet confidence in Cripps was weakened, and by 9 April Churchill was advising him that the mission should come home.

The biggest problem was whether the Executive Council would function like a British cabinet, or whether its powers were to be circumscribed by a powerful viceroy. Was the viceroy to be a constitutional George VI or an autocratic George III? Linlithgow was for a George III. According to Azad, the president of Congress, Cripps told him that the extended Executive Council, operating for the remainder of the war, 'would function as a Cabinet and that the position of the viceroy would be analogous to that of the King in England *vis-à-vis* his Cabinet'. When it transpired that this would not be the relationship of Council and viceroy – at least initially and formally – Cripps was accused of having been misleading. There is a good deal of doubt about whether Cripps did stretch his brief to this extent. Azad spoke little English. Jinnah said dismissively, 'He's like my bearer. He can understand a few words of English but he can only answer "yes" or "no"'.[188] Azad was accompanied at the meeting with Cripps on which he based his allegation by his secretary, acting as interpreter. He dictated his memoirs in Urdu during his final illness fifteen years later. There must be serious questions about his memory or indeed his understanding of what Cripps had said.

At any rate, Cripps was charged with having promised what he could not deliver. The charge was made by Congress, who effectively repudiated what they had already agreed. Cripps arrived seen as a friend of Congress. An article criticising the Muslim League which he had written in *Tribune* in May 1940 was very much remembered. He admitted that, 'My association in the past has been more close with my friends in the Congress than with the members of other parties or other communities, but I am duly impressed with the need in any scheme for the future of India to meet the deep anxieties which undoubtedly exist among the Muslims and the other communities.'[189] At his first meeting with Jinnah he told him that his views had changed in the course of two and a half years and that he now recognised the growth of communal feeling and the demand for a Pakistan. He never ceased to be closer to Congress than the League, but he was no longer as close as he had formerly been.

Cripps did frequently talk of the Executive Council as a cabinet. He told a reporter, for instance, 'You cannot change the constitution. All you can do is to change the conventions of the constitution. You can turn the Executive Council into a cabinet.' That was not to say, however, that the viceroy's powers could be equated with those of a constitutional monarch. He was asking the politicians to assume a degree of evolution.

American Influence

Just before the mission set off, Roosevelt wrote to Churchill saying (as well he might) that his views were 'based on very little first-hand knowledge of my part', but nevertheless taking it on himself to suggest that a temporary dominion government be set up. Churchill described the proposal as 'contemptuous' but kept his views to himself.

Roosevelt's representative in India, Colonel Louis Johnson, didn't help matters. He was brash, arrogant and ill-informed. Linlithgow said of another visiting American politician, 'my experience of peripatetic Americans, which is now extensive, is that their zeal in teaching us our business is in inverse ratio to their understanding of even the most elementary of the problems with which we have to deal'. But with the credulity of a recently arrived observer, Johnson listened to Nehru tell him that, 'In the recent history of India there has not been such a combination of fiercely anti-Indian freedom elements in the British Government as we have had during the past two years and still have today.' Johnson concluded that Cripps and Nehru could reach an agreement in five minutes if they were allowed to get together.[190]

Johnson had been a military man, but he also had a background in law and politics. In 1937 Roosevelt appointed him Assistant Secretary of War. In March 1942 the State Department announced that a mission would be sent to India under Johnson's chairmanship to assess India's need for war materials. Johnson's role was speedily changed from merely being head of a Productions Mission: he was appointed Personal Representative of the President. When Cripps met him at the Viceroy's House on 4 April, Easter Saturday, he saw at once that Johnson had been sent out 'post-haste' to try to engineer an Indian settlement. As Cripps' negotiations began to fail – which they did because of Congress's insistence on gaining a substantial element of control over defence – Johnson came to have an important role in the negotiations.

Cripps and Johnson had a shared background and they got on well. Cripps told Johnson what he wanted London to agree to on the defence issue. Various adjustments were made, and finally a Cripps–Johnson formula was prepared for passing on to the Congress Working Committee. It was clandestinely seen and approved by Nehru and then surreptitiously slipped under Johnson's door in the middle of the night. The intention was that Johnson would pass the formula on to the Working Committee.

So far so good, but they still had to get past the viceroy. First of all Linlithgow said he was too tired to look at the formula until the next day. Finally he looked at it at 10pm on Wednesday, 8 April 1942. He said he doubted if Congress would agree. 'Sir Stafford then said that he thought Congress would come in on this formula and Johnson had gathered that from them. I asked how Congress had come to know about this formula.' Cripps had to reveal that the document had been pre-approved by Nehru before being submitted to Linlithgow. Linlithgow was furious at having been kept in the dark and delayed his consent.

Finally he gave way and in the morning of the following day, 9 April 1942, it looked as if an agreement was imminent. The press reported widely that Congress was likely to join in the settlement with the government. Cripps was in high spirits and cabled Churchill with high hopes for success and asking in fulsome terms that Roosevelt be thanked for providing Colonel Johnson. But Linlithgow hadn't given up. While Cripps was cabling Churchill, Linlithgow was cabling Amery, communicating his 'strong feeling of grievance'. Later in the morning he felt compelled again to complain to Amery, while disclaiming any wish to sabotage the formula if Wavell and the War Cabinet accepted it.

Linlithgow didn't like the idea of emerging later as 'the bad boy responsible for wrecking at the stage of practice the wonderful settlement arrived at by Sir Stafford Cripps',[191] but he liked even less having been bounced into agreement on the defence issue. Moreover, he was determined not to accept any constitutional change which would weaken his control of his Council. He told Cripps at noon on 9 April that he and the War Cabinet were agreed on this point and asked him to emphasise it to the Congress politicians later in the day.

Cripps was to meet the Congress leaders at 5.30pm on 9 April. After their noon meeting Linlithgow sent him a note stressing that the constitutional position of the viceroy's Council could not be altered. At teatime

Cripps was still very excited. He thought that Linlithgow was vanquished and viewed his resignation with equanimity. He and Professor Reginald Coupland, a friend of Amery and a member of Cripps' staff, discussed who should stand in for the viceroy if he resigned.

But he had allowed himself to get carried away. Churchill, quite as much as Linlithgow, was adamantly against the sort of *quasi*-Cabinet which was at the nub of Congress's aspirations, and Congress was indubitably right to question the idea that the viceroy would allow his extensive powers to wither away.

The agreement that had seemed on the morning of 9 April to be so close was never achieved. For the rest of the day the sides started moving apart rather than closer, and before a day which had started so optimistically was out, agreement had proved to be unattainable The problem was not merely Linlithgow's intransigence, his insistence that the constitutional relationship between viceroy and Council could not be changed by an iota: Nehru and Congress had also started to go back to fundamentals. The claim for immediate Independence was revived. Confirmation of that and definition of the conventions of the Constitution was requested. As one goes through the detail of these negotiations, and again those surrounding the post-war Cabinet Mission, which is dealt with in Chapter 42, one is struck again and again by the propensity for Congress, with a practical solution within its grasp, to pull back, seize on minutiae and bog down the discussions, determined always to have nothing rather than something that was perhaps only insignificantly short of the ideal. It was frustrating for Western politicians, used to pragmatic fudge and uninterested in political theory. No one in Britain knew precisely what the rules of the British constitution were or was particularly interested in them, and the British couldn't understand the Congress focus on these theoretical problems. Cripps' advice was to work pragmatically: take power and make the most of it, knowing that the viceroy in practice couldn't do much to overrule them. Nehru was not prepared to do anything of the sort.

Nehru later claimed that Cripps had not been a free agent and that his hand had been forced by threats of resignation by Wavell and Linlithgow. There was no secret about Cripps' views of Linlithgow. He planned to have him replaced and told Nehru just that: 'I went so far as to assure Jawaharlal that I will not allow any British official, however highly placed he might be, to jeopardise a reasonable chance of a settlement'.[192] Politically, it was impossible to change the viceroy in advance of the agreement, publicly acknowledging that his advice was not being followed. But Congress would not risk accepting the agreement on the assumption that the viceroy would then be replaced with a more complaisant successor, who would surrender elements of his powers.

34

FAILURE OF THE MISSION

On 10 April 1942 Cripps sent a cable to Churchill, telling him that agreement had been rejected, not on the narrow matter of defence, but on wider grounds. 'There is clearly no hope of an agreement, and I shall start home on Sunday'.[193] He was returning empty-handed after just nineteen days in India.

Churchill's reaction is wryly recorded in his history of the Second World War, 'I was able to bear this news, which I had thought probable from the beginning, with philosophy'.[194] He went on with his wholly insincere reference to Cripps' having 'rendered a very important service to the common cause and the foundations have been laid for the future progress of the peoples of India'.[195]

Churchill's attitude had been hardening in the last days of the mission. He was irritated to hear of the Cripps–Johnson formula, and annoyed that it had been arrived at behind Linlithgow's back. He summoned a meeting of the India Committee, to be followed by a meeting of the War Cabinet. In the meantime he interviewed Roosevelt's personal representative in London, Harry Hopkins. Hopkins misrepresented matters. He said that Johnson wasn't working as a personal representative of the President and was being used by Cripps for his own ends. This was far from true: Roosevelt's implication in the matter was underlined by the fact that he cabled Churchill personally to try to save the Cripps Mission. But Churchill told the War Cabinet what Hopkins had told him, and the War Cabinet – even Attlee – was very critical of Cripps. They sent two messages to him, one objecting to the Cripps–Johnson formula and the other rebuking him for negotiating it behind the back of the viceroy. Cripps was upset to discover that Linlithgow had been reporting back to London in cables which he hadn't seen, despite the fact that he had shown the viceroy all of his. Everything had gone wrong for Cripps. His credibility had been blown by his secret negotiations with

Johnson, and the War Cabinet was coming solidly behind Linlithgow. They reassured the viceroy that there was no question of any convention limiting his powers under the existing constitution. 'If Congress leaders have gathered the impression that such a new convention is now possible this impression should definitely be removed'.[196]

Churchill hadn't needed to sabotage the mission because the mission collapsed of its own accord. That is not to say that he might not have sabotaged it if he had had to. In the early morning of 10 April, before he acknowledged defeat and said that he'd be coming home on Sunday, Cripps sent a telegram containing an implied threat of resignation. The India Committee was, however, already unimpressed by Cripps' performance. Cripps' telegram was swiftly followed by one from Linlithgow, complaining about a Cripps proposal that a constitutional convention regulating the working of the Executive Council should be promulgated. The meeting of the India Committee had begun with Attlee in the Chair; now it moved to Number 10 and Churchill presided. Amery was concerned by the public and political reaction that would follow if Cripps did resign and he had prepared a draft message for Churchill to send. Churchill rejected it at once. It was 'too conciliatory to Cripps and [expressed] a confidence which he, Winston no longer feels'.[197] The Committee rejected the idea of any erosion of the constitutional position by way of convention and minuted that Cripps had not been authorised before he left the country to discuss anything of this sort. The Committee agreed telegrams from Churchill to Linlithgow and Cripps, with copies to each other. They supported Linlithgow and reminded Cripps that he had never been given authority to negotiate. All he was supposed to do was to try to gain acceptance with 'possibly minor variations or elaborations' of what the British Government had already offered.

Churchill's cable to Cripps told him clearly and condescendingly that his mission had been a failure: 'We feel that in your natural desire to reach a settlement with Congress you may be drawn into positions far different from any the Cabinet and Ministers of Cabinet rank approved before you set forth . . . We are concerned about the Viceroy's position . . . You speak of carrying on negotiations. It was certainly agreed between us all that there would not be negotiations but that you were there to try to gain acceptance with possibly minor variations or elaborations of our great offer which has made so powerful an impression here and throughout the United States'.[198] It was a humbling dismissal for a man who had gone to India thinking he had so much discretion to negotiate.

'Not generous,' said Coupland when he read Churchill's cable. The evidence suggests that Cripps strayed very little beyond his instructions. While he was not sent explicitly to negotiate, he had after all been sent to see if a settlement could be agreed, which implied some movement from an established position.

When Amery heard that Congress was not going to buy a deal, his diary comment was, 'That certainly gets Cripps out of a pretty awkward tangle for I don't think he would have liked facing his Congress friends with definite Cabinet instructions to make clear to them that there could be no nonsense about a convention, but that if they came in it must be under the existing Constitution and that if they differed from the Viceroy they could only resign'.[199] Amery was not any more sincerely behind the mission than Churchill. His reaction to its failure was, 'On the whole I think we're well out of the wood. We can now go ahead with the war with a clear conscience'.[200]

Cripps was typically magnanimous in defeat. There were no recriminations. He had 'told Nehru that if they accepted my terms I should be such a Tremendous Figure in England that I could do everything'.[201] He did not exceed his authority in order to do a deal which would have so dramatically advanced his career.

What did Cripps think? His immediate reaction to the War Cabinet was to say, 'I am sorry that my colleagues appear to distrust me over this matter and I am quite prepared to hand the matter over if they would rather have someone else carry on the negotiations. I have throughout told you that I would not agree anything that was not satisfactory to Commander-in-Chief and Viceroy on a Defence question, but this you seem to doubt. Unless I am trusted I cannot carry on with the task'.[202] Cripps never blamed the War Cabinet – or indeed Churchill – for what had happened. He was inclined to blame Congress. As he waited for their decision on 10 April he told Coupland that 'the difficulty now was only distrust . . . "They have come to the very edge of the water, and stripped, but hesitate to make the plunge because the water looks so cold" '.[203]

While there were no recriminations, Cripps spoke much more frankly about Indian politicians, particularly Congress, than he had done before. He did his best to set out Britain's position in the best of lights for the United States. All that was holding India back from 'Indian self-government in its fullest form [was] the influence of Mr Gandhi and the Congress party. They were offered full participation but they refused it'. Cripps' spin was successful. America tended to feel that Britain had done its duty by India.

That success was Cripps' downfall. He was no longer needed and increasingly side-lined in Cabinet. This was a period when some of Churchill's best jokes about him began to appear: 'He has all the virtues I dislike and none of the vices I admire.' In July 1942, following the fall of Tobruk, there was a no-confidence motion in the House. Churchill easily survived, by 475 votes to 25, and there had been no attempt to supplant him with Cripps. Although Leader of the House, Cripps had no meetings at this time with Churchill, except in Cabinet, for seven or eight weeks. If Cripps had been a plotter – and if he had enjoyed greater support in parliament – he could perhaps have struck, but he did not. As Churchill had said to Stalin, 'The trouble is that his chest is a cage in which two squirrels are at war, his conscience and his career.'[204] Cripps realised he was no longer needed and proposed to resign. Churchill asked him to wait until the outcome of the North Africa landings was known. In the event the landings coincided with the second Battle of El Alamein. Suddenly Churchill was triumphantly ascendant. Approval of the Government's conduct of the war, which had been only 41 per cent in September 1942, shot to 75 per cent in November. Churchill's approval climbed to over 90 per cent and Cripps' declined to 51 per cent.[205] Cripps was removed from the War Cabinet and became Minister of Aircraft Production – a vital role, but not a base for interference in overall policy. There was to be no more 'chattering ourselves out of India'.

The mission had been a victory for opponents of change. The stolid viceroy had seen off the cerebral and nimble politician. Linlithgow could afford a touch of humour. When Cripps and he parted, the viceroy, remembering the popular film of 1939, said, 'Goodbye, Mr Cripps'.

35

QUIT INDIA

Following the failure of the Cripps Mission, Gandhi launched the Quit India campaign of civil disobedience which has already been referred to in the military context.

Rail and telegraph communications were struck at. In Madras, Bihar and the United Provinces, British servicemen were attacked and murdered. The emergency was massive. The Government responded with enormous force. Fifty-seven brigades of Indian and British troops supported the police. Rioters were fired at and aircraft were used to strafe saboteurs who were tearing up railway lines. In Bombay, demonstrators were beaten with rattan canes. Order was not restored for six weeks.

Linlithgow was alarmed. It's difficult to know how serious the challenge was. It is clear that large numbers did not respond to Gandhi's call. Churchill was particularly pleased that the 'martial races' had been loyal. Indeed, recruitment rose to 900,000 during 1942. The Muslim League did not participate, and Sikhs also declined to protest.

In hindsight, Quit India, and the Government's response to it, was not a propaganda coup for Congress, as Amritsar had been. In particular, the United States, which had been India's friend, and whose influence was very much behind Cripps' Mission, now tended to lose patience with Gandhi and Congress.

But at the time, for a short period it looked as if Quit India might well be successful. The estimate of Indian casualties in the crackdown ranges between 4,000 and 10,000, and it appeared to Indians that Britain was losing the war and that India would soon be invaded. Singapore and other disasters, including the virtual loss of Burma, had destroyed forever the image of British invulnerability. It was expected that the Japanese would infiltrate India with units of the INA, the fascist Indian National Army. William Joyce, 'Lord Haw Haw', broadcast that sepoys who had defected in

North Africa were being trained as parachutists and that Indian National Army paratroopers would soon be landing to assist the 'liberation'. Though American opinion may not have been affected unduly, Indian opinion was. The colonial power no longer looked invincible.

By the end of 1942 sixty thousand people had been arrested. On 31 August of that year, the viceroy told Churchill, 'I am engaged here in meeting by far the most serious rebellions since that of 1857, the gravity and extent of which we have so far concealed from the world for reasons of military security. Mob violence remains rampant over large tracts of the countryside'.[206]

By way of conciliation, two Indians, His Highness the Maharajah Jan Saheb of Nawanagar and Sir Ramaswani Mudaliar, were given seats in the War Cabinet (but any War Cabinet papers they saw were censored to remove anything of substance). When Churchill met them in the garden of number 10 Downing Street, he asked, 'What have we to be ashamed of in our government of India? Why should we be apologetic or say that we are prepared to go out at the instance of some jackanapes? . . . Look at the condition even now. An Indian maid with bangles on can travel from Travancore to Punjab all alone without fear of molestations. That is more than can be said in this country today, where our Wrens and Waafs cannot go two miles with the same feeling of safety . . . I am not going to be a party to a policy of scuttle'.[207]

Gandhi was arrested, and he and his household were taken by special train to the Aga Khan's palace in Poona. Their regime was very comfortable, and when his staff, concerned about his diet, discussed with the head jailer the fact that Gandhi was not eating much and might need goat's milk, they were told that a team of goats was already on standby.

Despite the loyal goats, Gandhi's health declined as he began a hunger strike. He looked as if he was going into a coma, Churchill wasn't too concerned: he asked Linlithgow to make sure that he wasn't getting glucose in his water, which he understood had happened on previous occasions. Linlithgow had to advise him that that was not the case. Churchill was still far from sympathetic, calling Gandhi an 'old humbug' and a 'rascal'. He told Field Marshal Smuts that he thought Gandhi had 'been eating better meals than I have for the last week'! Soundings were made about the likely effect of Gandhi's death and preparations were made. If he died, the governor of Bombay was to telegraph the word EXTRA to Amery, which would trigger the release of a statement: 'The government of India regret to announce that Mr Gandhi died while in detention at Poona at —— hours on —— from collapse/heart failure following a self-imposed fast'. He was attended by six doctors, three Indian and three British, including the Surgeon-General. They signed a daily bulletin. On 21 February his condition was critical and he was thought to be close to death. But from that day he suddenly began to improve and by 25 February was out of danger. On 3 March 1943 Gandhi took some fruit pulp mixed with goat's milk and had an enema. That was the end of that fast.

The Surgeon-General, amongst others, thought that he *was* being fed glucose, possibly without being aware of it. At any rate, between 24 February and 2 March, the last day of his fast, his weight had *increased* by a pound. Perhaps Churchill's suspicions were not all that wide of the mark.

36

GOVERNMENT POLICY POST-CRIPPS

By high summer of 1942 some sort of order had been restored. But the atmosphere was very tense. The Cripps Mission had excited expectations that were finally left unsatisfied. At the end of July 1942 Linlithgow concluded that the Government needed to set out its policy.

Amery drafted a statement which included a reference to attaining complete self-government after the war. Churchill tried to qualify this and indeed push back from Cripps by adding the words 'within the British Commonwealth of Nations'. Amery managed to eliminate that. Churchill saw the king shortly afterwards and resignedly told him that parliament was now prepared 'to give up India to the Indians after the war. He felt they had already been talked into giving up India'.[208] George VI was amazed. In his diary on 28 July 1942, he recorded that the Cabinet and most of parliamentary opinion was prepared to give up India to the Indians after the war. Churchill thought that too much had happened to make continued rule in India possible.

But Churchill's pessimism didn't last. Indeed even when Britain was offering, albeit on a post-dated basis, what Cripps had taken with him back in March 1942, Amery wrote to Linlithgow, telling him to be sure that 'whatever else you do or agree to', he was to keep in mind that a considerable area surrounding Delhi should be retained as the ultimate federal territory of an eventually united India, which was not to pass into the hands of any dominion that might temporarily emerge. The assumption was that an independent India would break up and that amongst the competing successor states there would be a place for Britain, militarily and otherwise. In a similar sense, in January 1942 Linlithgow stressed that nothing should be done to make it impossible for Britain after the war to regain any ground that she had given away in the course of working for victory. Consistently with all of this, Rab Butler, still a junior member of the government, had written to Amery, complaining that the draft Declaration did not make clear what he had understood was implicit: that Britain would continue to have a role to play in India after her control of the component parts had come to an end. Whether or not Cripps knew about these assumptions is not clear.

The bulk of the Conservative party had still not admitted to itself the possibility that the days of British rule were at an end, or that a continued role in India was not compatible with Independence. Churchill was only the most extravagantly outspoken. In the garden of 10 Downing Street in September 1942 he declared:

> I shall tell them that for the last twenty-five years the Conservative party has gone on the wrong tracks, it has lost confidence in itself, and it has given way perpetually until the present state of affairs has come about. It is all wrong, thoroughly wrong. If we have ever to quit India, we shall quit it in a blaze of glory, and the chapter that shall be ended then will be the most glorious chapter of that country, not merely in relation to the past but equally in relation to the future, however distant that may be. That will be my statement on India tomorrow. No apology, no quitting, no idea of weakening or scuttling. What do we gain from India? We have lost our trade and all our contracts, we have less than 500 civilians in the whole of the service there . . . and there is only one thing we are doing . . . and that is to do our duty there, and we are prepared to do that at any cost.[209]

On 10 November Churchill drew a line underneath Roosevelt's interference when he made the speech at the Mansion House that contained a famous phrase: 'We mean to hold our own. I have not become the King's First Minister in order to preside over the liquidation of the British Empire.' George VI's First Minister had recovered from his wobble.

Churchill's words amounted to the most public put-down he ever administered to his most important ally in the fight against Fascism. Considering how very circumspect he always was in his relations with Roosevelt, what pains he took to please and flatter, the Mansion House speech reveals how strongly he felt about the president's jejune anti-colonialist interfering.

As the war moved in Britain's favour, Churchill's thoughts on India turned from short-term expedients which he could subsequently ignore to the longer term, in which the jewel would remain firmly in the crown. In August 1944, for example, by which time it was possible to be certain of victory in the fairly near future over both Germany and Japan, Churchill told Amery about his plans for securing the Raj. There would be a purge of British officials who had lost the will to govern and had become 'more Indian than the Indians'. The power of the moneylenders and the land-lords would be reduced. There would be extensive land reform to benefit the peasants and the Untouchables, pretty much like collectivisation on 'Russian lines'. Britain would thus form a bond not with the educated elite of Congress, but with the masses. Amery told Churchill that he 'didn't see much difference between his outlook and Hitler's'.[210] Stalin would have been a better comparison. Churchill returned to proposals of these sorts in March 1945. He wanted to deprive Congress of what he regarded as the vital support of the landlords and moneylenders.[211] Linlithgow shared Churchill's belief that the masses of Indians had no interest in politics.

Churchill referred repeatedly to the extent of British expenditure on behalf of India. By June 1945 the cost of defence of India had risen to £1.292 million. He said in his war memoirs that, 'No greater portion of the world's population was so effectively protected from the horrors and perils of the World War as were the peoples of Hindustan. They were carried through the struggle on the shoulders of our small Island'.[212] He told Cabinet that Britain was creating a monster by putting modern weapons in the hands of the sepoys, who would shoot her in the back. He remained convinced, against the evidence, that the Indian Army was disloyal. His views were those of a man born just seventeen years after the Mutiny. They were not the views of all the Cabinet. In 1943 the Labour party had commit-ted itself to granting Independence to India immediately if it won the next general election.

As for the INA, some units were involved in the Battle of Arakan on the India–Burma frontier in 1943, but it was generally not effective. Its leader, Subhas Chandra Bose, had been educated at Cambridge. He was a former Indian civil servant who had been a Congress leader. He was duped by the Germans, to whom he initially fled, and then by the Japanese. He saw himself and his forces as liberators. Axis powers saw the INA as a small force, valuable more for propaganda than practical purposes, which would assist them in replacing one form of imperialism with another. He was despised by both his protectors.

37

WAVELL

Churchill had found Linlithgow a congenial viceroy. Both men were for doing nothing for as long as possible. Both thought that Independence could be postponed indefinitely. Even at a late stage Churchill dreamed that 'We might sit on top of a tripos – Pakistan, Princely India and the Hindus'.[213] Linlithgow similarly thought that Britain could 'carry on with some scheme of government imposed by ourselves with, of course, the inevitable corollary that we shall remain there to hold the balance'. He thought that British rule would last for at least another generation.[214]

So both of them were working to frustrate Independence. Intercommunal hostility was not a regrettable and negative factor, but rather a positive and welcome means of maintaining British rule. Here was the most explicit collusion in bad faith: despite all that had been promised, the tripos was to remain, a deliberately erected obstacle to progress to Independence. Thus Linlithgow remained in post for almost eight years, longer than any of his post-Mutiny predecessors.

But all good things must come to an end and a successor had to be found. One odd suggestion (from Amery) was Attlee. Of course Churchill couldn't let Attlee go, nor would Attlee or the Labour party have agreed. Next Amery suggested Eden.[215] Amery told Churchill that keeping India within the Commonwealth for the next ten years was crucial and should be 'the supreme goal of British policy'. He saw the continuation of British influence, through the Commonwealth if not through Empire, as critical for Britain's relationship with the Far East and he thought Eden could achieve that. He wrote to Eden himself in the same vein. Churchill liked the idea. Eden would be appointed as a commoner, so that he could return to his political career. The idea attracted Eden to some extent, although he was afraid that it might put him out of the running for the premiership. But on reflection Churchill decided he couldn't do without Eden and he told Wavell, still Commander-in-Chief in India, that Oliver Lyttleton would be appointed. (Oliver Lyttleton was only one of a huge range of candidates – including some bizarrely colourless mediocrities – that were considered before the final choice was made).[216] That was the last Wavell heard about the matter until the post was offered to him a month later.

Wavell had expected to continue as Commander-in-Chief in India or to be the new Supreme Commander, South-East Asia.[217] That was part of the reason that he became viceroy. Wavell was not the man Churchill and the Americans wanted as Supreme Commander. If he wasn't going to get the South-East Asia command it would be invidious for him to remain as Commander-in-Chief, India. He had to be got out of the way (to the benefit, as it happened, of the man who would become the South-East Asia Commander *and* who would supplant him as viceroy, Mountbatten). When Churchill appointed him viceroy he tellingly talked of Wavell's taking off his uniform and putting on civilian clothes.

Churchill didn't want a dynamic viceroy. He wanted a dull administrator who would avoid stirring things up. He chose Wavell precisely because he thought he was that kind of man. Wavell was well aware that his role was intended simply to keep India quiet until the end of the war. It came as a surprise to many that he had the motivation and the ability to address great political issues.

Thus Wavell came to be appointed viceroy on 1 October 1943. On the face of it, he seemed to be exactly what Churchill wanted. Wavell had been against Cripps, was for Linlithgow's policies and had no liking for the Congress politicians. But he was much more than he seemed and was in fact exactly what Churchill didn't want. He was highly intelligent and he had the best qualities of the military mind: a capacity to focus on the essentials of a problem and to seek severely logical solutions to it.

* * *

Immediately after Independence, Wavell's performance was contrasted unfavourably with that of Mountbatten. Wavell was seen as having been pessimistic and weak and as having run out of steam. And yet it was he who decided that India should be granted Independence within eighteen months. He also acquiesced in the conclusion that there would have to be partition. He didn't like that fact, but he was resigned to it and advised the Government accordingly. Before Mountbatten ever came out to India, Wavell had persuaded Congress and the Muslim League to accept difficult facts – that Congress would not get all of India and that the Muslim League would not get all of Pakistan. He advocated not scuttle but an orderly withdrawal against the eighteen-month timetable.

Wavell was and still is highly regarded by military historians. He was intellectually formidable, though he did not parade the fact. In 1938 he gave the Lees Knowles Lectures at Cambridge on 'Generals and Generalship'. Rommell carried a copy of the lectures with him throughout the North Africa campaign. Wavell was a scholarly soldier. He had been under consideration for the Chichele Professorship of Military Studies at Oxford when war broke out. Eventually he was the chancellor of one university and had honorary degrees from six.

Despite the prime minister's own enthusiasm for the verse of the popular Victorian anthologies and his love of the written and spoken word, he could never feel it appropriate for a warrior to profess a love of poetry. In 1944 Wavell published *Other Men's Flowers*, an anthology which he compiled during his viceroyalty of the poems he knew by heart. It was enormously successful and has been in print almost continuously since it first appeared. After the war Wavell was President of the Royal Society of Literature and of the Kipling, Browning, Poetry and Virgil societies and of the Edinburgh Sir Walter Scott Club: pretty remarkable. Yet all Churchill could say was: 'It may be my fault, but I always feel as if in the presence of the Chairman of a Golf Club.' This was below Churchill's usual form.

As a general Wavell had lacked a political touch. He had clung to the notion that war was the business of the soldiers and did not need to be discussed with the politicians. As Theatre Commander in North Africa he failed to take account of the fact that the prime minister was looking at a bigger picture than his. On one occasion, Wavell's independence resulted in Churchill's considering dismissing him for insubordination. Instead he ordered Wavell to proceed with the invasion of Syria and Lebanon 'and should you feel yourself unwilling to give effect to it, arrangements will be made to meet any wish you may express to be relieved of your command'.

Finally Churchill dismissed him from North Africa. Churchill said Wavell was 'tired'. His successor said he could see no signs of tiredness, and paid tribute to what Wavell had left behind him. Wavell took the dismissal well. The signal arrived while he was shaving, and it was read out to him. He said, 'I think the prime minister is quite right: this theatre wants a new eye and a new hand' and he went on shaving. The Chief of the Imperial

General Staff, Dill, thought that if Wavell were allowed home he might say that he was being blamed for the Government's mistakes (a serious misjudgement of Wavell's sense of duty). As a result, Wavell directly swapped offices with Auchinleck, the Commander-in-Chief in India. The swap was made against the wishes of Amery, who wanted to keep Auchinleck in India rather than the 'failed' Wavell, but it went ahead all the same.

Wavell may not have understood Churchill, but he did understand India. He had first served there in 1903, and when he was moved back from North Africa to become Commander-in-Chief he became a member of the viceroy's Executive Council, for two whole years the viceroy's right-hand man. So even before he became viceroy he had the benefit of close observation of the workings of British rule. He had a better apprenticeship for supreme office in India than any other viceroy. He also believed that India should achieve Independence.

He is not regarded as a success as viceroy, but he was very far from a failure either. He was the first man to hold the office to apprehend that Britain had been dishonest in what she had said to the Indian nationalists. He saw also that it was now too late to end the Raj in good order. His prescription was pretty much the same as that of his successor, Mountbatten, but he was in a much weaker position than Mountbatten, particularly in the shameful lack of support from London from which he suffered. He was intelligent, honourable and adaptable, though lacking some of the personal qualities that were needed. He was frequently tongue-tied, shy and restrained, and all this could, wrongly, be interpreted as proceeding from a lack of sympathy. At times his reticence amounted almost to an inability to speak. He 'tended to grunt, murmur and bump into things, caught off-balance by his bad eyesight and poor hearing'.[218] His difficulty in communication was exacerbated by the fact that he had only one eye (he lost his left eye at Ypres in 1915) and was almost totally deaf in one ear. King George VI described him as 'an oyster', despite the fact that he'd lost his eye in the service of his king and country. It is intriguing to picture the meetings between the awkward, stuttering George and the one-eyed, deaf and silent Wavell. No wonder the king found Mountbatten more congenial: charming, smooth and family.

Because he proceeded by analysis of a situation, formulation of plans to address the circumstances and implementation of that plan, he neither understood nor communicated with politicians, who tend to be intellectually lazy and to proceed by intuition and improvisation. Just as he hadn't found the knack of dealing with Churchill when he was a general, so as viceroy he failed to relate to him – or to Attlee when the latter became prime minister. He was prepared always to accept logic; he failed to see how little logic informs the course of politics.

It is true that Wavell made no attempt to smooth the demeanour of the bluff soldier which he considered himself to be. His manner with those to whom he did not warm was business-like rather than genial. He could be terse and silent. It was a pity for him, and perhaps for India, that he only revealed to his intimates his intellectual and temperamental resources. He wrote well and had read widely. He could deploy the extensive stock of poetry that kept in his head. He was a good and witty storyteller. A man who kept in mind the order of precedence for the five biggest princely states with the mnemonic 'Hot Kippers Make Good Breakfasts' (Hyderabad Kashmir, Mysore, Gwalior, Broda) must have been capable of fun.

He never enjoyed the support of his political masters as Mountbatten did, and he suffered from the fact that in his time there was a negligible degree of interest in India at Westminster. He was repeatedly disappointed to hear that at important Indian occasions in the House of Commons there were as few as twenty or thirty members present. He inferred from this a profound lack of interest within Parliament (and thus the Government) in the huge problems with which he was wrestling.

In addition to being a poor communicator, he was no dissembler and no politician. He failed to warm to Nehru, whose political approach he regarded as 'sentimental' and in Gandhi ('the old man') he saw only, and to an exaggerated degree, his bad qualities. He could never understand what his elliptical utterances meant. Wavell's fault may have been that rather than allow himself to be mesmerised by Gandhi's presence he sought, as others did not always do, to understand what he was saying. On one occasion he said at the end of an interview, 'He spoke to me for half an hour, and I am still not sure what he meant to tell me. Every sentence he spoke could be interpreted in at least two different ways. I would be happier were I convinced that he knew what he was saying himself, but I cannot even be sure of that.' That was a shrewd observation which few others were frank enough to record. One of Wavell's secretaries recalled of his chief, 'He would sit there while the little man prattled on, and the expression on his face was one of sheer misery. He would fiddle with his pencil and I could see his single eye gradually beginning to glaze, and at the end of it, all he could think of to say would be "I see. Thank you".'[219] On one occasion Wavell allowed himself to dream: 'I wonder if we shall ever have any chance of a solution till the three intransigent, obstinate, uncompromising principals are out of the way': Gandhi (just on 75), Jinnah (68), Churchill (nearing 70).[220]

Wavell could be very direct and ready to cut through red tape. In correspondence with London he could be very blunt: 'Cabinet's lack of imagination in dealing with India is sometimes astonishing.'[221] When Gandhi wrote from prison – he had been imprisoned as part of the clampdown on the Quit India movement before Wavell arrived – Wavell drafted a reply, even though he knew he shouldn't 'send anything so direct and open. I don't, however, see why I should refer home at all. Perhaps I'm unwise to enter into correspondence with Mr G, but I have not provoked it, and I must send some answer to his letter, and do not like the sort of grandmotherly stuff the Home Department produces.'[222] Wavell subsequently personally authorised Gandhi's release from prison. Technically this was inappropriate: Gandhi had been imprisoned by the Government of India and the Viceroy's Council resented the fact that Wavell had taken personal responsibility for his release.

Wavell never received a fair hearing from the Cabinet or much support from Amery. Sometimes he received no hearing at all. They did not want to listen to objective reporting, advice that was clear-cut and evidence-based. Linlithgow had said little to upset London. He was for keeping the lid on India and letting things simmer away. Wavell could see the dishonesty of British policy. He reported that the alternatives were staying on for another fifteen to twenty years and truly doing the preparation for peaceful transition which had not been done in the last thirty years, or getting out in as smooth a fashion as possible and accepting the consequences. He knew that policy before his time meant that the first alternative was not practical.

Before Wavell took up his new post, he had been preparing himself at the India Office. He was horrified by the double-speak from the Government which his research revealed. His conclusion was pretty much exactly what this book argues: 'We were proposing a policy of freedom for India, and in practice opposing every suggestion for a step forward'.[223] He came to the conclusion that when he got to India he should bring the principal politicians together, tell them that Britain wanted India to have self-government as soon as possible, and leave them alone, but with adequate secretarial backup, to come up with workable proposals. He said that when orthodox methods failed you should be prepared to fall back on unorthodox ones. Churchill and the Cabinet turned the proposal down at once.

Before he went to India as viceroy he and Churchill sailed together to New York on the *Queen Mary*. Wavell wasn't impressed by Churchill's views on India: '[H]e accused me [as Commander-in-Chief, India] of creating a Frankenstein by putting modern weapons in the hands of sepoys, spoke of 1857, and was really almost childish about it. I'd try to reassure him, both verbally and by a written note, but he has a curious complex about India and was always loath to hear good of it and apt to believe the worst. He has still at heart his cavalry subaltern's idea of India; just as his military tactics are inclined to date from the Boer War'.[224]

Amery reflected presciently that Wavell, although a soldier, might 'prove more radical before long than most politicians, witness Allenby in Egypt'.[225] When he made the appointment, Churchill did not know what Wavell had said in his biography of Field Marshal Lord Allenby, who finished his career as High Commissioner for Egypt and the Sudan, in which capacity he crossed swords with Churchill, then Colonial Secretary, and proved surprisingly progressive. Churchill only read the book after Wavell had been appointed and was shocked to learn that the new viceroy had approved of Allenby's liberalism. So shocked was he that he threatened not to attend the Cabinet dinner for Wavell on the eve of his departure for India. When he spoke at the dinner, 'Winston made a pure diehard speech, glorifying our past record in India', but saying nothing about the future except that his opposition to self-government was unchanged and that he expected to be proved right on this as he had been about Germany.[226]

38

WAVELL AS VICEROY

Wavell met Linlithgow in Delhi on 19 October 1943. The outgoing vice-roy's valedictory comment was memorably wrong-headed; in his opinion: 'Britain would have to continue responsibility for India for at least another thirty years'. He clunked on woodenly: Britain must avoid getting into the position where '[w]e could not get out of India because of the chaos it would cause but were unable to control and administer it if we remained'.[227] This was exactly the position that Britain had been in since at least 1935.

But Wavell could think for himself. As early as 10 September 1943, he had proposed to Amery that there should be a new attempt to secure a provisional central government, essentially, indeed explicitly, on the princi-ples that Cripps had proposed. It was typical of his approach that he was prepared to allow the facts of the situation, when they were open to him, to carry him to the same conclusion as Cripps, whom he had regarded as devi-ous in relation to Linlithgow.

Since Wavell was arguing for a return to the Cripps idea of a more or less representative executive, it is hardly surprising that Cripps himself supported the initiative, telling Churchill how important it was to keep India within the Commonwealth for economic and political reasons. Even those who were arguing for Indian Independence wanted to find a way to hang on to it indirectly as a means for perpetuating British power and reach.

Wavell's proposal arrived when Churchill was in North America. Attlee reconvened the India Committee. It was not greatly impressed by Wavell's suggestions. He had said that there were three possibilities: the continua-tion of 'the present policy of inaction'; an executive composed of individuals chosen for their personal qualities; or the revival of the Cripps idea of a National Government with a Representative Council working as a quasi-Cabinet. He favoured the last, though differing from Cripps in that he left the political leaders more scope for choosing the ultimate nature of the constitution.

Attlee came to the view that it was impractical to negotiate with political parties when one of them had been doing its best to weaken the defences of India. He preferred a less formal widening of the executive. The India Committee, by a majority, decided to ask the Cabinet to authorise Wavell to do much less than he wanted, and simply to consult with the political leaders. Churchill, now back from North America, quickly put a stop even to that. He issued a note to his colleagues and came fully into the attack at a War Cabinet meeting on 7 October. Inactivity won the day. There was to be no immediate initiative. Congress had to declare that they rejected their present position. There were to be no negotiations with Gandhi, and Churchill himself would issue a directive to Wavell. Amery commiserated with the new viceroy: 'You are wafted to India on a wave of hot air.'[228]

Wavell was not greatly surprised by Churchill. He had concluded in July that Churchill hated India and everything to do with it, and he agreed with the view that the prime minister knew as much about India as George III had done of the American colonies.[229] He was, however, surprised to discover that the Cabinet was collectively 'spineless, uninterested and dishonest'.

In informal conversation, Churchill told Wavell that negotiations with Gandhi would take place only over his dead body. On paper he directed that political initiatives were to be avoided 'lest the achievement of victory . . . should be retarded by undue concentration on political issues while the enemy is at the gate'. So Wavell's instructions were to do nothing to advance the cause of Independence.

At the end of 1943 Wavell reflected on his appointment: 'I accepted the viceroyalty in the spirit of the military appointment – one goes where one is told in time of war without making conditions or asking questions. I think I ought to have treated it in a political spirit and found out what the policy to India really was to be and I think I could have made my own conditions, for I think Winston was really hard put to it to find someone. However, here I am and I must do my best, though I am frankly appalled at the prospect of five years – hard to the mind and soft to the body'.[230] It's an interesting thought that if Wavell had made his own conditions – and if they had been accepted, a very much bigger 'if' – then he might have done what Mountbatten did, but some years earlier.

What he had discovered was that despite all the promises that had been made about Indian Independence, Churchill, and most of the Cabinet, had no intention of implementing them. Even Linlithgow had said that the main problem about Indian political progress was 'the dishonesty of the British'. Wavell also soon discovered that the Cabinet was not 'honest in its express desire to make progress.'[231] His first Secretary of State, Amery, *was* honest for the most part. He wrote to Wavell in 1944: 'You and I both genuinely mean to implement the Government's pledges, if they can be implemented, and at any rate to make quite clear that we are sincerely doing our best to promote a solution . . . The Prime Minister passionately hopes that any solution involving the fulfilment of our pledges can still somehow or other be prevented, and with that in view naturally makes difficulties at every stage.'

Wavell did not have to deal only with political crises. In 1943–44 there was a famine in Bengal which amounted to a massive catastrophe. Between 1.5 and 4.5 million may have died following a cyclone in October 1942 that flooded Bengal and Orissa and destroyed the harvest. The misery was compounded by the action of merchants, who hoarded stocks to inflate prices. Wavell described this as 'graft and knavery'.

It has frequently been alleged that Churchill deliberately interfered with famine relief.[232] The evidence simply doesn't support that allegation. There was certainly a grave humanitarian crisis, but it was not within the Government's power to make its consequences vanish. More could only have been done at the cost of diverting food and transport from other essential wartime destinations. That said, the Minister for War Transport, Lord Leathers, was unsympathetic, and thought that Indian demands for food were exaggerated. As so often Churchill did himself no good by ill-advised comments about the 'starvation of anyhow underfed Bengalis' being 'less serious than that of sturdy Greeks', or about Indians 'breeding like rabbits' and getting paid a million pounds a day for 'doing nothing about the war'. These remarks, disgraceful in their own time and even more offensive in today's judgement, have been the basis of a myth, but it is no more than a myth that Churchill altered decisions which were ultimately based on strategic priorities. Amery pleaded the case for famine relief and was supported by first Linlithgow and then Wavell as viceroys and by Auchinleck as Commander-in-Chief.[233]

On 20 October 1944 Wavell wrote in his diary, 'I have been Viceroy a year today, the hardest year's work I have done. In some ways I have done reasonably well, the food problem and getting some sort of a move on post-War development. I have found H.M.G.'s attitude to India negligent, hostile and contemptuous to a degree I had not anticipated, or I think I might have done more. Still the more one sees of the political problems and of the Indians, the more one realises that there are very dark days ahead for India, unless more wisdom and goodwill are shown, and I think they will have to begin from the top, from Whitehall'.[234]

Four days later he wrote to Churchill at length to give a résumé of his first year's experience. He didn't pull his punches: 'I propose to write entirely freely and frankly, as I know you would wish. I have served you now for over five years and we should know one another reasonably well. I know you have often found me a difficult and troublesome subordinate. I've not always found you an easy master to serve.' So far as his responsibilities for appeasing communal differences and making proposals for political advance were concerned, he conceded that he had made no progress whatsoever. He considered that it had probably been a mistaken course, twenty or thirty years earlier, to commit Britain to the political reform of India with a view to Independence. It would have been better to have prescribed economic development first. But the Cripps visit had put early Independence beyond doubt. India couldn't be held by force – not because Britain hadn't the means, but because ruthless force and coercion would be needed and these were not acceptable. He made the critical point that 'India will never, within any time that we can foresee, be an efficient country, organised and governed on Western lines. In her development to self-government we have got to be prepared to accept a degree of inefficiency comparable to that in China, Iraq or Egypt . . . [W]e cannot continue to resist reform because it will make the administration less efficient.' His conclusion was that a speedy move had to be made if India were to be kept within the Commonwealth – certainly before the end of the Japanese war.[235]

He continued:

[M]y primary reason for writing is that I feel very strongly that the future of India is the problem on which the British Commonwealth and the British reputation will stand or fall in the post-war period. To my mind, our strategic security, our name in the world for statesmanship and fair dealing, and much of our economic wellbeing will depend on the settlement we make in India . . . And yet I am bound to say that after a year's experience in my present office I feel that the vital problems of India are being treated by H.M.G. with neglect, even sometimes with hostility and contempt . . . There remains a deep sense of frustration and discontent amongst practically all educated Indians, which renders the present arrangements for government insecure and impermanent . . . The present Government of India cannot continue indefinitely, or even for long . . . If our aim is to retain India as a willing member of the British Commonwealth, we must make some imaginative and constructive move without delay.[236]

His proposal was for a provisional governmental institution. Again he was big enough to acknowledge that it would be based on Cripps. He wanted to call a conference of political leaders. Churchill did not reply for a month and then dismissed the matter. 'These very large problems require to be considered at leisure and best of all in victorious peace.' Wavell did not accept the rebuff: he appealed to Attlee and through him to the India Committee. Cripps was of course positive and wanted Wavell to come and talk to the Committee in person. The other members of the Committee were negative. They didn't like the fact that Wavell's approach did not predicate an agreement in advance by the Indian politicians on the ultimate constitutional settlement. They didn't want Gandhi brought back into prominence and they couldn't see that much had happened since Wavell's last proposal had been turned down a year earlier. The Committee did, however concede that there should be a review of what was to be done about India and Wavell should be involved in that review.

This was all agreed on 18 December but Wavell was told not to hurry over. Indeed Attlee did his best to discourage Wavell from coming back at all. Attlee was tending to lose his sympathy with Congress. He had come to dislike it and its capacity for domination. He expressed himself in terms which show his underlying sentiments, however favourable he was in theory to the idea of Independence. He spoke to the India Committee on 27 March 1945:

He was frankly horrified at the thought of the substitution for the present government of a brown oligarchy subject to no control either from Parliament or electorate . . . While in terms the proposals involved merely a change of personnel, once selection was based not on merits but on the fact that the individuals concerned represented organised political opinion, a constitutional change was surely involved. The new members would owe allegiance to an outside body and not to the Viceroy, who would be forced more and more into the position of a Dominion Governor-General. Effective control would pass to an Executive Council responsible only to party caucuses.[237]

That really was pretty reactionary stuff.

Wavell's visit was put off until March 1945. In the intervening period the India Committee spent a lot of time reviewing past initiatives and future possibilities. It is interesting and important to remember just how die-hard many members of the Committee were. Simon still thought that the Irwin Declaration of 1929 had been a mistake and could not believe that the viceroy could be reduced to the status of a mere governor-general of a dominion. Amery had doubts about whether the institutions of elective government were appropriate for India. He thought that an irreplaceable central executive would be a better idea. Butler thought that Britain would have to remain in place for a long time.

So when Wavell arrived in London he was met by a wall of opposition and negativity. He remained at home for more than two months. By now Labour had withdrawn from the coalition and Churchill led a Conservative caretaker government in the run-up to the General Election. Simon, Butler and Churchill remained hostile to allowing Wavell to take an initiative and ultimately agreed only because they thought that he would, like others, fail to bring Congress and the League together.

In April and May 1945, in London putting his proposals to the Cabinet and the India Committee of the Cabinet Wavell became very disillusioned. He was not a pompous man, but he did find it extraordinary that the India Committee, despite the fact that they had the viceroy at home and available, was attempting technical and detailed formulation of Indian policy without taking advantage of his advice. When he was invited to a meeting of the Committee on 14 May it was his first official contact with or communication from the Committee for exactly three weeks. Eventually he was moved to draft a letter, subsequently toned down, to Churchill on 24 May to point out that he had been home for eight weeks, and that he had heard nothing from the India Committee for over four weeks or from the prime minister for seven weeks. After a few more days without contact he and his family queued to get in to a News Theatre: '[T]he feeling was quite familiar after all these weeks of waiting on Ministers. But we did get into the theatre in the end; while I'm still in the queue for a decision on India'.[238]

What was eventually approved was a conference to be held at Simla, where political leaders would discuss the idea of forming a new Executive Council more representative of organised political opinion and including an equal number of Hindus and Muslims. Only the viceroy and the commander-in-chief would not be Indians. The important Home, Foreign Affairs and Finance portfolios would be in Indian hands for the first time. The members of the Council would, amongst other things, be working on the terms of the new permanent constitution.

39

THE SIMLA CONFERENCE

The Simla Conference of June 1945 was Wavell's policy initiative. If it had succeeded he would have been remembered as a great proconsul. He was well aware of that, but he was no more capable of misleading himself than he was vainglorious. He knew that his chances of success were minimal. He lacked the support of his masters in London. Congress was possibly ready to join his executive, but Jinnah would not participate if Congress were to have the power of nominating some of the Muslim members: there were to be four Hindus, four Muslims and two minor minority members.

Jinnah was by far the most influential Muslim spokesman of these years, though his adherence to the tenets of Islam may be slightly suspect. He was a man of great self-control. It was said that the only occasion on which he showed any evidence of human weakness was at the burial of his wife.[239] He had married a beautiful young woman, Ruttie. In 1929 she was on a trip to Paris with her mother when she became seriously ill and was brought back to India by sea. On 20 February, on her twenty-ninth birthday, Jinnah received a phone call to say that she had died. She was buried in Bombay's Muslim cemetery. At the end of the ceremony he broke down and wept uncontrollably.

For a time, Jinnah returned to England, where he lived in some state in Hampstead, with a large house in eight acres of garden. He was driven to his chambers and pursued a career at the bar, earning £25,000 a year. His daughter was sent to boarding school in England. He also had substantial financial interests in an empire of flats in Mayfair and properties throughout the world. He toyed with the idea of going into British politics as a Labour MP, but it is thought that he was rejected as being far too grand.[240] By the end of his life he owned over 300 suits. When he had been in England at the beginning of his career, he considered staying and taking up a career on the stage. He wore a monocle in imitation of Austen Chamberlain.*

Nehru and he despised each other. Nehru said of him, no doubt unfairly:

> You know the real reason why Jinnah left the Congress was because, about 1920, it suddenly broadened its base and began appealing to the masses. Jinnah did not like this. Congress was no longer a party for gentlemen. Jinnah always thought that membership should be confined to those Indians who had passed matriculation – a standard which would have been high for any country, but for India meant that the masses could never come in. He was a snob. When the peasants began to join Congress, he was annoyed. Why, many of them did not even speak English. They dressed in peasant clothes. It was no party for him . . .
>
> He had no real feelings about the Muslims. He wasn't really a Muslim at all. I know Muslims. I know the Koran. I have Muslim relatives and friends. Jinnah couldn't even recite a Muslim prayer and had certainly never read the Koran. But when he was offered the leadership of the Muslim League, he saw the opportunity and accepted it. He had been a comparative failure as a lawyer in England, and this was a way out.[241]

At the beginning of his political life, Jinnah held that Hindus and Muslims should work together to fight for Independence. Although he joined the Muslim League in 1913, he remained a member of Congress as well. But by the time of the Simla Conference this cohesiveness was far in the past. Now the aspirations of the Muslims had changed from what they had been even in the time of Cripps. Their constitutional goal involved a Pakistan. Wavell recognised this and thought that the best that could be hoped was that because of their association with Hindus during the war, Muslims might agree to federation rather than Independence after it. That was optimistic. Since the failure of the Cripps Mission the League had strengthened their organisation and had become the party of government in Sindh, Bengal, the

---

* I was tempted to say that this must have been the only time that Austen Chamberlain, the unimaginative son of the great Joe and the half-brother of the more able but unappealing Neville, had enjoyed the flattery of imitation, but it has recently come to my attention that when the students of Glasgow University – for reasons that are difficult to comprehend – elected him their Lord Rector in 1925, he was met at the railway station by a deputation of students, all wearing monocles.

North-West Frontier Province and even Assam, where there was a majority of Hindus.

At the conference, Wavell found Gandhi courteous but devious, Jinnah more direct but with much poorer manners. By 29 June 1945 the conference was getting nowhere and Wavell proposed that the party leaders should give him a list of names and he would try to form an acceptable council from them. Jinnah was particularly difficult and finally Wavell said to him, 'I am no dialectician and do not propose to argue. I have put to you a simple proposal which everyone else seems to understand. Are you or are you not prepared to submit me a list of names?' Jinnah asked for that proposal in writing, but when he had the written proposal, he refused even to discuss names unless he were allowed to select all the Muslim members and given a guarantee that any decision which the Muslims opposed in Council could only be passed by a two-thirds majority: what Wavell described as a kind of 'communal veto'. Wavell made his own choice of Muslim members. The choice was approved by the War Cabinet.

That was the end of the conference. Wavell was wonderfully magnanimous. He was certainly not to blame for the conference's failure, but he shouldered the blame all the same. In his final address he said, 'I wish to make it clear that the responsibility for the failure is mine. The main idea underlying the Conference was mine. If it had succeeded, its success would have been attributed to me, and I cannot place the blame for its failure on any of the parties'. His efforts to avoid recriminations were appreciated. Even Jinnah spoke appreciatively of his efforts. Gandhi wrote to him, saying, 'This time you have taken the blame on your shoulders. But the world will think otherwise. India certainly does.' M.A.K. Azad, a Congress elder statesman, said that the Simla Conference marked the start of a much more constructive phase in relations between Britain and India. It isn't easy to see evidence of that phase.

40

A New World

On 23 May 1945 the Labour party withdrew from the coalition government that Churchill wanted to be remembered as 'the Great Coalition'. There was a Conservative caretaker administration until the outcome of the general election of 5 July 1945 was known. Because of the practical problem of counting the votes of the men and women in the services around the world, the result was not announced until 26 July. Attlee became prime minister, a prime minister with an unusual interest in and experience of India, views which were very different from those of his predecessor. He saw India as an artificial conglomerate and had always felt that progress would be slow and gradualist, based on a fairly small Independence movement. By now he could see that Independence was imminent, and his main concern was that the outcome should be dominion status within the Commonwealth. As Churchill was replaced by Attlee, so Amery was replaced by Frederick Pethick-Lawrence.*

Until now, the story we have been studying has been played out against the background of the inter-war period and then the war years, when Britain still regarded herself as a very great power, controlling the greatest empire the world had ever seen. Indeed, as has been noted, the Empire, far from shrinking, had expanded its borders significantly after the First World War. While that war had hit the British hard in many ways, the implications were not immediately apparent, and the dominant purpose in political activity was not to adjust to changed circumstances, but to get things back to what they had been.

Political power in these years had resided for the most part in the Conservative party. There had been minority Labour governments, but for most of the time the Conservative party was dominant, even if

---

* Pethick-Lawrence is more fully introduced in Chapter 42.

sometimes in coalition, as in the National Government or the war-time coalition.

All that changed in 1945. The Labour party won a landslide election and came to power in a mood of great confidence, determined on real political change. The party had to address a world in which Britain's role was entirely novel. Britain had won the war, but that war had brought her almost to bankruptcy and she emerged from it with her authority mightily diminished.

Could she, should she, maintain an empire? The various effects of the Second World War profoundly altered Britain's attitude to India, and her colonial possessions in general. In this chapter I shall look at the post-war situation: at national morale and the wish to rule; concerns over Soviet Russia; and at attempts to rationalise policy.

Collapse of Morale

Thanks to the Labour landslide, the House of Commons of 1945 was the best educated in history. There were more graduates of Oxford and Cambridge and members of the Inns of Court than in any parliament since the time of the first Elizabeth. Most of the talented new recruits filled the Government back-benches. The Treasury Bench was occupied by much older men.* They were very different from the undistinguished conformists who had served Chamberlain. They probably made up the most able peacetime cabinet of the twentieth century – only the Liberal cabinets of Campbell-Bannerman and Asquith could compete – but they had been in office since 1940, discharging the heaviest of responsibilities in the most difficult of times. They were tired, and so was the country.

The state of British morale in the immediate post-war years is difficult for us now to understand. Even at the time there was a mood of incomprehension. Civilians and soldiers had risen to the challenge of the war, and the war had been won, but it didn't feel like a victory. Rationing continued – indeed it even extended to items that hadn't been rationed in the time of the U-boats, like bread.

---

* Attlee's cabinet members averaged fifty-five years of age at appointment, a post-war record apart from Churchill's gerontocracy of 1951 (fifty-five point six). Gordon Brown's cabinet was the youngest, which is perhaps not surprising, but Macmillan achieved the second-youngest, which is.

The country was effectively bankrupt. It was the most indebted nation in the world, dependent on American handouts and a US loan on which interest would continue to be paid. To make matters even worse, just five days after the Japanese surrender and without any warning, Truman peremptorily ended the Lend-Lease programme which had supplied Britain with essential military supplies. Although the supply ended abruptly, the capital and interest that Britain had to give the United States in return were not written off: the final payment was made in 2006.

In 1900 (and again in 2000), the national debt was about 30 per cent of GDP. In 1939, it was 115 per cent; by the end of the war it was at 238 per cent. The United States, now able to shape the world economy to its advantage, insisted on its debtor opening up trade to the Commonwealth. One of the conditions attached to US loans to Britain was that by July 1947 sterling had to be convertible. Keynes tried to argue against this, but as in many other matters at the Bretton Woods conference, the outcome was dictated by the States. A weak – very weak – pound was not readily convertible with a strong dollar. There was an immediate drain on dollar reserves, and a consequent monetary crisis. The convertibility of sterling against the dollar was suspended in August 1947, but devaluation followed all the same.

These macro-economic problems were compounded by micro-economic ones. Coal output fell in the winter of 1946/47, the coldest that Britain had endured for very many years. There was a fuel crisis. The first post-war winter saw the heaviest falls of snow for 133 years. February 1947 was the coldest February since records had first been collected. Britain was 'shivering with Shinwell [Manny Shinwell, the former Red Clydesider, was Minister for Fuel and Power] and starving with Strachey [Minister of Food]' as the Opposition had it. Later, when Shinwell became Minister of War, wits said that at least there would be no war; when he had been Minister of Fuel there had been no fuel. Aneurin Bevan bleakly joked that it was pretty strange that a country surrounded by sea and built on coal could find neither coal nor fish.

Against this background, Britain lost the confidence as well as the ability to continue as an imperial power. Indeed, back in January 1945 Amery, pretty well out of the blue, had suggested that India should more or less be given dominion status immediately, under the present constitution and with the present Executive Council in office. The idea was unrealistic, unworkable and politically quite unacceptable. Wavell's reaction was, 'S of S has a curious capacity for getting hold of the right stick but practically always the wrong end of it'.[242]

Scuttle was in the air. At midnight on 14 May 1948 Britain unilaterally surrendered her mandate authority over Palestine, 'leaving', as was said at the time, 'the keys under the mat'. In India a year earlier she did very much the same thing. The consequences in each case remain with the world.

The Red Peril

Palestine was a special case, not technically part of the Empire, but a territory entrusted to Britain to look after until it could manage on its own, and it's wrong to think that the Labour Government was set on a policy of wholesale abandonment of Empire. There was little talk until well into the 1950s about 'independence' as opposed to 'self-government': the assumption was that Britain would retain control over the security, defence and foreign affairs of ex-colonial possessions.[243] A similar process had been followed in the years between the wars in relation to Egypt, Iraq and Iran. This light control was a cheap way of maintaining the advantages of Empire. Herbert Morrison, Deputy Prime Minister, despite an attempt to topple Attlee immediately after the 1945 election, said that giving colonies even self-government (he wasn't talking about Independence) was like giving a ten-year-old child 'a latch key, a bank account and a shotgun.'[244] There was indeed talk of reviving Empire as an essential weapon in the Cold War.

The Communist menace had figured in British thinking long before the war. In the days of the Great Game, Russia had always been regarded as a threat to India, and this very traditional strand of policy was reinforced after the Bolshevik Revolution. There was a very important Intelligence Bureau in Delhi. Its chief in the 1920s was Sir David Petrie, who went on to become Director-General of MI5 from 1941 to 1946. He wrote a classified account of *Communism in India, 1924–27*. His views were not the product of 'reds under the bed' paranoia. From 1917 onwards, the Soviet Union consistently sought to destabilise the British Empire. In London MI5, working closely with British Intelligence authorities in India, constantly monitored the Indian political scene. Indeed, through the Indian Political Intelligence Unit in London, a part of the India Office housed within MI5, Indian nationalists in Britain were supervised as closely as their counterparts in India itself.[245]

Home Office warrants were frequently granted to keep an eye on nationalists. The Indian Political Intelligence Unit regarded Nehru, for example, as 'the second most powerful man in India' and whenever he was in Britain warrants were used to intercept his post and telephone conversations, and Intelligence Officers attended meetings at which he was speaking. The same thing happened when he was in India. In 1944 he wrote: 'During the last quarter of a century or more I have not written a single letter which has been posted in India, either to an Indian or a foreign address, without realising that it would have been seen, and possibly copied, by some secret service censor. Nor have I spoken on the phone without remembering that my conversation was likely to be tapped.'[246]

Thus those opposed to political advance in India were powerfully supported by the intelligence community which worked hard in the shadows to contain and check any movement towards Independence. The Indian Political Intelligence Unit wasn't happy when at midnight on 14 August 1947, three quarters of all British Empire subjects were removed, in their words, with 'the stroke of a pen in the twinkling of an eye'. Their concerns were understandable. They feared that the policy of scuttle would create a vacuum into which the Communist world, expanding rapidly in the years after the Second World War, would move. Indeed, when Mountbatten accelerated Attlee's original timetable for Independence, he exacerbated the subcontinent's vulnerability. If he had taken longer and strengthened the Indian army, the Punjab would arguably have been better protected against the bloodshed that took place there. Not that the British departure brought an end to British Intelligence activities. At the request of India and of Pakistan, British Intelligence Liaison Officers were posted in both countries.

Quite how critical the intelligence community in London or in Delhi was in obstructing legitimate Indian progress towards self-government will never be known, owing to the fact that they carried out a wholesale destruction of their records. The fact that they did destroy so much speaks for itself. Again, *res ipsa loquitur*.

Official Thinking after the Second World War

On 10 May 1948 H. T. Bourdillon, a Colonial Office official who had then been in charge of the Malayan department at the Colonial Office for just under a year, was about to return from his posting in the field. Before he did so he took it upon himself to write an interesting note for the Colonial Office Organisational Committee, which he called 'Reflections on Colonial Office organisation'.[247] He was writing, remember, after India – and Ceylon and Burma – had become independent, but he was reflecting on something which he saw as entirely novel. 'Previously,' he said, 'it was only the "white" territories in the empire – that is to say, the territories where white settlers of immigrant origin had become the dominant if not the most numerous section of the population – which had reached a stage of complete self-government. *Dominion status* [I stress this sentence] *for coloured colonial peoples, however sincerely professed as an objective, remained a castle in the air*. It has now come down to earth.'

Bourdillon could see that there had been a dramatic change in policy. 'Now,' he said, 'we are encouraging colonial territories to reach self-government *as rapidly as possible*' [and this time it was he who supplied the emphasis]. The reason for the change he saw as arriving directly from the war and 'a tide of conscious, militant nationalism' which had carried Ceylon, India and Burma to Independence and through these examples had encouraged other territories to follow their lead. At the same time there had been 'hardly less important developments amongst the spectators'. To that was added the publicity given to colonial questions in the arena of the newly created United Nations Organisation and the attack on Western democracies by militant Communism, 'ruthlessly prosecuted in the colonial sphere'.

Bourdillon's reaction is important for two reasons. First, he acknowledged that until then dominion status for 'coloured' colonial people *had* been no more than a castle in the air. Secondly, the sudden concession of Independence to India, Ceylon and Burma had been the result of politics and the war, policy departures that were quite extraneous to the thinking of the Colonial Office (or, for that matter, of the India Office). Indeed, Bourdillon's note was written precisely because he felt that the Colonial Office needed to change policy in order to meet a change in circumstances that had been imposed from outside.

His note was sent from the field to the centre, but at the centre, too, there was an awareness that colonial policy was expected to operate on entirely new lines. In March 1949 some 'Notes on British Colonial Policy' were addressed to the United States and the wider world.[248]

These Notes are written in language which would not be used today: 'At present the colonies are administered locally by over forty separate governments in all stages of advancement from the simple paternal government suitable for primitive tribal communities up to dyarchy [*sic*] as in Malta.' In these forty territories there were still, even after the removal of India, Ceylon and Burma, no fewer than 65 million people, who ranged 'from Europeans in Malta to unsophisticated tribesmen in tropical lands . . . Many of the territories are lands where the natural conditions, of jungle, swamp, or desert, make the lives of the people difficult and burdensome'. The tone is distinctly defensive: 'British colonial policy is often misrepresented and attacked both in this country and in foreign countries. Britain's critics accuse her of "selfish exploitation" of the colonial peoples; they give her no credit for past achievements; and they pay no regard to the fact that what we are trying to do in the colonial empire, namely to produce adequate conditions of life for mankind, is a task which others have been attempting in their own countries, often with indifferent success, for hundreds of years.' No explanation is given of why, or whether, it was for the British to try to improve the lot of foreign communities.

An attempt to answer that last question was made in a much longer paper published in May 1950.[249] This paper was prepared ahead of talks with the Americans. During the Second World War America had been highly critical of British Imperialism. Churchill had had to listen to harangues from Roosevelt on the subject and frequently American aid was only given in return for steps that were designed to fragment the Empire and the imperial trading benefits that Britain derived from it. Now Britain was resisting the idea that colonial possessions should be subject to some sort of supervision by the United Nations, rather in the way that its predecessor, the League of Nations, had supervised the mandates that were granted to the victorious powers after the First World War. Britain wanted to retain control of those nations which were not independent, and which must not be allowed to appeal to the United Nations over the head of the British Government. Britain emphatically wanted those nations that were independent consolidated within the British Commonwealth under the British Crown.

British aims, as set out in the paper, sounded wholly admirable: 'We are engaged on a world-wide experiment in nation building. Our aim is to create Independence – Independence within the Commonwealth – not to suppress it. No virtue is seen in permanent dependence. A vigorous, adult and willing partner is clearly more to be desired than one dependent, adolescent and unwilling.' Why 'within the Commonwealth'? Ostensibly because '[i]n this way there will be an ever-widening circle of democratic nations exerting a powerful stabilising influence in the world'. But did the Commonwealth represent at least the illusion of a continuing Empire? At any rate, the objective of strengthening the Commonwealth was explicitly set out as one of the targets of British policy.

In the section entitled 'The Size of the Job', the description of the state of the Empire which Britain had, apparently inadvertently, acquired, is interesting, both for its patronising tone and for its underlying argument that Britain was bound to stay on the imperial scene for some time. It is worth quoting at some length:

> [I]t is within living memory that we have come to grips with what are admittedly some of the world's most difficult and challenging problems. Africa was still 'The Dark Continent', and West Africa the 'White man's Grave', at the turn of the century. In his book 'The Martyrdom of Man' [the book which had so influenced Churchill's views on empire], Winwood Reade declared that the triumph of the Negro had been to survive his environment. Excessive heat, excessive rain, excessive drought: jungle, swamp and desert: poverty of soil: worm-infested water: pests such as the mosquito, the tsetse and the locust, destroying man, beast and plant – these were the conditions waiting to be conquered in 1900.
>
> Of the people of East Africa it has been said that at the time of the arrival of the British: 'They had no wheeled transport and (apart from the camels and donkeys of the pastoral nomads) no animal transport; they had no roads and towns; no tools except small hand hoes, axes, wooden digging sticks, and the like; no manufactures, and no industrial products except simple domestic handiwork; no commerce as we understand it and no currency, although in some places barter of produce was facilitated by the use of small shells. They had never heard of working for wages. They went stark naked or clad in the bark of trees, and they had no means of writing, even by hieroglyphics, or of numbering except by their fingers or making notches on a stick or knots in a piece of grass or fibre; they had no weights and measures of general use. Perhaps most astonishing of all to the modern European mind, they had no calendar or notation of time, and reckoned by the moons and seasons and the rising and setting of the sun . . . They are a people who in 1890 were in a more primitive condition than anything of which there is any record in pre-Roman Britain.'

The tone is still defensive: '[T]hese last 50 years have not been years in which we have been able to give undivided attention to the problems of our tropical dependencies: during that period we have ourselves had to fight two exhausting struggles for survival, and to face serious economic problems as a result.' All the same, 'our colonial policy rests upon a growing consciousness amongst the colonial peoples that they are moving steadily to a stage where they can stand by themselves'. The paper goes on to analyse the attitudes of the Soviet bloc and the 'anti-colonial countries' normally led by India, the Philippines, Egypt and Cuba. These countries appeared to feel that the colonial powers couldn't be trusted by themselves to adopt progressive policies, and sought to bring pressure through the General Assembly of the United Nations. The reasons why United Nations supervision was unacceptable were dealt with at some length.

The pace and scale of the reduction of Empire in such an incredibly short period after the end of the Second World War disproves the well-measured arguments that represent Independence for the colonies as being the planned and inevitable outcome of consistent and benevolent policies. It is untenable to suggest that suddenly and simultaneously such disparate possessions had reached the ideal moment for taking responsibility for their own affairs. What had happened was that external circumstances – economic, military, political and cultural – had obliged Britain to take a totally new line. What she did, for good or evil, was, using a word that everyone sought to avoid, to scuttle. The sophistry of the Colonial Office papers was an attempt to disguise that fact, but scuttle was what Britain did. She scuttled from all her colonies including the biggest and most important of them: India.

Some of what was said in the 1950 paper about Africa could be said about India – excessive heat, excessive rain, excessive drought, no wheeled transport, 'a people who in 1890 were in a more primitive condition than anything of which there was any record in pre-Roman Britain'. What was Britain to do with this subcontinent? What indeed *did* Britain do with it? There are still in India today inequalities in wealth and living standards perhaps even more glaring than in 1900. India has an atomic bomb and its technology is in advance of that of most of the world. Parliamentary democracy (of a sort and for most of the time) exists and the rule of law is not seriously challenged. Simultaneously, there is corruption on a massive and growing scale and millions are illiterate and underfed without proper access to health and welfare. Many argue that India is now controlled by an occupying power consisting of an economic and political oligarchy. Is India any more 'ready' for Independence now than it was in 1900, if fitness for Independence is to imply economic maturity, prosperity, a high level of educational attainment and the capacity for democratic government and political restraint on the United Kingdom model? Will it ever be? When would ever the Indian Civil Service, the India Office or the British Government truly have felt the moment had come to let go of the reins?

41

INDIA IN 1945

Despite the Cripps offer, the India that the new Labour Government had to deal with was not much changed from the India of ten years earlier, when the India Bill became an Act. The Hindus were looking for immediate Independence. The princely states didn't want to *lose* their independence. The Muslims wanted to be independent of the Hindus. The British couldn't see how these irreconcilable tensions could be resolved. There seemed no reason or logic to suggest that Independence would arrive in the next fifty years.

But the forces favouring separation from Britain had been strengthened by the war. Gandhi had said in 1942 that India's soldiers were not a national army but professionals who would have no objection to fighting for the Japanese if they were paid by them. And indeed at the end of the war the soldiers of the INA, who had fought with and for the Japanese, returned to India to be greeted with acclaim.[250] Their leader, Subhas Chandra Bose, was treated as a martyr after his death in August 1945 and is still regarded today as a patriotic freedom fighter. Although many Indians had fought – and fought bravely – for Britain, their contribution was devalued by the fact that their fellow countrymen had fought for the enemy.

There had been nothing of the national rallying to the British cause which had taken place in 1914. The viceroy's unilateral Declaration of War on behalf of India in 1939 was still remembered and resented. The Congress leaders had played no part in supporting the military effort and instead promoted the Quit India movement which left great tracts of the country ungovernable.

And if the Indians hadn't impressed the British, the British hadn't impressed the Indians by so nearly losing the war and by being thrown out of Singapore. By 1935 there had been only about 500 British in the Indian Civil Service and recruitment was difficult; ten years later the numbers were far less and India was substantially being governed by Indians. Now that the British had lost control of administration, and their army was desperately attenuated, it was difficult to say that Westminster truly controlled India any longer.

When Wavell was recalled to London in August 1945 to discuss matters with the new Secretary of State, he was disconcerted by the speed with which the Government wanted to proceed. He urged caution and pointed out that the position of the princely states had not even been discussed. In the first King's Speech of the new parliament, the government had said that they were determined to do their utmost to promote the early realisation of full self-government in India, and that after new central and provincial elections a constitution-making body would be convened to see whether the contents of the proposed Declaration of 1942 which had been the basis of the Cripps Mission were acceptable or some alternative scheme preferable. A new Executive Council, with the support of the main parties, would be formed as soon as the elections had taken place.

Despite this announcement, Congress leaders began to make inflammatory speeches which seemed to threaten a return to the violence of Quit India. Congress said they were not in favour of violence, but Nehru told Wavell on 6 November 1945 that he thought violence inevitable. Wavell feared that Congress would make use of the INA and try to suborn the Indian Army. He told the Government that they should be ready for what would amount to an attempt at a coup by Congress.

The INA had been of little fighting value to the Japanese but of good propaganda value. At the end of the war they were categorised by the British as 'blacks, greys and whites', depending on how far they had cooperated. Government policy was to prosecute the blacks. Auchinleck, the Commander-in-Chief, intended to discharge the greys from the army, but pay them for the whole time they had been prisoners of war. Wavell was against that. He couldn't stand the idea of paying people to fight against the British and thought it was unfair on those Indians who had been loyal.

In September 1945 Congress had resolved that returning INA soldiers could be 'of the greatest service in the heavy work of building up a new and free India'. The decision to prosecute some of these men for treason or indeed for war crimes turned INA men into heroes ready for martyrdom, a great propaganda possibility for Congress. There was a good deal of media manipulation. Twenty-five INA prisoners who had been prodded in the buttocks for singing *Jai Hind* ('Long live India') were reported in the *Hindustan Times* as having been bayoneted.

When the first batch of officers, a careful balance of one Hindu, one Muslim and one Sikh, went on trial at the Red Fort in Delhi there were widespread demonstrations and serious rioting. Wavell had to temper the attractions of clemency with the need to recognise the loyalty of those Indian soldiers who had become prisoners of the Japanese but had refused to transfer their allegiance. At the end of November the Viceroy's Council decided that no future trials would take place unless there were allegations of gross brutality against the accused. Those cases already in court would continue. Wavell had been urged to abandon these too, but thought it would be disastrous to do so. There was one bright moment for Wavell in the course of a pretty awful week. On 29 November he went to a railway board cocktail party. 'I asked the wife of some railway manager whether she had a family, and she replied, "No, I've tried frightfully hard, but I've only got a dachshund."'

The three INA officers who were the subject of the first trial were all found guilty, sentenced to transportation for life, to be cashiered and to lose all pay and allowances that had accrued while they were with the Japanese. Auchinleck remitted the sentences of transportation.

Of the new Labour Government, Attlee and Cripps were the more committed to seeing power transferred in India. Although Attlee had a special interest in India, dating from his time on the Simon Commission, his interest was more to do with management and efficiency and modernity than the ideal of self-government. During the war his attitude to the colonies in general was not advanced or particularly inconsistent with the views of Amery and Lord Cranborne, who favoured schemes for renewed colonial development and a defence policy associated with the colonies after the war. The most important consideration was money. The British garrison was costing money to run which was much needed in the bankrupt post-war home country. Attlee wanted to see an independent India which would be a member of the Commonwealth, a device which would enable Britain to retain influence in the region. He wanted trade with India to continue. In February 1947 he would tell Mountbatten that he was to secure 'the closest and most friendly relations between India and the UK. A feature of this relationship should be a military treaty'. At the end of his life, Attlee believed that what he had done in resolving the Indian dilemma would be remembered as his greatest achievement.

Ernest Bevin, the new Foreign Secretary, wrote emotionally of his reaction to Attlee's vision of keeping India within the Commonwealth, of moving into this new stage of British imperialism:

As I thought of the great men who had helped build this Commonwealth, I felt that Mr Attlee was filling a similar role. I thought of Durham who saved us Canada and united the French- and English-speaking peoples in the great Dominion. I thought of Camphell-Bannerman who created the Union of South Africa . . . I am glad it was a Labour Government that had the courage, the wisdom, to take this step regarding India. For in that Eastern territory [that is, in Asia] a great new area is being born.[251]

It's not easy to see Attlee as an empire-builder, but the age of empire-building clearly wasn't over.

After the confident proposals of the King's Speech the Cabinet took stock of the fact that progress towards a constituent assembly was, as ever, constrained by the inter-communal problem that had been reflected in the various undertakings – for example in the 1940 August Offer – not to impose a Hindu Government on the Muslims.

It was frustrating. In 1946 the new Secretary of State for the Colonies, Arthur Creech Jones, pointed out that as a result of the bi-partisan cooperation of the war-time administration, the Conservative party, now in opposition, was much more in tune with Labour's policy than before the war. But while the Conservatives had perhaps become rather less illiberal, Labour policy was far from a retreat from Empire. Ernest Bevin had already expressed his contempt for the 'ragged-arsed' Communists and agitators of the Trade Union movement. He was not now prepared 'to sacrifice the British Empire'. He claimed that was because the disappearance of the British Empire would mean 'that the standard of life of our constituents would fall rapidly'; in fact, he had a distinct weakness for what his cabinet colleague and arch-enemy, Herbert Morrison, called 'the jolly old Empire'.

On 14 January 1946 the India Committee had a long discussion on 'the extent to which the British Government could legitimately divest itself of responsibility for the future conduct of affairs in India.'[252] There was an alternative. It might be necessary to continue governing India even if that involved suppressing risings with the use of British troops. It was conceived that even if the United Nations had to be involved, they would simply ask Britain to deal with the matter on their behalf. There seemed a real possibility therefore, that however much Britain might want to be done with India, she might be compelled to remain there to keep the peace.

Ernest Bevin was concerned about the implications an announcement about Indian scuttle would have in the Middle East. Although Britain was going to scuttle from Palestine, he wanted to keep troops in place in Egypt until 1949. Other members thought that neighbours might take advantage of conflict in India to interfere and that the seeds were being sown of a future world conflict. Overall, there was little real debate. Holding on with bullet and bayonet was not really feasible. The question was largely a matter of presentation: 'Withdrawal from India need not appear to be forced upon us by our weakness nor be the first step in the dissolution of the Empire. On the contrary this action must be shown to be the logical conclusion, which we welcome, of policy followed by successive governments for many years.'[253] There is a fine dividing line between presentation and misrepresentation.

* * *

There had not been Central or Provincial elections in India since 1934 and 1937 respectively. In the elections that took place in December 1945 and January 1946 Congress hoped to get enough votes from the Muslims to put a stop to the campaign for a separate state of Pakistan. But the Muslim League campaigned vigorously, painting a picture of savage suppression by a Hindu majority. Jinnah's strategy proved sound. Muslims flocked to the League, which won 86.6 per cent of the vote for the seats reserved for Muslims in the Central Assembly and therefore won all these seats. In the Provinces the League's figures were not quite as good, but still not bad. Congress ended by controlling eight of the eleven provinces, the Muslim League two and the Punjab was ruled by coalition. The Muslim vote was now not split between the two parties to the extent it had been. The League could fairly claim to speak for Muslims. Britain now began to turn from dividing the communities to trying to find a way of binding them together.

The Government was moving much more slowly than the nationalists wanted. They thought their battle had been won and all that remained was for Britain to acknowledge that fact. They did not take account of the agonising that was going on in the British Cabinet about what to do or how it should be done. The Government's attention was, however, concentrated by the mutinies that broke out in 1946. The first of them was not initially a mutiny of Indians but of Royal Air Force servicemen who were upset by having to wait so long for demobilisation. The Indian Air Force followed the RAF. Next came the Royal Indian Navy. A four-day mutiny at the end of February 1946 involved 7,000 personnel, a quarter of the strength of the whole navy. This was largely attributable to the insensitive Commanding Officer of *HMS Talwar*, Commander F.W. King, whose usual form of address to his men was 'black buggers', 'coolie bastards' and 'jungli Indians'. The mutiny spread from his ship to others in Bombay, Calcutta and Madras. Congress and Muslim League flags flew from the Bombay ships, and order was only restored after British and Indian troops were deployed and bombers buzzed the rebellious craft. Two hundred and twenty-three were killed and over a thousand wounded. Communist agitation was suspected.

Wavell complained that he was being given no proper policy directives. He despaired of going on 'making promises to India with no really sincere intention of trying to fulfil them'. He concluded that Britain no longer controlled the subcontinent. The police threatened to mutiny as the navy had done. Clashes between the two religious communities were frequent. Jinnah said 'We shall have India divided or we shall have India destroyed', and Gandhi despairingly told the British, 'Give us chaos'.[254] Wavell gave up and prepared for military withdrawal, province by province.

Against this background the Government now announced the despatch of a delegation of senior cabinet ministers. This was 'the Cabinet Mission', the last of the bunches of parliamentarians that wandered around India in sweaty three-piece suits or linen jackets hurriedly obtained on coupon from the tropical outfitters, failing to find a way out of the dilemma their governments had created.

42

THE CABINET MISSION

Although Wavell and the press and others were aware that an important delegation was planned, the viceroy was not allowed to tell his governors about it, and he knew that the mission intended to have meetings which would not be under the aegis of the Viceregal Lodge. By February 1946 he was writing to the Secretary of State, complaining that he was being side-lined. 'I may be quite unjustified in my suspicions that there is an intention, not on your part I am sure, to treat the viceroy as a lay figure, and to keep him more or less outside the discussions, as was done at the time of the Cripps offer. If so, I should like to know.'[255]

The original idea was not for a multi-person mission, but a single plen-ipotentiary, the Scottish journalist and politician, Tom Johnston, who as Secretary of State for Scotland from 1941 to 1945 had presided over a Council of State of former Scottish Secretaries, effectively ruling Scotland independently of England in relation to domestic policy. Finally a trium-virate was chosen (of which Johnston was not a member). The mission was led by the new Secretary of State for India, Lord Pethick-Lawrence, 'pathetic Lawrence'.

Frederick Pethick-Lawrence, ennobled on his appointment as the Labour Secretary of State for India who replaced Amery, wasn't pathetic; nor was he, as Aneurin Bevan said, 'a crusted old Tory'. His prematurely aged appear-ance meant that he looked both, which was probably why Mountbatten insisted on his replacement when he became viceroy. He was business-like and effective but hopelessly unclubbable.

He achieved a double first at Cambridge, where, surprisingly for a high-minded youth who would devote his life to social reform, he played billiards for the university. (It may come as a surprise that one *could* represent a university at billiards.) His surname was an amalgam of his own, Lawrence, and that of his wife. She executed a similar name-change on their marriage, and they formed a union that was modern for their times, and in which she retained an unusual degree of independence. She was a suffragette, and he supported the movement, devoted to Christabel Pankhurst, whose nickname for him was 'Godfather'. His wife was a member of the India Conciliation Group, set up on Gandhi's advice at the second Round-table conference, as was Cripps' step-mother. He had visited India in 1926–27 and had been a member of the Round-table conference and of its Federal Structure Committee.

His religious beliefs were a complicated fusion of Christianity and oriental traditions. He was always in favour of Indian Independence. For years he wrote a weekly contribution in *New India*, published by Annie Besant, and twelve months before his appointment as Secretary of State he clashed with Amery over the latter's negative response to nationalism. All the same, he didn't enjoy the Cabinet Mission. He was frustrated by the nationalists' sophistry. He told his wife, whom he missed greatly, that he had 'nearly reached the limit of human endurance'.

The mission left Britain on 19 March 1946. The Cabinet's Directive to the mission stressed British self-interest. One of the mission's objectives was to secure Britain's defence interests in India and the Indian Ocean area. Britain still had significant interests in the east, from Aden to Singapore, and India was to fulfil her traditional role of protecting these interests, although from now on at her own expense. There was great secrecy surrounding the mission's departure. After perusal, the directive was handed back for destruction or confidential preservation. Pethick-Lawrence's tropical clothing coupons were issued under an anonymous name. He used some of them to buy a topee of enormous size. It didn't do much for him and he fainted in the sun. When he did so in temperatures of 46 degrees Celsius, he endearingly apologised for his 'stupid weakness'.

The other members were Cripps (if he was counting, he was on his third mission) and A. V. Alexander, a Cooperative-sponsored MP with, like many of the traditional Left, an affection for the Empire.

A major part of their brief was to work out how an independent India could look after itself in terms of both internal security and against outside aggression. Before the mission left, Pethick-Lawrence asked for an appraisal by the chiefs of staff. Their analysis was given less than a week before the mission left for India: 'It is of very great importance that there should be coordinated machinery for defence of geographical India, and that there should be a single common defence authority with whom His Majesty's Government could deal'.[256]

Wavell was not at the centre of their negotiations. A special code, 'Novic', was used to denote cables between London and the mission which were not to be seen by him. Wavell didn't think much of Pethick-Lawrence's negotiating skills. He found his approach vague and his drafting poor. He complained about 'waffling' and 'woolliness'. 'He is curious. Sometimes he makes quite concise, sensible, even statesmanlike contributions: and then suddenly seems to turn into a gushing babbler, unable to control his tongue and quite incapable of stopping.'[257] Cripps on the whole he thought much better, though partisan and much too friendly with Congress, with whom he had 'continued and daily contacts'. 'Cripps was much the ablest of the party, with an extremely acute legal intellect, very quick to seize on a point . . . But he is an ambitious man and was quite determined not to come away empty-handed this time; and this made him over-keen and not too scrupulous'.[258] Alexander's knowledge of India he thought scanty, but in time he came to like him. He found him intelligent, honest and amusing and he discovered to his surprise that Alexander shared his own enthusiasm for poetry.

He was critical of the deference shown to Gandhi. When Gandhi asked for a glass of water the secretary to the mission himself went off to fetch it and when he took some time over his task, Cripps himself rushed off. 'G. is a remarkable old man, certainly, and the most formidable of three opponents who had detached portions of the British Empire in recent years, Zaghlul [of Egypt] and de Valera being the other two. But he is a very tough politician and not a saint'.[259]

He always believed that Gandhi's 'professions of non-violence and saintliness are political weapons against the British rather than natural attributes'. At a meeting with Gandhi on 27 August 1946, the Mahatma, according to the editor of Wavell's journal, thumped the table and said, 'If India wants her bloodbath she shall have it.' Wavell did not use precisely these words in his journal, simply saying that Gandhi said that if a bloodbath were necessary, it would come about in spite of non-violence.[260] Towards the end of the mission, Wavell picked up a copy of *Alice through the Looking Glass* and wrote a parody of Jabberwocky which contained verses such as:

> And as he mused with pointed phrase,
> The Gandhiji, on wrecking bent,
> Came trippling down the bhangi ways,
> And woffled as he went.[261]

Cripps tried to revive his friendship with Nehru. Not an easy task. Quite apart from the reciprocal insults which had followed the collapse of the Cripps Mission, each effectively calling the other a liar, Nehru had spent most of the intervening period as a prisoner of the British. Wavell and others still felt that the Labour party were unthinking friends of Congress, but Cripps realised that the Muslim League was now a very significant force. His first visit to an Indian politician was to see Jinnah. His great objective was to get Jinnah and Gandhi together. Gandhi arrived in Delhi on a special train provided by the Government. He contributed the cost of a third-class railway ticket. When he reached Delhi he took up residence in a hut in the sweepers' quarter, where Cripps joined him on 31 March 1946, taking off his shoes before entering. Eventually Cripps' efforts were rewarded by the prospect of negotiations at Simla, the first face-to-face negotiations since Wavell's conference, also in Simla, in 1945. What was to be discussed was a government for all India, but with two groups of Muslim and Hindu provinces. Ultimately, the way provinces were to be grouped caused the failure of the conference.

Gandhi increasingly irritated the delegation and the viceroy, though Cripps continued to defend him. At times even he was taken aback. He recorded in his diary on 20 May 1946: 'Then just as we were considering answering Gandhi's first letter we got a second one purporting to set out a whole lot of points gone over in our talks and representing wholly wrongly what we had said or promised. That made the Viceroy and Albert [Alexander] go completely off the deep end and decided the mission that in future we must all see him together or none of us. It's a very serious matter as it means I can't see the Old Man and keep him on our side. I feel we shall lose him in consequence'.[262] Wavell said, 'I have never seen three men taken more aback by this revelation of G in his true colours.' He saw particularly that Cripps had been 'shaken to the core'.[263]

Whether as a result of the strain of these events or not, Cripps now suffered from one of his illnesses, either a return of his frequent colitis, as the Western doctors thought, or because of an imbalance of the flora in his gut, as Gandhi's doctor thought. He went into hospital and there enjoyed the ministrations of both Western and complementary medicine, the latter involving ingesting six pints of buttermilk a day. He was absent from meetings from 21 May until 3 June.

Gandhi's uncompromising, absolutist approach made him an impossible negotiator. He saw no need for compromise: indeed he abhorred it and while over his lifetime he had advanced the cause of Independence hugely, at this stage more pragmatic dealing was required. He did not evince that approach. Writing from his sick bed, Cripps begged Gandhi for trust and cooperation. Gandhi replied, 'I entirely agree with you that the State Paper demands and commands trust. Yet it, like everything coming from the British, creates nothing but distrust'.[264]

In the days that followed, Gandhi continued, as so often in the past, to produce new ideas and to refine old ones. He could focus on the most minor of issues. In June, Congress appeared to be altering its position to allow it to accept places in the interim government. Gandhi then took exception to the nomination forms to be used for elections to the Constituent Assembly. Even Cripps was irritated by this departure 'by the Old Man arising out of a perfectly harmless paragraph in the Governors' instructions'. At some critical meetings, Gandhi was in one of his twenty-four hours of silence. Alexander reported that Gandhi 'had removed all but his loin cloth and then sat right up in a divan chair, with his legs crossed, nodding and waggling his head as the case might be!'. He would then scrawl comments on small pieces of paper which were handed to someone else to be read out. Cripps was not sure that Gandhi was taking things in correctly. When he received a letter from Gandhi on 25 June 1946 Cripps 'couldn't make head or tail of it except that he was going to advise the Congress to reject the whole thing'.

Wavell got on well with Alexander, whom he regarded as the best of Britons and the best of Trade Unionists. They golfed together in Simla and dined together in the Viceregal Lodge. They both felt that too much attention was being given to appeasing Congress. Wavell threatened resignation if there were any more concessions. Meanwhile Pethick-Lawrence and Cripps threatened to resign if there were *not*.

The mission's Simla Conference came to nothing, as had Wavell's, a year earlier. Cripps blamed the failure on Jinnah; Wavell thought that he was unreasonable and prejudiced in doing so. At any rate, it became clear that the Indian representatives could not put forward any agreed plan, and in these circumstances the mission formulated its own, and set it out in a formal statement on 16 June. There would be a union of India with a central legislature which would deal with foreign policy and defence and would have responsibility for finance. Communal issues would also be decided by the central legislature if need be, but would require a majority of votes in each community before the legislation could be passed. Other powers would rest with the provinces. There were detailed provisions about the grouping of provinces into communal blocs.

On 16 June Wavell invited fourteen men to serve as members on an interim government. It was implied that if Congress or the League wouldn't play ball, Wavell would proceed without them. It looked as if this would work until Gandhi insisted that there must be a *Congress* Muslim (as well as any *League* Muslims). Wavell and the mission knew that this would be unacceptable to Jinnah: Jinnah held that the Muslims, as the weaker community, had to be united and that the inclusion of Congress Muslims would be divisive.

The subsequent manoeuvring was intricate and tiresome. When Congress seemed ready to join the Government, the League would not. When Congress declined to participate, Jinnah was ready to join in. There were in particular competing interpretations of one paragraph, paragraph 8, of the Mission Statement of 16 June.

That statement of 16 June was accompanied simultaneously by the publication of a White Paper in London. Together they were intended to combine enough opt-out groupings to satisfy the Muslim League with enough union to satisfy Congress. Gandhi proved very difficult. Initially, he appeared to welcome the statement (it would 'convert this land of sorrow into one without sorrow and suffering'); but he also said that since the proposed constituent assembly would be a sovereign body, it could change its rules anyway.

Inter-communal violence intensified. The Muslim League called for a Direct Action Day, a Muslim *hartal*, on 16 August 1946. In four days of riots, 4,000 were killed and 10,000 wounded. The British General who restored order compared the episode with the Somme. Calcutta riots sparked off massacres in Bombay, where 1,000 died and over 13,000 were wounded. On Direct Action Day, Nehru, at Wavell's prompting, had driven to Jinnah's residence on Malabar Hill, outside Bombay, to try to achieve reconciliation. Nothing came of it. Jinnah described Nehru as 'an arrogant Brahmin who covers his Hindu trickiness with the veneer of Western education. When he makes promises, he always leaves a loophole, and when he cannot find a loophole, he just lies'. Nehru said Jinnah 'had no real education. He was not what you would call an educated man. He had read law books and an occasional work of light fiction, but he never read any real book'.[265]

Finally Congress made some concessions and on 2 September 1946 an interim government was sworn in. Nehru added '*Jai Hind*' ('Long live India') at the end of his oath. Wavell had succeeded in bringing Congress representatives into the Government of India for the first time – and without making constitutional concessions. For the first time national politicians and not nominees ran the important ministries. Although Wavell could overrule decisions of his Council, he only did so once, and only on a minor matter. On 16 September he began to negotiate direct with Jinnah to try to bring the League into a coalition government. There were immense difficulties and technical objections to be confronted but after six weeks of negotiations about the intricacies of procedure and membership Wavell succeeded. By the end of October he had the coalition that he wanted. But the League's entry was conditional on its accepting the statement of 16 June. That they would not do, and the coalition did not last. The mission had failed.

In the aftermath there were riots and violence and intercommunal atrocities in many provinces. By 20 November 1946, Wavell was writing to Pethick-Lawrence, now back in London, saying that something pretty close to open civil war between the communities was taking place. On 27 November he pointed to the Government's responsibility: 'The absence of a definite policy on the part of His Majesty's Government is a very serious matter indeed at a critical time like this'.[266] Attlee summoned the Indian leaders to London for urgent talks. Nehru, Jinnah, Liaquat,* Baldev Singh, representing the Sikhs, and Wavell flew out on 1 December. Nothing came of the meeting. Reassuringly, both Congress and the League thought that Wavell was against them.

Jinnah and Liaquat were convinced that Britain would acquiesce in a Congress scheme that would deprive the League of real power. They were wrong. At a Governors' Conference on 2 August 1945 only one governor had advocated bypassing the League and forming an Executive Council without it. On 6 December the British Government made a strong statement to the effect that they would not force on India a constitution which would deprive a significant part of the population of representation. This was Wavell's achievement. He wanted to make it clear that Congress would have to face up to agreeing to a deal that was fair to the League. It is argued that Wavell should not have gone so far to woo Jinnah, who at the end of the day could not afford not to be represented on the Council. But if Jinnah *had* continued to stand apart, a Congress-dominated Council would have been unthinkable.

Little more happened before Wavell was dismissed.

---

* Liaquat Ali Khan, often just Liaquat, the first prime minister of Pakistan.

43

AFTER THE FAILURE OF THE MISSION

So the Cabinet Mission had returned to London without solving the problem. The Government was pretty much back where it had been before the mission went out, and had run out of ideas. At a meeting on 10 December 1946 Attlee said that there was no evidence that the Indian political parties were trying to reach any agreement. Nehru was using his position as President of Congress to try to secure party domination throughout India. If Britain imposed a constitution on India that reflected that state of affairs, the Muslims would simply refuse to play. The prime minister was concerned about the prospects of civil war and bloodshed. Some of his colleagues were irritated by the fact that the Indians seemed to think that they would be protected from the consequence of their actions by the army. In reality there were limited British forces in India and the Indian army was unreliable.

There was a crude division between those who thought that the only option was to get out and leave the Indians to sort things out for themselves and those who considered that it would be dishonourable to leave India in chaos and with no guarantee of fair treatment of the Muslims. 'That would indeed be an inglorious end to our long association with India. World opinion would regard it as a policy of scuttle unworthy of a great Power.' Faced with this dilemma the uninspired conclusion was that more thought was needed. The only concrete decision was that Britain was not in a position to 'put back the clock and introduce a period of firm British rule'. The implication of the discussions was that finally Britain would have to give up without being in a position to secure the future.[267]

Three weeks later, on New Year's Eve 1946, the Cabinet met again to think about India and to consider a memorandum from the prime minister[268] and also one by the Minister of Defence.[269] The background to the discussions was that Wavell had concluded that he would be unable to continue British rule beyond 31 March 1948.

Even if by now there was no alternative to scuttle, there were practical problems to face, as well as some emotional resistance. Many members of the Cabinet were loath to mark the great Labour victory by precipitate surrender. Wavell saw that even Aneurin Bevan, about as far to the Left as any member of the Cabinet, 'hates the idea of our leaving India but like everyone else has no alternative to suggest'.[270]

By the time the Cabinet next met to discuss India, on 8 January 1947, although Congress had said that they would accept the interpretation placed by the Government on the Cabinet Mission Statement, and the Muslim League in return was considering whether to collaborate in the work of the Constituent Assembly, it was inescapably evident that the aims of the two communities were irreconcilable. For a hundred years Britain had openly exploited Hindu/Muslim antagonism. Now that Independence was imminent, Britain didn't want that hostility to result in partition. A united India, tied into the Commonwealth, was a more useful tool for Britain than a divided subcontinent with a weak Pakistan in the north. The effect of a strong Pakistan might be even worse.

The viceroy still wanted the Government to declare a date for withdrawal, but the Cabinet's views were increasingly diverging from his. He saw the last phase of the Raj as requiring a military plan for evacuation from hostile territory and wanted to do so province by province. In the autumn of 1946 he had drawn up operation BREAKDOWN to this end. The Cabinet's India and Burma Committee, on the other hand, still wanted a friendly transfer 'with an increasing acquiescence between the viceroy and British officials in the wishes of the Indian governments'. In other words, Britain was to appear to acquiesce in a transfer of power which was fundamentally not in tune with established policy.

Attlee, as always, had very clear views and the Cabinet was entirely with him in agreeing that as the viceroy couldn't be brought to heel by telegram, he should be called back to London for consultations.[271]

Wavell under Attlee

Attlee had inherited Wavell. As deputy prime minister he hadn't been impressed by him, and as prime minister he became increasingly irritated. Cripps, and the Government generally, was anxious to retain the goodwill of Congress and declined to support Wavell when he wanted to present it with *ultimata*.

On 1 September 1946 Wavell wrote to the Secretary of State with the final draft of BREAKDOWN. This involved a phased withdrawal from southern India, to be followed by *complete* withdrawal by 31 March 1948. In other words, the Raj was to be dismantled within eighteen months. In submitting this plan to the Cabinet, Wavell said that the alternative would be a declaration that Britain would remain in India for another fifteen to twenty years. That of course was the nub of the problem: fulfilling Britain's obligations properly, transferring power peacefully, could not take place for another generation, because Britain had still not prepared for it. The alternative was abdication. Wavell could see this clearly.

Years later Attlee was still horrified by Wavell's proposal: 'An extraordinary plan ..., [the] combined thinking of Wavell and his ICS advisers. They were going to move all the British out of India, up the line of the Ganges, and put them on ships in Bombay. Winston would have been right to call it "Operation Scuttle". Out of the question. Indians would have assumed the Raj was on the run.'[272]

When Attlee received the plan, he noted, 'While it is reasonable for the Viceroy to want us to have a Break Down plan, it is unreasonable of him to expect us to envisage failure.' His apprehension was that setting a specific date of withdrawal would create a scramble for power. Wavell replied that as a military man he had some knowledge about retreats and that 'our present position in India is analogous to that of a military force compelled to withdraw in the face of greatly superior numbers . . . If HMG is unable to accept my plan, on what plan am I to base our withdrawal?'[273]

As usual, there was no great sense of interest among the public at large. In January 1946 a polling organisation put the question, 'Concerning India, should Britain get out now, leaving the Indians to work out their own constitution, or should we stay until the new constitution has been agreed?' A strong majority, 58 per cent, wanted Britain to stay, 24 per cent were for getting out, and 18 per cent didn't know. Intriguingly, there was a powerful class element to the responses: about 80 per cent of the middle class wanted to stay, as against 55 per cent of the working class.[274]

The deadlock between Wavell and the Government had been clear when he was in London in December 1946. He was demanding to be given a fixed policy to work to and a deadline for the transfer of power. Ultimately the Government would dismiss him because of that and appoint Mountbatten, who insisted on both points as a pre-condition for accepting office.

Attlee had fought bravely in the First World War, at Gallipoli (where he supervised a rear-guard operation at the evacuation of Suvla Bay), in Mesopotamia and in France, twice wounded and attaining the rank of major. The war had an important effect on his character, developing his leadership skills and stimulating his self-confidence; but he was not impressed by the military mind, and he didn't like soldiers dealing with political matters. He encouraged Wavell to appoint a political advisor. Wavell took this badly. He resented Attlee's suggestion that he didn't have experience of political matters. By the time Attlee was making the suggestion, Wavell had already been involved in India for five years and had political experience in the Middle East. He told Attlee that if they wanted a politician they should replace him. He had no wish to be a figurehead. 'I have no personal ambition, I have already reached a position far above my expectations or merits.'

He ended his 1946 journal on a sombre and pessimistic note, finishing with characteristic humility: 'It is a great strain on a small man to do a job which is too big for him, if he feels it too big. Health and vitality suffer. I am afraid that 1947 may be even more difficult, and more of a strain.'[275]

Attlee, usually blunt and straightforward, was uncharacteristically slippery in his dealings with Wavell. By his silence when Wavell said that the Government should replace him if they wanted a politician rather than a soldier and by his subsequent failure to demur when Wavell said that he assumed that the silence meant that the Government wished him to continue, Attlee gave a clear impression in 1946 that the viceroy had the Government's confidence. And yet at the very same time he was discussing Wavell's replacement with Mountbatten. Attlee was perfectly entitled to replace Wavell if he did not think he was up to the job. It is surprising, however, that he lacked the courage and decency to do the thing openly.

When Wavell was back in London in December 1946 he wrote to the prime minister saying that if he were to return to India he'd need to have assurances on various points, including the fact that the Government recognised that arrangements had to be made with a view to the transfer of power not later than 31 March 1948. Again he received no response. On 19 December he attended a 'disastrous' Cabinet meeting when Attlee was overtly hostile to the BREAKDOWN plan. When he met Attlee on the following day, the prime minister told him that he could accept the plan if it were put in a form which would not require parliamentary legislation. It became evident that this was technically impossible. Attlee was not prepared to admit publicly that the Government was presiding over failure. Wavell noticed Attlee seemed ungracious when they said their goodbyes. The reason no doubt was that two days earlier Attlee had asked Mountbatten to take over as viceroy. On 4 February 1947, 'just after lunch I had a letter from the PM by special messenger, dismissing me from my post at a month's notice. Not very courteously done'.[276]

Wavell was dismissed at extraordinarily short notice. Normally a retiring viceroy was given six months' notice of his replacement. Wavell had repeatedly been led to understand by the Government's failure to say otherwise that his dismissal was not in contemplation. Just a week or two before Attlee wrote his letter, Wavell had been with the prime minister in London and had been given no reason to think that his tenure of office would be curtailed. When he was appointed in June 1943, Churchill told him that he wished to be free to make another appointment after three years, if that proved necessary, but that he hoped it would not be. The three-year period had passed without event and the normal period in post was five years.

Wavell was very far from being a pompous man and he didn't stand on his dignity, but he was stung by the method of his dismissal, and made that very clear in his reply to Attlee on 5 February 1947. In the course of a dignified letter, he said, 'You are causing me to be removed because of what you term a wide divergence of policy. The divergence, as I see it, is between my wanting a definite policy for the Interim period and HMG refusing to give me one. I will not at this time enter into further argument on this'.[277]

He had been an attractively human viceroy, instinctively usually right. Lord Listowel, Pethick-Lawrence's Under-Secretary of State and soon his successor, spoke of the 'abject and humiliating thraldom' which was Wavell's relationship with London. His successor, Mountbatten, was sympathetic, but he was not the kind of man who could understand why Wavell had put up with the restrictions which fenced him round. When Wavell told Mountbatten that he had not been allowed to have an informal talk with Gandhi, Mountbatten could not understand why Wavell would even have asked for permission. But circumstances were different for Mountbatten, as we shall see.

44

THE LAST VICEROY

Ever since his membership of the Simon Commission in 1928, Attlee had kept up to date with Indian affairs. Even before the war and the disintegration of morale in India that came with it, he had been arguing for a promise of dominion status at a fixed date. He had not felt able to make much progress as long as Wavell was in post. He found him negative, and wrote him off as imperceptively as Churchill had done: 'A curious silent bird'. He cast around for a successor. 'I thought very hard, and looked all around. And suddenly I had what I now think was an inspiration. I thought of Mountbatten.'

Wavell's Private Secretary, George Abell, told the Cabinet that he estimated that the chances of getting agreement with the Indian leaders were one in ten. Attlee told the king that the odds were six to four against success. He was clear, however, that Mountbatten, whose name had first been put forward by Amery in 1942 as successor to Linlithgow, would be a better jockey than Wavell: 'Dickie Mountbatten stood out a mile. Burma showed it. The so-called experts had been wrong about Aung-San [the Burmese Nationalist leader], and Dickie had been right'.[278] 'He and I agreed entirely. I told him I wanted a man to end the British Raj.'[279] Wavell of course had wanted to end the Raj, saw no alternative, but when he asked Attlee to allow him to do so, the prime minister took fright.

Mountbatten's official biographer, Philip Ziegler, wrote of his subject, 'his vanity, though child-like, was monstrous, his ambition unbridled. The sheer vulgarity of that vanity can obscure his very real and considerable abilities'. Ziegler recorded that 'there was a time when I became so enraged by what I began to feel was his determination to hoodwink me that I found it necessary to place on my desk a notice saying: "REMEMBER, IN SPITE OF EVERYTHING, HE WAS A GREAT MAN"'.[280*]

---

* When I have been dealing with Churchill in this book, I have had to refer to a

Mountbatten had suggested that Cripps should become Secretary of State – largely to avoid having him come out to India with him to hold his hand. Indeed, he was horrified when Cripps offered to resign from the Cabinet and accompany him. Mountbatten told Attlee that he didn't want to be reduced to a figurehead because of the presence of a man of Cripps' prestige. He also wrote to his cousin, the king. He said that he had been terrified by the prospect of Cripps breathing down his neck.[281] He told the king, 'I don't want to be ham-strung by having to bring out a third version of the Cripps Offer!!!'[282]

The current Secretary of State, Pethick-Lawrence, was seventy-four years old and found his responsibilities onerous: he had to retire after just eighteen months in office. Mountbatten and Attlee had not thought much of him. At Mountbatten's request he was replaced by the Under-Secretary of State, Lord Listowel.*

The last viceroy had enormous charm, style, a capacity for hard work and was wholly committed to success. Did that make him a great man, as Ziegler believed? It's hard to know what amounts to greatness. The problem is the one that bothered Gray in Stoke Poges Churchyard. Can a man be great if he does not play a part in a large theatre, his decisions affecting large numbers of men? If not, and the status depends on quirks of time and place, it doesn't mean a great deal. Both in South-East Asia, as Supreme Commander, and in India as viceroy, Mountbatten was able to make decisions of enormous significance, hobbled by few of the constraints that normally exist in parliamentary democracies.

He had been appointed Supreme Commander in South-East Asia at the age of just forty-three. He was not daunted by the scale of the challenge. He

---

similar if only imagined notice about him, to remind me that his failure to put aside his primeval assumptions in regard to India must not detract from one's appreciation of his sublime capacity in general to rise to the level of events.

* Listowel is an intriguing figure. He was always a problem to his father because of his left-wing views. At Eton he shared these views with his headmaster's wife. When he reached Balliol College, Oxford, he continued to disappoint. His father thought the problem might be the influence of the Master, A. D. Lindsay, so he was moved to Magdalene College, Cambridge. There things were even worse: he chose to be known as Mr W. F. Hare, rather than by his courtesy title, Lord Ennismore. That was too much, and his father disinherited him. In consonance with his radical views, his wives were (1) a Hungarian political activist, (2) the jazz singer Stevie Wise and (3) the former wife of a middleweight boxer.

exulted in the range of his responsibilities. He didn't get on well with Auchinleck, the Army Commander. He thought that Auchinleck suffered from an inferiority complex. The Auk certainly didn't, but he did want to retain his autonomy as Army Commander, and to be responsible for deciding on what units should be allocated to the South-East Asia command. But Mountbatten could be magnanimous. In May 1946 he wrote to the king to press for a peerage for Auchinleck – 'the man who made my victory in Burma possible . . . I would gladly and willingly stand down in favour of him if only one can be spared for this theatre. He is a great man.'[283]

He had trouble too with the navy's wish for Independence. The conflict between Mountbatten and Auchinleck was not as bitter as the conflict between the Supreme Commander and his naval Chief, Admiral Somerville, a 'cantankerous old bugger'.

His relations with his initial deputy, the American Lieutenant-General 'Vinegar Joe' Stilwell, an intemperate Anglophobe, started surprisingly well. 'Louis is a good egg,' Stilwell initially reported to the US General Marshall, one of the combined Chiefs-of-Staff. That impression didn't last. By 1944: 'The Glamour Boy is just that. He doesn't wear well and I begin to wonder if he knows his stuff. Enormous staff, endless walla-walla.' Later Mountbatten was 'a fatuous ass', 'childish Louis', 'publicity crazy', 'a pisspot'.[284]

Overall, reactions to Mountbatten tended to polarise. There were those, such as Admiral Cunningham, who found his 'film star work made me physically sick'. Others responded very positively to his charm and flamboyance. The casual intimacy which he affected, particularly when addressing junior ranks, almost always reassured and inspired.

It must be remembered that whereas now Mountbatten is often seen as a meretricious, self-serving figure, extraordinarily charming but essentially shallow, that was not the perception at the time. As Supreme Commander in South-East Asia, he had exercised a degree of power in the last months of the war that is difficult to comprehend. Even if he *had* been promoted above his own ability, he played his hand well. He had unusually able commanders operating below him; he intervened when he needed to and intervened to good effect. It was his finest hour. Accordingly, he came to India with a golden reputation and with peculiar prestige; and his impeccable aristocratic pedigree as Queen Victoria's great-grandson was balanced by a known sympathy for the Labour party's politics. The story is that when Labour party activists canvassed the Mountbattens at Broadlands they were received very sympathetically but that when they asked if they might talk to the staff, Mountbatten said, 'I'm afraid you'll find them frightfully Conservative.'

Along with prestige and a formidable reputation he brought with him an unequivocal commitment to Independence not later than June 1948.* Mountbatten referred to himself as the last viceroy, but in a sense Wavell was more truly the last. He was the last man to rule the Raj. By Mountbatten's time the Raj was dead. He was the undertaker. He claimed he had been given plenipotentiary powers by Attlee. When he met Nehru, the latter asked him, 'What is different about you from your predecessors? Can it be that you have been given plenipotentiary powers? In that case you will succeed where all others have failed.' Mountbatten replied that he *did* have such powers. He certainly liked the idea that plenipotentiary powers had been conferred on him. Whether they were is not entirely certain. His account was challenged in 1968. Admiral Brockman, who was in a position to know, having been very close to Mountbatten in India, often working with him until the early hours, said he had never heard the phrase used during Mountbatten's time as viceroy.[†] Mountbatten continued to maintain that Attlee had given him such powers, although Brockman remained unconvinced. There certainly is no reference to special powers in the official records or in Attlee's correspondence.

But even if he didn't formally have such powers, that didn't much matter. The reality was that he could in practice do what he wanted. With a

---

* The need for a definite withdrawal date had penetrated government thinking, as a result of Wavell's advocacy and didn't come from Mountbatten. The choice of the actual date was more difficult. Many of the Cabinet, led by Bevin, were against an early date. Bevin thought that an early date would cause problems in Malaya, Ceylon and the Middle East; Pethick-Lawrence and Cripps though an early date would prejudice Congress as against the League. The practical arguments that pointed to a speedy exit were not accepted without lengthy debate.

† Sir Ronald Brockman was a 'secretary bird', a supply and secretariat officer (the bird was the emblem of the Royal Naval Staff College), one of those naval officers who in their time were attached to senior commanders in their successive roles. Brockman was attached as Secretary to two Sea Lords, Sir Roger Backhouse and Sir Dudley Pound, before working with Mountbatten, as he did for twenty-two years. Mountbatten was eventually Brockman's third First Sea Lord, when the former was appointed to the position from which his father had been dismissed in 1914. Secretary birds could reach exalted rank without having spent much time at sea, and Brockman finished his career as a vice-admiral. When he died in 1999 he was the last surviving Companion of the Order of the Star of India.

commitment to departure by a fixed date, his job was to wind things up as best he could, and nothing he did could have been disowned by the Government. The powers that he did have were wide ones. He could do a great deal without referring to the Indian Office. Strangely, previous viceroys had not been allowed to meet politicians without prior consent. This did not apply to Mountbatten.[285]

There was an enormous emphasis on publicity. The viceroy's staff, an entourage known as the Dickie Birds, were frequently minuted, 'Press advisor to arrange for photographers to be present to photograph the meeting'. His daughter, the honourable Pamela Mountbatten, was told that she would be 'doing the young people'. Lady Mountbatten was told to 'establish early contact with the women who matter in India'. All of this was what the Mountbattens called the 'good-will campaign'. The tone was very relaxed. An extraordinarily diverse range of guests were 'invited' (not as before 'commanded') to attend meals at the Viceregal Lodge. The Mountbattens would drop in on the Nehrus and eat strawberry ice-cream in the garden. Gandhi had tea on the lawn at the Viceregal Lodge, declining the cakes and sandwiches, and eating from a bowl of goat's curd which he'd brought with him. He persuaded Mountbatten to try it.

45

Mountbatten's Instructions

By the time Wavell received his letter of dismissal, Attlee had been in correspondence for six weeks with Mountbatten about the terms on which he'd accept office. His years in India were not to count against promotion in the Royal Navy. He wanted continued use of the aircraft that he had enjoyed at South-East Asia Command (a typical Mountbatten touch). Moreover, although in mid-January 1947 Attlee was still telling Wavell that it wouldn't be advisable to fix a day for the British to leave India, he had already told Mountbatten that he would make a statement to the House naming 'a definite and specified date' for departure. But Mountbatten, just as Wavell had been, was conscious of a vacuum at the heart of official policy. For all the talk of Independence as a generality, there was no detail: 'I am not really sure . . . what HM Government wish me to try and achieve in India.' This was exactly the problem that Wavell had had to deal with.

Eventually the Government did give some instructions to Mountbatten, albeit pretty vague ones. He was to reach an accommodation with the princely states, to keep the Indian army together and to end British rule by June 1948. Later this was fleshed out: 'to obtain a unitary government for British India and the Indian states, if possible within the British Commonwealth'. In truth, Attlee already recognised that a united settlement was out of the question.[286] But the Commonwealth dimension was crucial: if India remained bound in to the protection of Britain's strategic interests, imperial reach would be preserved. Keeping India within the Commonwealth was the critical issue that underlay policy between the 1945 general election and Independence. If that could be achieved, the military and economic nexus would be perpetuated. Even if formal control over India were coming to an end that did not mean that Britain's role in the Far East was ending – that would not be accepted for another generation. Informal control over India was the key to an ongoing mission east of Aden. On the other hand, if the Commonwealth dimension were to disappear, Britain's whole eastern presence, of which India had been the pivot, would be over.

Mountbatten was bound to succeed to some extent, in that the commitment to immediate departure was known. He could not fail to hand over power to India by June 1948. Whether he could succeed in transferring power to a peaceful India and in keeping that India within the Commonwealth was another matter.

His confidence, his arrogance, was an advantage. He admitted that he thought he could do anything. Furthermore, he had glamour – perhaps too much of it. He and his wife Edwina brought a Hollywood feel to the Viceregal Court, and he loved being at the centre of the trappings that surrounded the representative of the king-emperor. The Mountbattens were a very different couple from the Wavells. Wavell was sensitive and shy. In her advanced, classless way Lady Mountbatten said that Lady Wavell dressed like her maid. Mountbatten's grandeur, as a Battenberg, a representative of high European nobility, meant that he had no need of the formality that had surrounded his predecessors. Half the guests in the Viceregal Lodge were Indians, and to the dismay of traditional courtiers he mixed freely and without affectation with Indians of all classes. Edwina also did her bit. She and Nehru were very close, possibly lovers.

Mountbatten threw himself into political discussions. He became, it can truly be said, a friend of Gandhi – though he could still be irritated by him. When he first met Gandhi he was charmed: 'an old poppet'; a more favourable and less accurate assessment than that of Wavell, who regarded Gandhi as tiresomely evasive. In Mountbatten's case, one master of personality-projection respected another. He was delighted on the occasion when Gandhi arrived for a meeting holding a finger to his lips to signify that it was his day of silence.

Mountbatten's appointment was thought in Westminster to imply a change in communal preference. Wavell had been felt to have a considerable degree of sympathy with the Muslims, whereas Mountbatten was understood to have close links with Nehru and his supporters. It is true that his closest contact amongst the political leaders was of course Nehru, with whom relations were on the whole very warm. Jinnah was cold by contrast. But the perception of bias was and still is exaggerated. It is not the case that Mountbatten was in Congress's pocket. Emotionally he may have been sympathetic to them, but he did his best to be neutral. When a remark reflecting Muslim intransigence by Jinnah's sister was reported to him, he responded, 'I might add that the Hindus are nearly as bad, and that the determination, from the highest to the lowest in the land, to make out that the opposite religionists are devils incarnate as well as crooks, makes any sensible solution out of the question'.[287]

Jinnah, on the face of it, was the leader most similar to Mountbatten. He was very English, with his house in London, his monocle, and Western suits quite as smart as Mountbatten's. Despite all of that, he was not seduced by Mountbatten and Mountbatten found him difficult to deal with, a malevolent wrecker. Perhaps because he was perceived as close to Nehru, who did some early briefing against Jinnah, Mountbatten's initial meetings with Jinnah didn't go particularly well. Jinnah's intransigence was inevitable, given the hostility of the two communities. Its consequence was that an all-India union was impossible: there was no alternative to partition, the creation of two dominions, with the princely states being asked to decide which they wanted to join.

Congress realised that Britain was going to go even at the cost of partition. Congress could cope with the idea of a Pakistan, but greater fragmentation was a challenge to their dominant position. Even Pakistan itself had to be pared down: the Congress Working Committee resolved that there should be 'a division of Punjab into two provinces, so that the predominantly Muslim part may be separated from the predominantly non-Muslim part'. There might be a Pakistan, but not the great Pakistan that Jinnah wanted. Jinnah of course refused to accept that the Punjab and Bengal needed to be partitioned.

The relationship between Mountbatten and Nehru was temporarily upset by 'Plan Balkan'. This was a last attempt, made as a matter of form, because Mountbatten didn't really expect it to work, for a unitary settlement more or less on the basis of the Cabinet Mission Plan. Power would be devolved to the provinces, including the princely states. The provinces and princely states could then form what groupings they wanted and negotiate arrangements with a central government. Some sort of union would follow. He put the plan to a small conference on 2 June 1947 consisting of leaders of the Congress party, the Muslim League and the Sikhs. Nehru was infuriated: the plan would have meant that the power of Congress would be drastically reduced, that the resultant union would be weak and that there might have been up to six independent governments within the union.

Mountbatten wasted no time flogging a dead horse. Plan Balkan was quickly forgotten and he turned to more serious suggestions. He was clear that if the Government did not declare immediately how power was to be transferred, there would be uncontrollable disturbances, especially in the North-West Frontier Province and the Punjab. He announced that the British Government had now abandoned its attempt to secure a union of the whole of India. Power would therefore be transferred to more than one authority. Provinces and princely states would have the right to withdraw from the union.

Mountbatten took advantage of his friendship with Churchill to persuade him not to attack these proposals in parliament. Churchill was well disposed to Mountbatten, effectively his sponsor. Some think this was because of feelings of guilt. Mountbatten's father, Prince Louis of Battenberg, had been First Sea Lord, the professional head of the navy, in the First World War, when Churchill, as his political chief, had with great reluctance been obliged to dismiss him because of popular attacks arising from Battenberg's German connections. It is more likely that Churchill simply admired his dash and glamour and lack of convention, in the same way as he favoured others with more charisma than ability: Lawrence of Arabia, Sir Roger Keyes, General Freyberg and Wingate. Churchill was far from happy with the way events were moving in India. But he was not prepared or indeed able to rally opinion. Moreover, busy working on his history of the Second World War, he had no more time than inclination to spend his days in parliament.

Congress accepted the amended plan and so, to Mountbatten's relief, did Jinnah, who had earlier entertained reservations. The urbane Jinnah gave his response in a speech on radio which he chose to make in English. At a press conference, Mountbatten announced that Britain would in fact be going not in 1948, but in 1947. He hadn't yet chosen a date in that year, but under pressure from reporters he grabbed at one: the anniversary of the Japanese surrender. Britain would leave in just seventy-three days, on 15 August 1947. Many had thought that a united India couldn't be given its freedom even by June 1948. Could a divided India be given its freedom ten months sooner?

The decision to accelerate Independence was made because it was apprehended that even more bloodshed and rioting would take place if there were delay. The Government was also afraid that if Independence were not given speedily, Congress might fragment and Communism would take control of the subcontinent. Some still argue that Independence could have been delayed until it could have delivered without the cost in blood that was paid in 1947.[288] But too many mistakes had been made by then to make further delay possible.

After the inter-communal riots in March and April 1947, Lady Mountbatten, genuinely well-disposed to India and Indians and free from prejudice, made a tour of the Punjab. She reported to the St John Ambulance Brigade on her visits to hospitals and village communities. She had seen a child with its hands chopped off, a disembowelled pregnant woman, a tiny baby the sole survivor of its family. She was greatly distressed and like Mountbatten concluded that partition was the only solution to the inter-communal hatred of which she had seen so much evidence.

Mountbatten sent his wife to see Nehru. He had also been to the Punjab at the same time, after the deaths of some 2,000 people there. They shared their sense of horror in the face of the depths to which inter-communal hatred could bring the nation. Nehru wrote that he had 'seen ghastly sights and I have heard of behaviour by human beings which would degrade brutes'.[289] A few days after his meeting with Lady Mountbatten, Nehru called on M.A.K. Azad, one of the Congress Old Guard, and asked him 'in despair, what other alternative was there to accepting partition'. He asked Azad to give up his opposition: 'It would be wisdom not to oppose what was bound to happen. He also said that it would not be wise for me to oppose Lord Mountbatten on this issue.' These retrospective comments by Nehru, when his image had become that of a more or less benevolent elder states-man, have to be read with caution, but there is probably something in his claim that, '[t]he truth is that we were tired men, and we were getting on in years too. Few of us could stand the prospect of going to prison again – and if we had stood out for a united India as we wished it, prison obviously awaited us. We saw the fires burning in the Punjab and heard every day of the killings. The plan for partition offered a way out and we took it'.[290]

For Congress as for the British, partition was a compromise. But it represented a bigger failure for the imperial power that had so strongly defended the unity of India as its great achievement, indeed the justifica-tion of its policy. What was really unforgiveable was not partition in itself, but the failure to prepare for the consequences of partition. Not until June, for instance, were plans made to divide the army, just six weeks before Independence. Above all no consideration of the borders of the two new countries had taken place, with the terrible consequences we shall encounter.

46

THE VIEW FROM WHITEHALL

In February 1947, when Attlee told the House of Commons of Mountbatten's appointment and announced a definite departure date – at this stage June 1948 – after which Britain would no longer have responsibility for the subcontinent, the news created a sense of shock. *The Times* thought that the announcement of the time limit was miscalculated. The *Daily Telegraph* said that it was 'reckless folly' to abandon India in the absence of prior agreement. What was proposed was a reversal of every precedent in setting up dominions, where acknowledgement of status had followed agreement about who would take power. To declare unconditional withdrawal at a pre-fixed date was to jettison any concept of responsible trusteeship. The statement was intended to concentrate Indian minds, but it was truly an abdication of responsibility. No one knew whose hands would receive the symbols of power.

The Cabinet received a memorandum from Attlee dated 22 May 1947. Whoever wrote the memorandum for Attlee had a good grasp of his peremptory, business-like style. It summarised the conclusions that followed from a series of discussions in the India and Burma Committee, first with Mountbatten's Chief of Staff, Lord Ismay, and later with Mountbatten himself. Mountbatten had been told to do his utmost to secure general acceptance of the Cabinet Mission's plan. If this proved impossible he was to report by 1 October on the steps that he thought necessary for handing over power in June 1948.

Attlee acknowledged that the intention was 'to thrust upon Indians the responsibility of deciding whether or not India shall be divided and in what way'. Jinnah privately acquiesced despite public protests against any proposal to partition Bengal and the Punjab. Mountbatten thought that the Muslim League would go along with the process.[291]

Attlee and his Government took the Commonwealth very seriously indeed: surprisingly so for an ostensibly radical regime. Attlee himself took enormous pains to see that the Commonwealth developed as a viable and dynamic body. If the Empire was to go, the Commonwealth must continue. The new Foreign Secretary, Ernest Bevin, saw the Commonwealth as a bulwark against Communism and a mini-United Nations Organisation.

Ernest Bevin ended up a thoroughly Palmerstonian figure in foreign affairs. He was strongly patriotic with firm, almost nineteenth-century, views about Britain's role on the world stage. As Britain's strength and pre-eminence had been so totally eclipsed by America and Russia it seemed to him and his adviser, Sir Orme Sargent, that Britain could only appear as a respectable world power by virtue of being the dominant European power. The implication of this was, while of necessity shedding those bits of Empire which could not be sustained, consolidating what remained and enhancing the status of the Commonwealth. He saw America as 'a well-intentioned but inexperienced colossus'.[292] He believed, remarkable as it may seem, that British power and influence could be equal with those of the United States and Russia: the basis for this lay in making use of the material resources of 'the Colonial Empire'.[293] Accordingly, he was initially against the breakup of the Empire. He complained to Attlee about 'this awful pessimism'. Attlee responded, 'I am not defeatist but realist'. [294]

Part of the motive for accelerating Independence was the cost of maintaining the British presence. Dalton, the Chancellor of the Exchequer, saw the matter in fairly blunt terms: 'If you are in a place where you are not wanted, and where you have not got the force, or perhaps the will, to squash those who do not want you, the only thing to do is to come out'. [295]

Servicemen had to be got home. There were two reasons to this. One was that it cost money to keep them abroad as a garrison. The other was that their presence was required in the civilian labour force: in 1946 18.6 per cent of the country's manpower was in the services. By June 1946 there were 44,537 civilians and 10,837 service wives and children in India, together with British army personnel and British officers in the Indian army.[296]

There was a huge and uncounted number of Anglo-Indians at home in Britain. English residents had always been transient visitors to the subcontinent. They went out, made their money in trade or profession, in the civil service or the army, and retired early to enjoy their wealth and reduced health at home. Only a very small minority chose to see out their days in the subcontinent. Some of this vast array of old India hands were idealistic enough to salute the new India and wish it well. For the most part, however, they regretted the defeatist taste of the handover, an abandonment of a task not fully completed which diminished their achievement and that of their predecessors. Their views are interesting, but were of little significance.

47

THE PRINCELY STATES

The problem of the princely states was not fully resolved before Independence. In his 'Report on the Last Viceroyalty', the document which he handed to the king on his return to England, Mountbatten claimed that he had been told nothing in London before he took up the viceroyalty that alerted him to the fact that dealing with the princely states was going to be at least as hard as dealing with British India, if not harder. He exaggerated the difficulties. But it is indeed the case that the Government in London had seen the princely states as very much a minor appendix to a much bigger problem. Mountbatten had to spend a great deal of the brief time left to him on persuading the princes that their future lay within the union, rather than as a series of mini-Pakistans.

Sir Conrad Corfield, Head of the Political Department of the Government of India, was the man charged with responsibility for dealing with the princes. He saw his principal duty as being to look after the interests of his clients. Mountbatten saw Corfield's role differently, that of a sheep dog whose task it was to round up the errant princes and bring them within the Indian flock. Corfield came to irritate Mountbatten enormously – and also Congress and to an extent the League.

The princely states were independent of British India. What bound them to Britain and had compromised their independence was that they had conceded paramountcy to the British Crown. Paramountcy would lapse when the Crown surrendered control of India, and the states would in theory therefore become independent once more. Nehru ignored the theory of reversion of powers, and argued that the princely states couldn't regard themselves as truly independent since they had already surrendered the right to declare war or conduct their own foreign affairs. At a practical level, few could defend themselves.

Corfield secured the inclusion of a clause in the India Independence Bill which provided that paramountcy would lapse only at the exact time that

India became independent. On that date, 15 August, an array of nearly 600 states containing 100,000,000 people would exist alongside and independent of India and of Pakistan. Corfield knew that *most* of the states would have to join the Indian union, but he did intend some to be truly independent. The original nationalist position was that paramountcy would not lapse, but automatically transfer to the new government of a united India. Cripps had vetoed that idea in 1942.

When Mountbatten arrived, he consulted not with Corfield, but with V.P. Menon.* Menon argued that the princely states should sign treaties of accession to the new Government, in terms of which responsibility for foreign affairs and defence would transfer to the Indian Government, in return for domestic autonomy and retention of their subventions, the privy purses.

Menon's plan was that in the case of those states which did not accede to the union, London should automatically transfer paramountcy to the successor government in the subcontinent. There was an objection to this in terms of law. Gandhi described this objection, the intransmissibility of paramountcy, as a 'vicious doctrine'. Mountbatten tended to side with the Menon formula.

Corfield had wanted as many as possible of the states to become independent entities, so that they could thereafter negotiate with India and Pakistan. Mountbatten wanted them to be part of a Constituent Assembly from the start. Corfield knew that most states could not remain independent for long, but he maintained later that he considered that the *threat* of ongoing Independence could be used to negotiate better terms. Corfield saw his role as the princes' independent advocate very clearly: 'My job was to look after the interests of the princely states. It was no part of my job to make things easier for India'.[297] Mountbatten had a different job, and Corfield kept his distance in order to safeguard his independence. Nehru and others thought that Corfield and the political department were undermining the interests of the new state.

Corfield, feeling the weight of personal responsibility for fair dealings with his clients, flew to London in May 1947 to obtain instructions from Listowel. He did so without getting permission from Mountbatten. The viceroy was not pleased. Corfield was a 'son of a bitch'. His excursion to London did nothing for the princes.

They were asked to meet Mountbatten on 25 July 1947. For the occasion

---

*   Whose brief biographical details were given in Chapter 27.

he dressed up in full viceregal uniform to impress them. His father had been a prince. He was one of them. The viceroy was convinced that accession was the only possible course open to them. He ignored Corfield and the political department. He told the Secretary of State that Corfield had not understood that on the lapse of paramountcy 327 owners of small states would have power of life and death over their subjects, whereas the gravest punishment they could currently impose was three months' imprisonment. He used every ounce of his charm and authority to persuade the princes to accede, reminding them that after 15 August he would no longer be in a position to attend to their interests. On the other hand, he said, he would persuade Congress that if the princes did accede, they would be allowed to go on receiving titles and honours. Corfield gave in his notice and flew home 'with a feeling of nausea'.

Mountbatten worked his way through the princes, telling them that his kingly cousin, George VI, would be upset if they did not accede and remain within the Empire, as India and Pakistan were to become dominions within it. There were 561 princely rulers to get through. Mountbatten wasn't particularly attracted by the anachronism of the princely states. He wanted them subsumed without delay. Some of the princes, Bhopal, Travancore and Hyderabad amongst them, wanted to be separate dominions. Mountbatten told them that this wouldn't be on the cards. He even declined to discuss whether London would maintain relations with any independent state after 15 August.

The exercise wasn't concluded when Independence arrived. Nehru accepted dominion status in part because he thought that as governor-general of the dominion, Mountbatten would be able to persuade the princes to accede. V.P. Menon and Vallabhbhai ('Sardar') Patel spent two years bribing the princes, pretty much as the British had done. The rulers were offered a privy purse, and the appearance of power in return for surrendering the reality. The annual subventions were ended in 1971. When powerful leaders thought they could stand apart, different tactics were used. The Indian army blockaded Junagadh, part of Gujarat, where the Muslim ruler had acceded to Pakistan. Kashmir and Hyderabad were brought within the Indian Union only by threats of force from Pakistan in the first case and the application of force by India in the second.

Indians didn't think much of the princes. Gandhi described them as 'British Officers in Indian dress' and Nehru called them 'sinks of iniquity'. Quite how iniquitous they were will never be known, because Corfield told his officials to extract from the files any evidence of what were called 'eccentricities' on the part of the princes. No fewer than four tons of eccentricities were burned, to the annoyance of both Mountbatten, who knew just how eccentric royals could be, and Nehru. The path to Independence would have been simpler if the princes' interests had not required consideration. Their importance lay in the fact that their existence could be used to weaken the position of Congress, and to an extent the League, and for that reason they were courted. It was reasonable to assume that by offering them distinctions and baubles, they might be pleased to remain on cordial terms with London, which many of them knew better than their own territories.

48

The Final Plan

Hastings ('Pug' and now Lord) Ismay, accompanied Mountbatten to India. We last met Ismay when as Military Secretary to Lord Willingdon he was concerned for the viceroy's safety. During the war he had served with great distinction as Secretary to the Chiefs of Staff. He ranks only behind Churchill and the Chief of the Imperial General Staff, Alanbrooke, in forging Britain's military contribution to victory. In 1946 he retired from the army; but he volunteered to accompany Mountbatten for two reasons. First, he loved India. Secondly, he was afraid that Mountbatten might rush things.

In the event, after only a month back in the subcontinent, he reappraised the situation and told Mountbatten that he must make haste. He wrote to a friend, 'The communal feeling I have found, I just did not believe possible. It tore at you, all the time. There was slaughter everywhere. We British had all the responsibility and none of the power. The police force was already undermined, and the civil service were frustrated and madly anxious. They were blamed by both Nehru and Jinnah for everything that went wrong. This was one reason why to delay partition would be to increase the disasters.' *This* was the extent to which Britain had prepared India for Independence by 1947.

At Mountbatten's request Ismay visited London on 3 May 1947. He took with him the plan for partition. Choices would be offered: Bengal and the Punjab could be split between India and Pakistan; or could join with one another; or could be independent. The destiny of the princely states was still uncertain at this stage. Mountbatten urged the Cabinet to approve a plan quickly. He appeared confident that it would be acceptable to the politicians in India. The Cabinet did indeed act quickly, and gave their approval within the week. The only changes were an emphasis on the right of different parts to decide their own future and a further opt-out for the North-West Frontier.

Mountbatten had been working seventeen hours a day for six weeks. He went off to Simla to recuperate and prepare for Ismay's return from London and the release of the plan to the politicians. He invited Nehru and Krishna Menon to stay with him and, on a last-minute hunch, as he called it, that Nehru might not like the plan, gave it to him, against the advice of his staff, to look at overnight. In the morning Nehru delivered what Mountbatten called the 'Nehru bombshell'. He had been prepared for the necessity of partition, but the extent of the non-Indian area appalled him. This turnaround was reminiscent of so many other episodes in negotiations over the years. Nehru had appeared to endorse the plan earlier, and the minor changes made in London don't explain why it was unacceptable now.

It was Krishna Menon who saved the day. He suggested that if India and Pakistan joined the Commonwealth, the apparent unity of the subcontinent would be preserved. Mountbatten convinced himself that not only had his 'hunch' been a brilliant piece of intuition, but that getting India into the Commonwealth had been his own coup. He ended a self-congratulatory letter to his daughter, 'I think I can get Congress back into the Commonwealth!!! Hush!'

But the idea of incorporating India into the Commonwealth was very far from new. It went back as far as the Balfour Report of 1926. The Commonwealth was a much more coherent entity than it is today, and much more controlled by Britain. It continued the imperial bond through strong economic and military commitments. It was precisely for that reason that Nehru had hitherto tended to see the Commonwealth as a limitation of India's Independence. Moreover, the preponderant sense of the policy urged on Mountbatten by both the service chiefs and the politicians had been to bring India within the Commonwealth nexus. It is indeed argued by his supporters that he had been quietly working towards this end from the start. But his reaction to the Nehru Bombshell was despair at the rebuff of the plan which he had so confidently commended to London, and what saved the day at Simla wasn't any negotiating triumph by Mountbatten. It was the way in which Krishna Menon found a way of saving Nehru's face. It was typical of Mountbatten that he could pocket someone else's success and believe it had been his all along.

That he did. Henceforth Mountbatten committed himself wholeheartedly to the Commonwealth solution. 'Towards the achievement of this objective, he revealed a steely determination, and often resorted to dubious diplomacy. It was a stunning performance,' says M.N. Das.[298] On the basis that as soon as something can't easily be had, it becomes the more desirable, he made the prospect of Commonwealth membership all the more attractive by pretending to Krishna Menon that he had been told by London *not* to attempt to keep India within the Commonwealth. Although Nehru didn't like the idea of membership, he recognised that the concept might keep some states from opting for Independence and reduce the Balkanisation risk. I shall return to the complicated implications of Commonwealth in the next chapter.

By 11 May Mountbatten was able to send a telegram to Ismay, still in London, saying that Independence would have to be granted in the course of 1947, on the basis of dominion status and with Commonwealth membership for both India and Pakistan. The Cabinet was taken aback to learn that the pre-Commonwealth plan which they had just approved and which they had been told would be acceptable to all parties was to be replaced by another one.

On 18 May Mountbatten returned to London, the amended plan apparently accepted by Congress and at least not objected to by the Muslim League. The Government could not hope to get the necessary legislation through parliament before the recess without the agreement of the opposition. Mountbatten visited Churchill, not yet out of bed for the day.

Churchill was mollified by the idea that 'Independence' would be moderated by membership of the Commonwealth and didn't oppose the legislation. It would be wrong, however, to think that by now Churchill had simply acquiesced in Indian developments, either out of regard for Mountbatten (whom Attlee may well have appointed to spike Churchill's guns), or because he thought the cause was lost. His views on India, however wrongheaded, were deeply felt, and he did not abandon them. He was distressed about the Attlee Government's abandoning of a continued British role in India. In speeches right up till Independence he continued to rumble darkly about what was happening. Even after Independence, on an occasion when Mountbatten approached Churchill, full of bonhomie, he was rebuffed bitterly: 'Dickie, stop. What you did in India is as though you had struck me across the face with a riding whip'.[299]

On 31 May Mountbatten returned to India, having been given 'a large measure of discretion to amend the details of the plan, without prior consultation with His Majesty's Government'. His plan was accepted by Congress and Jinnah said that he would recommend it to his League. It was now that the new fixed date emerged. Mountbatten gave a press conference to 300 journalists, speaking without notes for three-quarters of an hour. He faced fierce questioning about how the plan would work and he responded time and time again by indicating that this was no longer Britain's problem: 'Every time you ask me whether I am going to decide a question for you I say "No". If you put the same question in a second and third way, I still say my answer is "No". I am quite sincere when I say to you that you have got to make up your minds'.[300] In answer to another question, and apparently without any great reflection, he said that Independence could be achieved 'about 15 August [1947]'. The 'about' was immediately forgotten.

49

COMMONWEALTH AND INDEPENDENCE

When Mountbatten spoke to his daughter as if the Commonwealth dimension were no more than an inspired afterthought he overlooked the fact that in the Statement of Instructions which he had been given there was a paragraph that dealt with the ongoing relationship between Britain and India. The first sentence made it clear that Commonwealth membership was desired. The rest of the paragraph touched on the relationship between Britain and an India that chose to remain apart and reflects the fact that for strategic reasons India remained very important:

> HMG hope that India will remain a free and independent member of the British Commonwealth of Nations. If, however, this does not eventuate, HMG is most anxious, after the transfer of power, that there should be the closest and most friendly relations between India and the UK. A feature of this relationship should be a military treaty. At the appropriate time delegates from the Chiefs of Staff will be sent to India to assist you in framing it.[301]

This paragraph was inserted as an addition to the original draft, probably by Ismay. The fairly real possibility that India would not consent to become a member of the Commonwealth does not appear to have concerned the British Government unduly; but they were insistent on a treaty for the defence of the area as a precondition for Independence. In course, the notion of the treaty as a precondition gave way to the idea that a treaty could follow Independence and was more likely to do so if it were not pressed too hard by Britain.

Britain was prepared to scramble out of *running* India, but the military were intent on retaining a presence there for strategic reasons. The best chance of keeping that presence would involve binding India into the

Commonwealth. At a Chiefs of Staff meeting on 20 May 1947, the Chief of the Air Staff, Lord Tedder, said that if the RAF were compelled to withdraw completely from India that would have an adverse effect on communications and bases which would affect both the Middle East and South-East Asia. On 20 June the Joint Planning Staff concluded that as a strategic Commonwealth requirement, it was essential that India remained as a support area, with personnel and material capable of expansion in wartime. The Chiefs of Staff Committee didn't think that the politicians understood the importance of an ongoing relationship with India from a defence point of view. Ismay was authorised to advise Attlee that 'from the military point of view . . . it was as clearly vital as anything could be to ensure that India remained within the Commonwealth'.

But there were those in London who could not see that a relationship with India could be informed by the same idea of racial kinship as in the case of the existing dominions. India might be more of a nuisance than an asset – rather like Southern Ireland – if it remained in the Commonwealth. Maybe something special would be required for this exotic entity, not *membership* of the Commonwealth, but *agreements* with the Commonwealth. How could the Commonwealth possibly extend 'its "club spirit" to include peoples of oriental race and modes of thought'.[302] These views were echoed by Sir Gilbert Laithwaite in the Burma office: India could not have the same 'natural link with the Empire' as the 'white dominions'. The India Office saw 'no reason to suppose' that India would accept the gentlemanly 'broad unwritten obligations' of Commonwealth membership. She could not be relied on and would weaken 'the cohesion of the Anglo-Saxon club'. Such statements illuminate the remarkable survival of offensive and antique modes of thought.

Indeed, the India Office thought that despite the unsatisfactory nature of the Irish connection, Southern Ireland had at least some affinities with Britain, whereas Indians would be 'a disturbing and not a welcome element'. Their links were with Asia. India was 'so flaky and unreliable that even if she did come into the Commonwealth, she must enter into a Treaty binding her to cooperate with it in matters of foreign affairs and defence'.

While there had been no mention of the Commonwealth in the plan that Ismay originally took to London, after the Nehru bombshell and the Krishna Menon initiative, Mountbatten's telegram to Ismay sent at 9pm on 11 May 1947 shows how near the surface the issue truly lay: 'I consider that the main advantages which the United Kingdom would gain are briefly: a) the terrific world-wide enhancement of British prestige and the enhancement of

the prestige of the present government. b) The completion of the framework of world strategy from point of view of Empire defence.'[303]

On 3 July 1947 the Chiefs of Staff sent a memorandum to the Secretary
of State, urgently pressing for discussions with 'the Indians on our long
term strategic requirements in that country'. By now the treaty approach
was beginning to be replaced by the idea that India and Pakistan were to be
'temporary dominions', and that the 'no-treaty' practice should be followed.
The Chiefs of Staff were uncomfortable with this. They did not think that
matters could be left on the same basis with the Indians as with the reliable
white dominions: 'The fact that we do not arrange formal Treaties with
dominions must not blind us to the necessity for taking early and concrete
steps to obtain our defence requirements should, at a later stage, either
Pakistan or Hindustan decide to leave the Commonwealth. It may in fact be
most desirable to have written agreements with these temporary dominions'. Mountbatten agreed that there should – in due course – be written
agreements, but didn't like the term 'temporary dominions'. He thought
that seeking agreements at this stage would 'inevitably give impression that
we did not trust future governments of new dominions to negotiate to our
satisfaction when they are set up'.

After Independence, India came to feel that the Commonwealth might
have some value. Liaquat Ali Khan, the first prime minister of Pakistan,
thought that with India, Pakistan and Ceylon in the Commonwealth, that
institution would have a new shape and direction. A Congress meeting on
18 December 1948 at Jaipur took the view that a free association with the
independent nations of the Commonwealth would be good for common
welfare and the promotion of world peace. The problem was India's republican values. Britain could see that it would be a mistake to demand that
India pay allegiance to the Crown. King George was told by his Private
Secretary, Sir Alan Lascelles, that she would 'then go – with the consequence
which anybody can foresee'.

After Independence, Mountbatten remained in India as governor-general
until June 1948, when he was succeeded by Chakravarti Rajagopalachari.
With the departure of the king's cousin, it rather looked like time to cut the
link with the king. Finally a formula was reached amongst the Commonwealth
prime ministers in April 1949, largely as a result of Attlee's work. The
Government of India, notwithstanding her republicanism, declared that she
wished to continue membership of the Commonwealth and that she
accepted the king as 'the symbol of the free association of its independent
member nations, and as such the Head of the Commonwealth'. Nehru said

with wonderful disingenuousness that he was a bad bargainer not used 'to the ways of the marketplace' but that he had thought it 'far more precious to come to the decision in friendship and goodwill than to gain a word here or there at the cost of ill-will' – a remarkable change of policy.[304] India's ties to the Commonwealth were maintained by allowing her to become its first republican member. The Republic of India was born on 26 January 1950.

50

ENDGAME

Drawing Lines on the Map

Although it had been accepted that India would be divided into two parts, until astoundingly late in the day no one seems to have realised that precise boundaries were needed between Pakistan and India. In another viceroyalty, Wavell had thought about it. In a telegram of 7 February 1946 he had told Attlee that a 'detailed demarcation' of the projected Pakistan was necessary. He submitted suggestions for boundaries, but nothing much happened, and all through the ensuing negotiations, no one knew what they meant when they discussed 'Pakistan'. In March 1946 there were no papers in the official archives in Delhi dealing with the practical implications of partition until one, and only one, arrived from Lieutenant General Sir Francis Tuker, GOC, Eastern Command. He suggested that partition seemed likely and that some planning should take place for it.[305]

Eventually Sir Cyril Radcliffe, QC, a leading member of the Chancery Bar, was sent out on 8 July 1947 – thirty-eight days before Independence – to draw the lines. His qualifications for the task were not obvious, but he became so helpful to governments in fixes, chairing so many public enquiries, that the wit and Member of Parliament A.P. Herbert talked of 'government by Radcliffery'. The systematic failure of British governments to contemplate or prepare for any planned transfer of power to India is epitomised by the fact that a man of Radcliffe's background and lack of experience (he had never been east of Gibraltar before he came to India) should have been asked to embark on such a fundamental task so very late in the day. He was only in India for six weeks. He was supposed to operate on a forensic, apolitical basis, independent of Hindus, Muslims and the British Government. There was in fact a degree of contact between him and Mountbatten, though both denied it later.[306] It was not significant.

Radcliffe was originally asked to preside over a commission which would not only decide the future frontiers of the two countries but also assess and distribute their joint assets. It was then thought that the combined operation was too much for one committee and Radcliffe was told that his only job would be to divide the country. 'Otherwise, you will have nothing to worry about.'

When he reached India Radcliffe asked how long he had got. Mountbatten said, 'five weeks'. Before Radcliffe could protest that this was grossly inadequate, Nehru intervened: 'If a decision could be reached in advance of five weeks, it would be better for the situation.' Jinnah and the others agreed.

Initially, it was envisaged that boundary disputes between India and Pakistan would be referred to the United Nations, but that did not happen. Radcliffe presided over two boundary commissions, one for Punjab and one for Bengal, each to have two Muslim and two non-Muslim High Court judges. The two Muslim and two Hindu judges appointed to assist Radcliffe made it clear from the outset how they would interpret their role: 'We did not volunteer for this task. We were drafted into it. You must realise that we cannot possibly be associated with any decisions you may make on the question of dividing the Provinces. It is not simply that our careers would be harmed. Our very lives would not be worth a scrap of paper if we were involved in decisions where the division of territory is disputed. We will help you all we can with advice. But they will be your decisions, and yours alone.'[307]

In practice the judges voted on communal lines, and the effective decision in every case was that of Radcliffe himself. In delineating the 'Radcliffe line' Sir Cyril took advantage of the sketched 'detailed demarcation', such as it was, left from Wavell's time. The boundary shown on the Second Schedule to the Indian Independence Act* is very close to that proposed by Wavell. The Schedules were, however, merely provisional, and not detailed maps, simply lists of districts. In his five weeks, Radcliffe and his secretary, Christopher Beaumont, had little time to embark on extensive new research. The monsoon was late that year and in the Punjab, in particular, it was unbearably hot and humid. Radcliffe said later that he thought that his greatest achievement as Chairman of the Boundary Commission was the physical one of surviving.

---

* The First Schedule provisionally listed the districts to be included in East Bengal, the Second those to be included in West Punjab.

Surviving not only meant surviving the climate, but also surviving assassination. He found he could trust no one and that everyone he met had an axe to grind. His young Indian ADC was leaving India after the transfer of power and was instructed not to discuss politics. Radcliffe had a huge Punjabi bodyguard who wore only a nightshirt and a bandolier around his waist with two pistols stuffed into it. He hovered outside Radcliffe's bathroom or near his bed and Radcliffe could only hope that they were both on the same side.

Radcliffe beat the five-week deadline. His Awards, as his decisions were known, were bound to be wrong whether he took five weeks or five years. He tried to take account of irrigation canals and water supplies so that there was enough water in the central Punjab, but on the scale with which he was dealing, he was bound to make mistakes. If villages weren't bisected by the boundary they were separated from the villagers' fields, railway stations from the towns they served and communities from the resources on which they relied. He found his task hateful and lonely and he could not wait to leave the subcontinent. He flew off on Independence Day itself. 'They had absolutely no conception. They asked me to come in and do this sticky job for them, and when I had done it they hated it. But what could they expect in the circumstances? Surely, they must have realised what was coming to them once they had decided on partition. But they had made absolutely no plans for coping with the situation. Strange chaps. Just didn't do their homework'.[308]

Last Days

There was an enormous amount to be done in the seventy-three days between Mountbatten's press conference and the renunciation of sovereignty. The administrative logistics of partitioning the material of Empire – railways, finance, properties, military forces – had to be sorted out at ludicrous speed. In parliament the passage of the India Independence Bill was equally accelerated: it went through its parliamentary stages in just one week in July 1947, just a few weeks before India and Pakistan became independent – how very different from the timetable for the 1935 Act.

All of this was evidence of failure. The British achievement, so it was claimed, had been to take a disunited land-mass and fuse its myriad peoples into a single union. That great object was now surrendered. The Indian princes were abandoned, the alliances in which the British had promised them the protection of the Crown disavowed. As far as the ideal of achieving

Independence without bloodshed was concerned, all that can be said is that things might have been very much worse. They were in truth bad enough. The violence in the last days of the Raj and the first days of the new India and Pakistan was greater than anything seen in the Mutiny.

Mountbatten had a calendar marked up to show the days left before Independence. As the pages of the calendar were torn off the pressure on him and his staff became unbearable. He told the Secretary of State, Listowel, 'It is almost impossible to describe the atmosphere in which we are living or the strain to which everyone has been subjected'.[309] Ismay was in bed with dysentery. Brockman was an invalid. At times in the past Mountbatten had been so confident that things were going well that he was able to spend two hours a day working on his family tree. Now he too was periodically played out and occasionally succumbed. He lapsed into exhausted silence whenever the pressure was relieved.

It was all incredibly difficult. Take Hyderabad as an example. Hyderabad had a Muslim ruler but only 10 per cent of the population was Muslim. It was thus an extraordinarily difficult model for Independence. And yet little thought had been given to the problems posed by such states.

Mountbatten thought that the problems of Hyderabad and Kashmir and Junagadh, for example, would be more capable of being resolved if he remained as governor-general of both dominions, India and Pakistan.* Jinnah was not in favour of a single governor-general, although he did want Mountbatten to stay on in some capacity after Independence. Mountbatten tried to persuade Jinnah that even if there were two governors-general, there could be an overriding arbitrator. Jinnah did not respond favourably. In any event London had said it would be constitutionally difficult.

Finally Jinnah announced that *he* proposed to be Pakistan's governor-general. He was accused of megalomania and vanity. That is unfair. He was probably correct in recognising that an independent Pakistan would be diminished if it shared a governor-general with its larger neighbour. He declined the conventional K.C.M.G. that dominion governors-general received.

Mountbatten had pressed Radcliffe to postpone delivery of the Awards until after the transfer of power. Radcliffe refused, but under pressure agreed not to release them one by one. All the Awards were delivered to the

---

* In retrospect, Attlee held, as Mountbatten and others had done at the time, that if Mountbatten had been the initial governor-general of both dominions there would have been a good chance of avoiding the tragedies of the Punjab and Kashmir.

viceroy on 13 August. It was intended that they should be disclosed ahead of the transfer of power, but typically Mountbatten didn't want to spoil a party. He ruled that the Awards would not be promulgated until 16 August, the day after Independence. Indeed, by the time that Radcliffe arrived to hand over the Awards, Mountbatten had already left for the Independence Day celebrations in Karachi. The charitable explanation for three days' delay was that Mountbatten did not want the launching of the new nations to be marred by recrimination. A more serious charge is that he delayed issuing the Awards so that he could have discussions with Nehru and amend them in favour of India. Such evidence as exists to support the charge relates mainly to just two instances, Ferozepur and Gurdaspur, and it is far from conclusive.

Liaquat Ali Khan, Nehru and Sardar Patel, and Baldev Singh for the Sikhs, gathered in the Council Chamber of Government House on 16 August at 5pm, just three hours after the Awards had been sent to them. The fact that every party was equally annoyed took some of the immediate force out of their protests and the Awards were accepted and published.

It's pretty amazing that the celebrations about the establishment of two new countries could take place without anyone's knowing precisely what these countries were. It has been suggested that delaying the announcement somehow exacerbated the subsequent bloodletting. It is not obvious that this was the case. The argument is that if the content of the Awards had been known in advance this would have allowed last-minute movements of troops into the areas where disturbances were expected ahead of the transfer of power. But there weren't many troops to be deployed, and the Indian army couldn't be relied upon in what was really civil war. Those who thought that there were bound to be disturbances and not much could be done about it were probably right. Mountbatten frankly said that the release of the Awards was bound to cause 'controversy and grief' and that he didn't want Independence Day spoiled. Alan Campbell-Johnson, Mountbatten's press attaché, described Mountbatten at his desk as midnight struck and a subcontinent fractured: 'Mountbatten was sitting quietly at his desk. I have known him in most moods; tonight there was an air about him of serenity, almost detachment. The scale of his personal achievement was too great for elation; rather his sense of history and the fitness of things at this dramatic moment, when the old and the new order were reconciled in himself, called forth composure.'

That's one way of looking at it. The other is to marvel that Mountbatten could be serene, composed, satisfied with himself, when he knew that the

Awards which he had in his pocket would cause the death of a million people and the misery of a million more within the next few weeks. Later he would say, 'What really did anything matter to the Indians except Independence?'[310]

After the Awards

Before the announcement of the Boundaries Awards, Mountbatten wrote to M.A.K. Azad saying, 'I shall see to it that there is no bloodshed and riot. I am a soldier not a civilian. Once partition is accepted in principle, I shall issue orders to see that there are no communal disturbances in the country . . . I will order the army and the air force to act and I will use tanks and aeroplanes to suppress anybody who wants to create trouble."[311] This breezy declaration meant nothing. Mountbatten's main interest was in getting out as quickly as possible and before the bloodletting began. He had already announced that British forces would be withdrawn at the earliest opportunity, so they were not going to be there to take the blame for enforcing partition.

Mountbatten knew very well how dangerous the situation was. On 8 April 1947 the viceroy suggested to Jinnah that he and the Congress leadership should join in an appeal against provocative acts which might lead to bloodshed. Jinnah agreed until he found that as well as Gandhi, the President of Congress, Jivatram Kripalani, was to sign. He would not see the standing of the Muslim League diminished by associating his name with that of an 'unknown nobody'. Next, Nehru too stood on his dignity. Congress would not be told who was to sign on their behalf. It looked as if the uncontentious declaration would never be signed until Mountbatten hit on the solution of having just Jinnah and Gandhi sign.

The Punjab was the scene of the worst repercussions of the lack of preparation. One in six of the population of the Punjab was a Sikh, and the Punjab was to be split between India and Pakistan. The Sikhs rejected the idea of subordinating themselves to the Muslims who had for so long been their persecutors and Sir Cyril Radcliffe hated the task of drawing a demarcation line which could never fulfil its objective. He was haunted by the experience for the rest of his life.

Mountbatten had been warned in very explicit terms of the dangers by Sir Evan Jenkins, the governor of the Punjab, but he chose to pay little attention. Tension was seething, even ahead of the Awards by the Boundary Commission. There had already been atrocities. There was a massacre of

2,000 Sikhs in Rawalpindi in March by Muslims. Since then there had been sporadic killings. Things intensified during the last fortnight before Independence. Evidence accumulated of plans for sabotage, the destruction of the canal system, attacks on trains, and for the assassination of Jinnah. On 9 August 154 Muslim soldiers and officials were hacked to death by Sikhs on the train that was taking them to Pakistan.

Countless villages in the Punjab were in flames and the population was already on the move before the midnight hour. The Punjab Boundary Force under Major-General Thomas ('Pete') Rees was thrown together at the last minute by Auchinleck, responsible for 38,000 square miles of territory including 17,000 villages. They faced, for instance, Sikh *jathas*, hard-fighting and well-equipped units under the command of former Indian Army or INA soldiers. They also faced Muslim squads, much less organised in rabble bands. On 14 August they found thirty-eight Sikhs knifed at Lahore Railway Station. On the following day in Amritsar they arrived to find that Muslim women had been dragged from their homes, paraded naked outside the Golden Temple, then raped and hacked to death.

On 14 August, Auchinleck met General Rees and Sir Evan Jenkins at Lahore Airport. Jenkins told Auchinleck that his force was now partisan and could no longer be trusted. Sikhs queuing for a train at the station had been stabbed while the force looked on. A tenth of the houses in Lahore had already been destroyed. Jenkins returned to England for good on the following day.

Rees and the Punjab Boundary Force did its best. It was mainly commanded by British officers and the 55,000 troops were mostly Gurkhas. Initially both Muslim and Hindu thought it was a force for good; soon, however, each side thought the force favoured the other and by 29 August it was agreed that it would be disbanded. Mountbatten's operational responsibilities had ended. He went on holiday to Simla: 'lazed in bed all morning'.

The holiday didn't last for long. V.P. Menon took it on himself to send a telegram asking the governor-general, as Mountbatten now was, to come back to Delhi. Nehru and his deputy, Patel, were glad to see him back, as he directed an Emergency Committee which took enormous over-arching powers to try to contain the crisis. Now that Mountbatten was no longer the symbol of an occupying power, Nehru's relationship with him became even closer than it had been before. Mountbatten wrote that Nehru 'has come suddenly to see me alone on more than one occasion – simply and solely for company in his misery; to unburden his soul; and to obtain what comfort I have had to give. He has lately written me two or three letters indicating that he does not know why he is writing, except that he feels he must write to someone to get his troubles off his chest'.[312]

51

CONCLUSION

Lieutenant-Colonel P.S. Mitchison, GSO, 4th Indian Division, described a typical scene in these final days: 'Motoring from Beas to Lahore, at a time when 100,000 Mussulmans on foot were making their way westwards through Amritsar, in the course of fifty miles I saw between 400 to 600 dead. One attack on the refugees went in from thick crops while I was nearby. In a few minutes fifty men, women and children were slashed to pieces while thirty others came running back towards us with wounds streaming'.[313]

Women and girls were particularly badly treated. Rape was a matter of humiliation and breaking the blood-line, as much as of lust. By 1952 about 30,000 abducted women from both sides had been recovered and returned to their peoples as a result of a political agreement, but many women could never return and many of those who did were killed or killed themselves because of their 'dishonour'. Patrick French narrates many heart-rending examples of the events of these days. One man killed twenty-five female relatives, decapitating his own daughter. In the same village eighty women jumped into a well to their deaths to avoid rape or conversion to Islam.[314] British officers told Louis Heren of *The Times* that the slaughter was 'a thousand times more horrible than anything we saw in the war'.

Auchinleck had wanted to keep British troops behind to reduce the violence, but Mountbatten did not agree. He may have been right. It is doubtful if a small remaining British force could have done much to halt the killing, and the responsibility for trying to do so would have been a horrible one. None of this greatly bothered Mountbatten and when he was back in Britain he minimised what had happened and said that nothing that had happened had surprised him.

Auchinleck, the Commander-in-Chief, said long before the end that any Indian officer worth his salt was now a nationalist (and that he too would have been in their circumstances).[315] At Independence he wanted to see India and his Indian Army remain united. The rush of the end made this impossible, and the army essentially collapsed as a consequence of intercommunal antagonism.

In these unhappy circumstances Auchinleck stayed on as commander of both the Indian and the Pakistani forces, but his relations with Mountbatten were not good and in September 1947 Mountbatten asked him to resign. Without children, abandoned by his wife, who had left him for a brother officer, and dismissed by his country, he withdrew finally to Morocco to lead the life of a countryman.

On Independence Day Mountbatten was made an earl for his services as viceroy. Of course he accepted the honour. Auchinleck was to be made a baron. This supremely honourable, humble man declined the peerage in case it were associated with a period in Indian history where he felt the British role had been less than honourable. Ismay understood. Ismay was to receive the order of the Grand Cross in the Order of the Star of India. Ismay was a true servant of India. He had served the Empire and India for thirty-five years. He did not think it appropriate to receive an award for playing a part in the end of British rule, given the nature of that end. He crossed his name out and told the viceroy what he had done. Mountbatten said that it was too late. Ismay said that if Mountbatten didn't cancel it then he would decline it. Against the king's wishes, the award was cancelled.

Auchinleck and many other experienced officers despised Mountbatten for what seemed to them shallowness and exhibitionism. Lieutenant General Sir Richard Savory, Adjutant General of the Indian Army, said Mountbatten had 'tried to make it appear to India and the world and to ourselves that we were committing a noble deed'.[316] The steadiness of such officers, and their solid sense of responsibility, contrasts well with Mountbatten's hyperactive showmanship. But for all his egregious brashness, the deed he did, and to a large extent the way he did it, were what Britain wanted.

In November Mountbatten was back in London. He made a speech at India House at which he sought to minimise the scale of the disaster. He said that 'only' a hundred thousand people had died, and only a small part of the country had been affected. Ismay wrote to his wife, 'I was horrified at Dickie's speech. It seems to me immaterial whether one hundred thousand or millions have actually died: or whether only three per cent of the country is in turmoil. The essential facts are that there is human misery on colossal scale all around and millions are bereaved, destitute, homeless, hungry, thirsty – and worst of all desperately anxious and almost hopeless about their future'.[317]

Mountbatten did not want the disasters to detract from his achievement. He blandly told Attlee on 17 November 1947 that he had never supposed 'that the Indians could achieve self-government without the risk of further grave communal disasters'.[318] The admission goes to the heart of the charge that Britain had done nothing over the longer term to prepare India. At a press conference on 4 June, asked about mass movement in the aftermath of partition he had replied that he did not expect any such movements 'because of the physical difficulty involved . . . but I equally think that a measure of transfer of population will come about in a natural way; that is to say, people will cross the boundary or the government may take steps to transfer populations'. There was nothing 'natural' about this calamitous collapse of civilisation.

Mountbatten has been accused of precipitating, or at least exacerbating, the carnage, by the speed with which he moved to Independence. It has even been suggested that his desire to get back to his career in the Royal Navy dictated his timetable. That is unfair and facile, but we shall never know whether the decision to accelerate Independence was flawed, whether preparation for partition, both moral and material, would have worked. No attempt was made to prepare by way of reassuring people, publicising what was happening, seeking to alleviate the fears that turned into panic. No attempts were made to police the movements of population, to provide safe convoys and to plan the logistics.

The end-game of the Raj was always going to be foreshortened, whether or not Mountbatten presided over it. But his reaction is fairly telling. In reply to a letter in which his correspondent says how glad he was that the massacres occurred after Britain had handed over, the governor-general replied, 'I agree, but only provided it had happened well after my departure and not two or three days after. In fact I do not know how I would have faced the situation if I had arrived home on 16 August to read of this appalling massacre'.[319] It is immaterial, for the judgement of history, whether it happened two or three days or two or three years after he had left the scene.

Most of Mountbatten's contemporaries, British and Indian, took the view that delay would not have helped, and would indeed have made matters much worse. Mountbatten's replacement as governor-general, the first Indian head of state, said, 'If the viceroy had not transferred power when he did, there could well have been no power to transfer.' H.M. Patel, an Indian representative on the Partition Council which arbitrated on practical issues ahead of Independence, believed that every day's delay would have added to the toll in lives. Ismay wrote to Mountbatten, 'You, and all of us who are with you, were not blind to the dangers of rushing things, but we were completely convinced that every day's delay was fraught with the utmost danger; and we felt that the wisdom of your decision was absolutely vindicated by events.'[320] It is futile to speculate about whether things might have been better or worse if Mountbatten had given himself another year; what is in question is not the decisions that were made in the last six months, but the decisions which had been taken, and not taken, over thirty years.

There was much self-congratulation around Independence. Today, looking back at these last thirty years of the Raj with all their tragedies and misery, their culmination in the suffering and deaths of the massacres of 1947, their corrosive and continuing legacy of hatred, it's difficult to see much to celebrate, difficult to imagine any other episode in history in which the outcome is so at odds with professed aims.

Remember Macaulay. When the day came when India was ready to take her place as an independent nation that would 'be the proudest day in English history. To have found a great people sunk in the lowest depths of slavery and superstition, to have so ruled them as to have made them desirous and capable of all the privileges of citizens, would indeed be a title to glory all our own'. Was 15 August 1947 such a day? Was it the outcome of steady and responsible planning, the honourable discharge of a great fiduciary responsibility? Or was it the end of a shabby tale of procrastination, and deceit, an end that was finally cobbled together in panic and despair? *Res ipsa loquitur*.

NOTES

The notes which follow indicate the books that I have found useful. I don't think that it would be particularly helpful for me to supply a bibliography. The literature of Indian Independence expands at a rate that reflects the interest in the subject, particularly in India itself, and a printed bibliography is no more than a snapshot which very speedily wrinkles and fades. Online resources are generally up to date. One which concentrates on the period 1914 to 1947 is a bibliography of books, articles and dissertations on British-Ruled India 1757–1947 available at *www.houseofdavid.ca/Ind_uni.htm*.

1   Leonard Mosley, *The Last Days of the British Raj*, p. 243.
2   CO537/5698, number 69, 'The Colonial Empire Today: Summary of Our Main Problems and Policies': CO International Relations Department Paper with Annex: 'Some Facts Illustrating Progress To Date'.
3   Seeley, *The Expansion of England*, p. 17.
4   Jan Morris, *Farewell the Trumpets*, p. 112.
5   Jan Morris, *Farewell the Trumpets*, p. 115.
6   Lawrence James, *The Rise and Fall of the British Empire*, (pbk edn), pp. 232–3.
7   G. Younghusband, *Forty Years a Soldier*, p. 5.
8   Judd, *Empire: The British Imperial Experience, from 1765 to the Present*, pp. 236–7.
9   See S.R. Wasti, *Lord Minto and the Indian Nationalist Movement, 1905–1910*.
10 Judd, *Empire: The British Imperial Experience, from 1765 to the Present*, p. 239.
11 G. Martin, 'The Influence of Racial Attitudes etc', *Journal of Imperial and Commonwealth History*, 14, p. 106.

12 Patrick French, *Liberty or Death: India's Journey to Independence and Division*, (pbk edn), p. 36.

13 David Reynolds, *The Long Shadow*, p. 185.

14 Knaplund, *Britain, Commonwealth and Empire 1901–1955*, p. 215.

15 Judd, *Empire: The British Imperial Experience, from 1765 to the Present*, p. 267.

16 Lawrence James, *The Rise and Fall of the British Empire*, (pbk edn), p. 415.

17 Second Earl of Birkenhead, *The Life of F.E. Smith, First Earl of Birkenhead*, p. 507.

18 Quoted, Hyde, *Lord Reading*, p. 353.

19 Lawrence James, *The Rise and Fall of the British Empire*, (pbk edn), p. 420.

20 M. Newman, *Harold Laski: A Political Biography*, p. 118.

21 Lawrence James, *Churchill and Empire: Portrait of an Imperialist*, p. 139.

22 Lawrence James, *The Rise and Fall of the British Empire*, (pbk edn), p. 417.

23 Lawrence James, *Churchill and Empire: Portrait of an Imperialist*, p. 143.

24 A. Draper, *The Amritsar Massacre: Twilight of the Raj*, pp. 90–91.

25 Judd, *Empire: The British Imperial Experience, from 1765 to the Present*, p. 259.

26 M. Diver, *Far to Seek*.

27 *Hansard*, V Series, 383, pp. 302–5.

28 Lawrence James, *The Rise and Fall of the British Empire*, (pbk edn), p. 419.

29 Lawrence James, *The Rise and Fall of the British Empire*, (pbk edn), p. 419.

30 Judd, *Lord Reading: Rufus Isaacs, First Marquess of Reading*, Vol II, p. 306.

31 Judd, *Empire: The British Imperial Experience, from 1765 to the Present*, p. 266.

32 Templewood, *Nine Troubled Years*, p. 29.

33 Birkenhead, *Halifax: The Life of Lord Halifax*, p. 172.

34 Roberts, *'The Holy Fox': A Biography of Lord Halifax*, pp. 23–4.

35 See Birkenhead, *Halifax: The Life of Lord Halifax*, p. 220.

36 Roberts, *'The Holy Fox': A Biography of Lord Halifax*, p. 19.

37 Second Earl of Birkenhead: *The Life of F.E. Smith, First Earl of Birkenhead*, p. 209.

38 Malcolm Hailey, 'India – 1983', in *The Asiatic Review*, 29 (1933), p. 631.

39 Private letter from Lord Birkenhead to Lord Reading, 4 December 1924, quoted Birkenhead, *Halifax: the Life of Lord Halifax*, p. 206.

40 Birkenhead to Reading, 10 December 1925, quoted Birkenhead, *Halifax: The Life of Lord Halifax*, p. 222 and see Veerathapa, *British Conservative Party and Indian Independence 1930–1947*, p. 12.

41 Judd, *Lord Reading: Rufus Isaacs, First Marquess of Reading*, Vol II, p. 301.

42 Templewood, *Nine Troubled Years,* p. 47.

43 Patrick French, *Liberty or Death: India's Journey to Independence and Division*, pbk ed, p. 53.

44 Judd, *Empire: The British Imperial Experience, from 1765 to the Present*, p. 220.

45 Walker, *The Commonwealth*, pp. 86–7.

46 Lord Butler, *The Art of the Impossible*, (pbk edn), p. 37.

47 Birkenhead, *Halifax: the Life of Lord Halifax*, p. 268.

48 Middlemas and Barnes, *Baldwin. A Biography*, p. 698.

49 Middlemas and Barnes, *Baldwin. A Biography*, p. 698.

50 Roberts, *'The Holy Fox': A Biography of Lord Halifax*, p. 27.

51 Quoted, Mansergh, *The Commonwealth Experience*, p266.

52 Roberts, *'The Holy Fox': A Biography of Lord Halifax*, p. 27.

53 Walker, *The Commonwealth*, p. 47.

54 Templewood, *Nine Troubled Years*, p. 46.

55 Baldwin Papers, E5/109, quoted Roberts, *'The Holy Fox': A Biography of Lord Halifax*, p. 28.

56 Peel, 'A Note on Lord Irwin's Declaration', *Journal of Imperial and Commonwealth History*, I (1972–73), p. 331.

57 Birkenhead, *Halifax: The Life of Lord Halifax*, p. 274.

58 Lawrence James, *Churchill and Empire: Portrait of an Imperialist*, p. 186.

59 Gilbert, *Winston S Churchill*, Vol V, p. 353 *et seq.*

60 Quoted *'The Holy Fox': A Biography of Lord Halifax*, p. 30.

61 Judd, *Lord Reading: Rufus Isaacs, First Marquess of Reading*, Vol II, p. 352.

62 Gilbert, *Winston S. Churchill*, Volume V, pp. 352–9.

63 Patrick French, *Liberty or Death: India's Journey to Independence and Division*, pbk ed, p. 55.

64 Birkenhead, *Halifax: the Life of Lord Halifax*, p. 282.

65 D.A. Lowe, *Lion Rampant: Essays in the Study of British Imperialism*, p. 161.

66 Roberts, *'The Holy Fox': A Biography of Lord Halifax*, p. 36.

67 Quoted Birkenhead, *Halifax: The Life of Lord Halifax*, p. 297.

68 Lord Irwin to the Secretary of State for India, quoted Birkenhead, *Halifax: The Life of Lord Halifax*, p. 296.

69 G. Studdert-Kennedy, 'The Christian Imperialism of the Die-Hard Defenders of the Raj', *Journal of Imperial and Commonwealth History*, 18, (1990) pp. 349–50.

70 Birkenhead, *Halifax: the Life of Lord Halifax*, p. 299.

71 Earl of Birkenhead, *Halifax: the Life of Lord Halifax*, p. 247.

72   Birkenhead, *Halifax: the Life of Lord Halifax*, p. 307.

73   Birkenhead, *Halifax: the Life of Lord Halifax*, p. 314.

74   Gilbert, *Winston S. Churchill*, Volume V, pp. 375–7.

75   Jan Morris, *Farewell the Trumpets*, pp. 293–5.

76   D.A. Lowe, *Britain and Indian Nationalism: The Imprint of Ambiguity 1929–1942*, p. 238.

77   D.A. Lowe, *Britain and Indian Nationalism: The Imprint of Ambiguity 1929–1942*, p. 173.

78   Quoted Stewart, *Burying Caesar: Churchill, Chamberlain and the Battle for the Tory Party*, p. 71.

79   Hoare to Willingdon, 3 December 1931, quoted John Charmley, pbk edn, *Churchill: The End of Glory, A Political Biography*, p. 267.

80   Gilbert, *Winston S. Churchill*, Volume V, pp. 370–1.

81   Knaplund, *Britain, Commonwealth and Empire 1901–1955*, p. 164.

82   John Charmley, pbk edn, *Churchill: The End of Glory, A Political Biography*, p. 274.

83   Lawrence James, *Churchill and Empire: Portrait of an Imperialist*, p. 192.

84   Walter Reid, *Churchill 1940–1945: Under Friendly Fire*, p. 354.

85   Middlemas and Barnes: *Baldwin. A Biography*, p. 536.

86   Addison, 'The Political Beliefs of Winston Churchill', *Transactions of the Royal Historical Society*, 5th Series, Vol XXX (1980), p. 26.

87   A. Warren Dockter, *Men of a Martial Nature: Winston Churchill and British Indian Muslims,* www.academia.edu.

88   Middlemas and Barnes, *Baldwin. A Biography*, p. 700.

89   Lord Moran, *Winston Churchill: The Struggle for Survival 1940–1965*, p. 370.

90   Patrick French, *Liberty or Death: India's Journey to Independence and Division*, pbk edn, p. 92.

91   Addison, 'The Political Beliefs of Winston Churchill', *Transactions of the Royal Historical Society*, 5th Series, Vol XXX (1980), p. 28.

92   PRO, CAB 23/39, Minutes of a Conference of Ministers held at 10 Downing Street, 5 February 1922, quoted Addison, 'The Political Beliefs of Winston Churchill', *Transactions of the Royal Historical Society*, 5th Series, Vol XXX (1980), pp. 41–2.

93   Quoted, Randolph S. Churchill, *Winston S. Churchill*, vol II, p. 100.

94   Randolph S. Churchill, *Winston S. Churchill*, vol II, p. 115.

95   Richard Toye, *Churchill's Empire: The World that Made Him and the World He Made*, p. xii and pp. 54–5.

96   Quoted in A. Warren Dockter, *op cit.*

97 For an interesting discussion of this topic see A. Warren Dockter, *op cit*.

98 Moore, *Escape from Empire. The Attlee Government and the India Problem*, p. 3.

99 Knaplund, *Britain, Commonwealth and Empire 1901–1955*, p. 150.

100 Knaplund, *Britain, Commonwealth and Empire 1901–1955*, p. 157.

101 Knaplund, *Britain, Commonwealth and Empire 1901–1955*, p. 158.

102 Knaplund, *Britain, Commonwealth and Empire 1901–1955*, p. 154.

103 Hoare to Willingdon, 3 December 1931, quoted John Charmley, pbk edn, *Churchill: The End of Glory, A Political Biography*, p. 270.

104 Charmley, pbk edn, *Churchill: The End of Glory, A Political Biography*, p. 273.

105 Charmley, pbk edn, *Churchill: The End of Glory, A Political Biography*, p. 275.

106 Templewood, *Nine Troubled Years*, p. 98.

107 See Knaplund, *Britain, Commonwealth and Empire 1901–1955*, p. 177.

108 Templewood, *Nine Troubled Years*, p. 99.

109 Templewood, *Nine Troubled Years*, p. 48.

110 See Knaplund, *Britain, Commonwealth and Empire 1901–1955*, p. 188.

111 Knaplund, *Britain, Commonwealth and Empire 1901–1955*, p. 192.

112 Knaplund, *Britain, Commonwealth and Empire 1901–1955*, p. 198.

113 Gallagher, *The Decline, Revival and Fall of the British Empire*, p. 121.

114 Bridge, *Holding India to the Empire: The British Conservative Party and the 1935 Constitution*, pp. ix-x.

115 Gowher Rizvi, *Linlithgow and India: A Study of British Policy and the Political Impasse in India, 1936–1943*, p. 3.

116 Commons, 4 June 1935.

117 Parliamentary debates, House of Commons, Vol 302, Columns 824–8, 4 June 1935.

118 Gowher Rizvi, *Linlithgow and India: A Study of British Policy and the Political Impasse in India, 1936–1943*, p. 77.

119 See Gowher Rizvi, *Linlithgow and India: A Study of British Policy and the Political Impasse in India, 1936–1943*, p. 78.

120 See Veerathapa, *British Conservative Party and Indian Independence 1930–1947*, p. 110.

121 Panikkar, *Asia and Western Dominance*, p. 273.

122 Lawrence James, *The Rise and Fall of the British Empire*, pbk edn, p. 423.

123 Lord Butler, *The Art of the Impossible*, pbk edn, p. 1.

124 Lord Butler, *The Art of the Impossible*, pbk edn, p. 57.

125 Jan Morris, *Farewell the Trumpets*, pp. 479–80.

126 Patrick French, *Liberty or Death: India's Journey to Independence and Division*, pbk edn, p. 102.

127 Gowher Rizvi, *Linlithgow and India: A Study of British Policy and the Political Impasse in India, 1936–1943*, p. 3.

128 John Glendevon, *The Viceroy at Bay: Lord Linlithgow in India 1936–1943*, p. 55.

129 John Glendevon, *The Viceroy at Bay: Lord Linlithgow in India 1936–1943*, p. 58.

130 John Glendevon, *The Viceroy at Bay: Lord Linlithgow in India 1936–1943*, p. 94.

131 John Glendevon, *The Viceroy at Bay: Lord Linlithgow in India 1936–1943*, p28.

132 John Glendevon, *The Viceroy at Bay: Lord Linlithgow in India 1936–1943*, p121.

133 Quoted, Lord Zetland, *'Essayez': The Memoirs of Lawrence, Second Marquess of Zetland*, p. 292.

134 Gowher Rizvi, *Linlithgow and India: A Study of British Policy and the Political Impasse in India, 1936–1943*, p. 86.

135 Menon, *Transfer of Power*, p. 437.

136 Gowher Rizvi, *Linlithgow and India: A Study of British Policy and the Political Impasse in India, 1936–1943*, p. 112.

137 Gowher Rizvi, *Linlithgow and India: A Study of British Policy and the Political Impasse in India, 1936–1943*, p. 114.

138 Gowher Rizvi, *Linlithgow and India: A Study of British Policy and the Political Impasse in India, 1936–1943*, p. 119–21.

139 Lawrence James, *Churchill and Empire: Portrait of an Imperialist*, p. 236.

140 Linlithgow to Zetland, 18 September 1939, quoted Moore, *Churchill, Cripps, and India, 1939–1945*, pp. 18–19.

141 Zetland to Linlithgow, 26 October 1939, quoted Moore, *Churchill, Cripps, and India, 1939–1945*, p. 20.

142 John Glendevon, *The Viceroy at Bay: Lord Linlithgow in India 1936–1943*, p. 164.

143 See Cabinet Discussions, War Cabinet Conclusions 30 (40) 4.CAB 65/5 dated 12 February 1940.

144 Amery, *My Political Life*, Vol 3, p. 109.

145 Louis, *In the Name of God, Go!*, p. 20.

146 Amery, *My Political Life*, Vol I, p. 253

147 John Barnes and David Nicholson, eds, *The Empire at Bay: The Leo Amery Diaries 1929–1945*, p. 1034.

148 Patrick French, *Liberty or Death: India's Journey to Independence and Division*, pbk edn, p. 131.

149 John Glendevon, *The Viceroy at Bay: Lord Linlithgow in India 1936–1943*, pp. 180–1.

150 John Glendevon, *The Viceroy at Bay: Lord Linlithgow in India 1936–1943*, p. 182.

151 See Mansergh, *The Commonwealth Experience*, p. 304.

152 Letter, 31 May 1941, quoted Moore, *Churchill, Cripps, and India, 1939–1945*, p. 41.

153 Amery, *My Political Life*, Vol 3, p. 178.

154 Lawrence James, *The Rise and Fall of the British Empire*, pbk edn, p. 425.

155 Lawrence James, *Churchill and Empire: Portrait of an Imperialist*, p. 237.

156 Amery, *My Political Life*, Vol 3, p. 174.

157 Amery, *My Political Life*, Vol 3, p. 175.

158 John Barnes and David Nicholson, eds, *The Empire at Bay. The Leo Amery Diaries 1929–1945*, p. 367.

159 *Hansard*, V Series, 383, 302–5.

160 House of Commons Debates, 22 April 1951.

161 Clarke, *The Cripps Version: The Life of Sir Stafford Cripps 1889–1952*, pbk edn, pp. XIV–XV.

162 See Clarke, *The Cripps Version: The Life of Sir Stafford Cripps 1889–1952*, pbk edn, p. 121.

163 Moore, *Escape From Empire: The Attlee Government and the Indian Problem*, p. 8.

164 Clarke, *The Cripps Version: The Life of Sir Stafford Cripps 1889–1952*, pbk edn, p. 123.

165 Clarke, *The Cripps Version: The Life of Sir Stafford Cripps 1889–1952*, pbk edn, p. 138.

166 Clarke, *The Cripps Version: The Life of Sir Stafford Cripps 1889–1952*, pbk edn, p. 139.

167 Linlithgow to Zetland, 21 December 1939, quoted Clarke, *The Cripps Version: The Life of Sir Stafford Cripps 1889–1952*, pbk edn, p. 141.

168 Cripps to Orme Sargent, 2 February 1942, quoted Clarke, *The Cripps Version: The Life of Sir Stafford Cripps 1889–1952*, pbk edn, p. 241.

169 Moore, *Churchill, Cripps, and India, 1939–1945*, pVI.

170 Linlithgow to Amery, 16 February 1942, quoted Moore, *Churchill, Cripps, and India, 1939–1945*, p. 58.

171 Linlithgow to Amery 21 January 1942, TOPI, Vol I, p. 23.

172 Attlee to Amery 24 January 1942, TOPI, Vol I, p. 35.

173   Amery diary, 26 February 1942.

174   Moore, *Churchill, Cripps, and India, 1939–1945*, p. 70.

175   Churchill to Linlithgow, 10 March 1942, quoted Moore, *Churchill, Cripps, and India, 1939–1945*, p. 74.

176   Quoted, John Glendevon, *The Viceroy at Bay: Lord Linlithgow in India 1936–1943*, p. 225.

177   Lawrence James, *Churchill and Empire: Portrait of an Imperialist*, p. 293.

178   Gilbert, *Winston S. Churchill*, Vol VII, p. 70.

179   Amery, *My Political Life*, Vol 3, p. 205.

180   *New York Times*, 31 March 1942.

181   Figures supplied by Dr James Tilley, Associate Professor, Department of Politics and International Relations, University of Oxford.

182   See Alan Campbell-Johnson, *Mission with Mountbatten*, p. 38–114.

183   See Moore, *Churchill, Cripps, and India, 1939–1945*, p. 81.

184   Penderel Moon, ed, *Wavell: The Viceroy's Journal*, p. 33.

185   See Moore, *Churchill, Cripps, and India, 1939–1945*, p. 90.

186   Churchill to Cripps, 2 April 1942, Moore, *Churchill, Cripps, and India, 1939–1945*, p. 96.

187   Moore, *Churchill, Cripps, and India, 1939–1945*, p. 98.

188   Clarke, *The Cripps Version: The Life of Sir Stafford Cripps 1889–1952*, pbk edn, p. 296.

189   Press statement, Delhi, 23 March 1942, TOPI, Vol I, p. 463.

190   Patrick French, *Liberty or Death: India's Journey to Independence and Division*, pbk edn, p. 143.

191   TOPI, Vol I, p. 711.

192   PRO, CAB 127/81, quoted Clarke, *The Cripps Version: The Life of Sir Stafford Cripps 1889–1952*, pbk edn, p. 319.

193   TOPI, Vol I, pp. 730–1.

194   Churchill, *The Second World War*, Vol IV, p. 192.

195   Gilbert, *Winston S. Churchill*, Vol VII, pp. 87–8.

196   War Cabinet to Linlithgow, 10 April 1942, in Moore, *Churchill, Cripps, and India, 1939–1945*, p. 122.

197   Amery diary, 10 April 1942.

198   Churchill to Cripps, 10 April 1942, in Moore, *Churchill, Cripps, and India, 1939–1945*, p. 122.

199   John Barnes and David Nicholson, eds, *The Empire at Bay. The Leo Amery Diaries 1929–1945*, 10 April 1942.

200   John Barnes and David Nicholson, eds, *The Empire at Bay. The Leo Amery Diaries 1929–1945*, p. 795.

201 Quoted Gupta, *Imperialism and the British Labour Movement*, p. 270n. and Clarke, *The Cripps Version: The Life of Sir Stafford Cripps 1889–1952*, pbk edn, p. 335.

202 Cripps to War Cabinet, 10 April 1942, in Moore, *Churchill, Cripps, and India, 1939–1945*, p. 119.

203 Moore, *Churchill, Cripps, and India, 1939–1945*, p. 126.

204 Quoted Moran, *Churchill*, p. 94.

205 Quoted Clarke, *The Cripps Version: The Life of Sir Stafford Cripps 1889–1952*, pbk edn, p. 367.

206 TOPI, Vol II, p. 853.

207 TOPI, Vol III, p. 3.

208 Wheeler-Bennett, *King George VI*, p. 703.

209 TOPI, Vol III, p. 2.

210 Amery, *Empire at Bay*, p. 872.

211 John Barnes and David Nicholson, eds, *The Empire at Bay. The Leo Amery Diaries 1929–1945*, pp. 1032–3.

212 Churchill, *The Hinge of Fate*, pp. 304–5.

213 R. A. Butler, *The Art of the Possible*, p. 111.

214 Linlithgow to Lumley, 25 November 1942, TOPI, Vol III, p. 218.

215 Amery to Churchill, 16 April 1943, TOPI, Vol III, p. 654.

216 See John Barnes and David Nicholson, eds, *The Empire at Bay. The Leo Amery Diaries 1929–1945*, p. 893.

217 Penderel Moon, ed, *Wavell: The Viceroy's Journal*, p. 3.

218 Patrick French, *Liberty or Death: India's Journey to Independence and Division*, pbk edn, p. 174.

219 Leonard Mosley, *The Last Days of the British Raj*, p. 19.

220 Penderel Moon, ed, *Wavell: The Viceroy's Journal*, 11 July 1944, p. 79.

221 Penderel Moon, ed, *Wavell: The Viceroy's Journal*, p. 49.

222 Penderel Moon, ed, *Wavell: The Viceroy's Journal*, p. 61.

223 Jan Morris, *Farewell the Trumpets*, p. 481.

224 Penderel Moon, ed, *Wavell: The Viceroy's Journal*, pp. 4–5.

225 John Barnes and David Nicholson, eds, *The Empire at Bay. The Leo Amery Diaries 1929–1945*, p. 893.

226 John Barnes and David Nicholson, eds, *The Empire at Bay. The Leo Amery Diaries 1929–1945*, p. 945.

227 Penderel Moon, ed, *Wavell: The Viceroy's Journal*, p. 33.

228 Wavell, *Journal*, 8 October 1943, p. 23.

229 Penderel Moon, ed, *Wavell: The Viceroy's Journal*, p. 12.

230 Penderel Moon, ed, *Wavell: The Viceroy's Journal*, p. 45.

231 Penderel Moon, ed, *Wavell: The Viceroy's Journal*, p. 452.

232 See Mookerjee, *Churchill's Secret War*.

233 Lawrence James, *Churchill & Empire: Portrait of an Imperialist*, pp. 304–305.

234 Penderel Moon, ed, *Wavell: The Viceroy's Journal*, p. 93.

235 Penderel Moon, ed, *Wavell: The Viceroy's Journal*, pp. 94–9.

236 Wavell to Churchill, 24 October 1944, TOPI, Vol V, p64, also quoted in Moore, *Churchill, Cripps, and India, 1939–1945*, p. 141.

237 TOPI, Vol V, p. 345.

238 Penderel Moon, ed, *Wavell: The Viceroy's Journal*, pp. 129–33.

239 Patrick French, *Liberty or Death: India's Journey to Independence and Division*, pbk ed, p. 63.

240 Patrick French, *Liberty or Death: India's Journey to Independence and Division*, pbk ed, p. 88.

241 Leonard Mosley, *The Last Days of the British Raj*, pp. 26–7.

242 Penderel Moon, ed, *Wavell: The Viceroy's Journal*, 20 January 1945, p. 111.

243 See Calder Walton, *Empire of Secrets: British Intelligence, The Cold War and the Twilight of Empire*, p. xxiv.

244 See Calder Walton, *Empire of Secrets: British Intelligence, The Cold War and the Twilight of Empire*, p. xxiv.

245 See Calder Walton, *Empire of Secrets: British Intelligence, The Cold War and the Twilight of Empire*, p. 16 *et seq*. The book merits extensive reading: it reveals an aspect of British government activity in relation to the empire which has not been widely explored.

246 See Calder Walton, *Empire of Secrets: British Intelligence, The Cold War and the Twilight of Empire*, p. 131.

247 CO866/49, no 1, COOC/1, Part 1.

248 CO875/24, number 8: 'Notes on British Colonial Policy': CO Circular Memorandum number 28, with Annex: CO Information Department Circular Outline (CO857/24, number 22).

249 CO537/5698, number 69, 'The Colonial Empire Today: Summary of Our Main Problems and Policies': CO International Relations Department Paper with Annex, 'Some Facts Indicating Progress to Date'.

250 Jan Morris, *Farewell the Trumpets*, p. 476.

251 Allan Bullock, *Ernest Bevin: Foreign Secretary 1945–1951*, p. 234.

252 India Committee Meeting, 14 January 1946, TOPI, Vol VI, p. 355.

253 CAD 128/8, CM 108 (46): 'India: Constitutional Position': Cabinet Conclusions (Confidential Annex), Part 1, In Series, *British Documents on the End of Empire*.

254   Jan Morris, *Farewell the Trumpets*, p. 483.

255   Penderel Moon, ed, *Wavell: The Viceroy's Journal*, 17 February 1946, p. 214.

256   India Committee Meeting, 14 January 1946, TOPI, Vol VI, p. 521.

257   Penderel Moon, ed, *Wavell: The Viceroy's Journal*, 23 June 1946, p. 301.

258   Penderel Moon, ed, *Wavell: The Viceroy's Journal*, pp. 267 and 310.

259   Penderel Moon, ed, *Wavell: The Viceroy's Journal*, 3 April 1946, p. 236.

260   Penderel Moon, ed, *Wavell: The Viceroy's Journal*, p. 341.

261   Penderel Moon, ed, *Wavell: The Viceroy's Journal*, p. 316.

262   Quoted Clarke, *The Cripps Version: The Life of Sir Stafford Cripps 1889–1952*, pbk edn, p. 434.

263   Wavell, *Diary*, 20 May 1946.

264   Gandhi to Cripps, 27 May 1946, PRO, CAB 127/128.

265   Leonard Mosley, *The Last Days of the British Raj*, p. 30.

266   TOPI, Vol IX, p. 197.

267   CAB128/8, CM 104 (46) 3: 'India: Constitutional Position': Cabinet Conclusions (Confidential Annex), Part 1.

268   CP (46) 456.

269   CP (46) 468.

270   Akbar, M.J., *Nehru: The Making of India*, p. 366.

271   CAD 128/11, CM 4 (47) 1: 'India: Constitutional Position': Cabinet Conclusions (Confidential Annex) Unrevised Draft Statement about Transfer of Power, Part 1.

272   Kenneth Harris, *Attlee*, p. 371.

273   TOPI, Vol VIII, pp. 621–3.

274   Figures supplied by Dr James Tilley, Associate Professor, Department of Politics and International Relations, University of Oxford.

275   Penderel Moon, ed, *Wavell: The Viceroy's Journal*, 31 December 1946, p. 403.

276   Penderel Moon, ed, *Wavell: The Viceroy's Journal*, p. 417.

277   Penderel Moon, ed, *Wavell: The Viceroy's Journal*, p. 498.

278   Francis Williams, *A Prime Minister Remembers*, pp. 209–10, 373.

279   Kenneth Harris, *Attlee*, p. 373.

280   Ziegler, *Mountbatten, The Official Biography*, p. 701.

281   TOPI, Vol IX, pp. 248 and 340, n2.

282   Ziegler, *Mountbatten, The Official Biography*, p. 356.

283   Ziegler, *Mountbatten, The Official Biography*, p. 311.

284   Ziegler, *Mountbatten, The Official Biography*, p. 247.

285 Patrick French, *Liberty or Death: India's Journey to Independence and Division*, pbk edn, p. 278.

286 Patrick French, *Liberty or Death: India's Journey to Independence and Division*, pbk edn, p. 277.

287 Ziegler, *Mountbatten, The Official Biography*, p. 368.

288 See Leonard Mosley, *The Last Days of the British Raj*.

289 Leonard Mosley, *The Last Days of the British Raj*, p. 104.

290 Leonard Mosley, *The Last Days of the British Raj*, p. 248.

291 CAB 129/19, CP (47) 158: 'Indian Policy': Cabinet Memorandum by Mr Attlee: Proposed Statement on Partition.

292 FO 371/65589 number 8399, 20 November 1947.

293 CO 936.

294 PREM 8/564, Bevin to Attlee, 1 January 1947 and Attlee to Bevin, 2 January 1947, reprinted in TOPI Vol IX pp. 431–433 and pp. 445–6.

295 Dalton diary, 24 February 1947, reprinted in H. Dalton, *High Tide and After: Memoirs, 1945–60* (London, 1962) D211.

296 Lawrence James, *The Rise and Fall of the British Empire*, pbk edn, p. 555.

297 Mosley, *The Last Days of the British Raj*, p. 162.

298 Manmath Nath Das, *Partition and Independence of India*, p. 265.

299 Stephen Roskill, *Churchill and the Admirals*, p.281.

300 Ziegler, *Mountbatten, The Official Biography*, p. 387.

301 TOPI, Vol IX, p. 385.

302 Moore, *Escape from Empire: the Attlee Government and the Indian Problem*, p. 227.

303 Ziegler, *Mountbatten, The Official Biography*, p. 383.

304 See Mansergh, *The Commonwealth Experience*, p. 335–7.

305 Leonard Mosley, *The Last Days of the British Raj*, p. 17.

306 Patrick French, *Liberty or Death: India's Journey to Independence and Division*, pbk ed, p. 322.

307 Leonard Mosley, *The Last Days of the British Raj*, pp. 195–6.

308 Leonard Mosley, *The Last Days of the British Raj*, p. 200.

309 Listowel Papers, quoted, Mosley, *The Last Days of the British Raj*, p. 416.

310 Mountbatten to Leonard Mosley, Leonard Mosley, *The Last Days of the British Raj*, p. 229.

311 Leonard Mosley, *The Last Days of the British Raj*, p. 210.

312 Mountbatten to George VI, 11 September 1947, quoted in Mosley, *The Last Days of the British Raj*, p. 433.

313 Leonard Mosley, *The Last Days of the British Raj*, p. 237.

314 Patrick French, *Liberty or Death: India's Journey to Independence and Division*.

315 Jan Morris, *Farewell the Trumpets*, p. 487.

316 Ziegler, *Mountbatten*, p. 297.

317 Ismay Papers, 17 November 1947, quoted in Mosley, *The Last Days of the British Raj*, p. 437.

318 TOPI, Vol IX, p. 741.

319 Ziegler, *Mountbatten, The Official Biography*, p. 439.

320 Ziegler, *Mountbatten, The Official Biography*, pp. 439–41.

INDEX